Through the Heart of Patagonia by H. Hesketh Prichard

Illustrator: John Guille Millais

TEHUELCHE HUNTING SCENE

On our precious globe, oceans spill their majestic waters across 70% of the Earth's surface. Over the continents, land untainted by the presence of man is becoming ever more elusive and scarce.

One area that almost retains its pristine, unspoiled look is Patagonia in South America.

This sparsely populated region is located at the southern end of South America and displays itself across the vast lands of Argentina and Chile. As a whole it comprises of the southern section of the Andes mountains as well as the deserts, pampas and grasslands east of this. Patagonia has two coasts: to the west it faces the Pacific Ocean and to the east the Atlantic Ocean.

The Colorado and Barrancas rivers, which run from the Andes to the Atlantic, are commonly considered the northern limit of Argentine Patagonia. For Chilean Patagonia it is at Reloncaví Estuary. The archipelago of Tierra del Fuego marks its abrupt southern frontier and the famed end of the world.

The name Patagonia comes from the word patagón, which was used by the Spanish explorer Magellan in 1520 to describe the native people that his expedition thought to be giants. He called them Patagons and, we think now, they were from the Tehuelche people, who tended to be taller than Europeans of the time.

Patagonia encompasses some one million square kilometers and is home to a rich and diverse landscape of plants, fauna and wildlife. It is a spectacular wilderness full of life and full of history.

Early explorers and travellers faced a sometimes difficult and uncomfortable journey to reach there. The words and pictures they brought back bear testament to a remarkable land and remarkable people.

These are their stories.

Index of Contents

Index of Illustrations

INTRODUCTION

Patagonia is a country about which little is known to the world in general, books dealing with it being few and far between, while the aspect of that quaint tail of South America and its wild denizens has practically never before been pictorially brought under the eye of the public. The following pages have been written with the idea of familiarising my readers with the conditions of life in Patagonia, and of reproducing as strongly as possible the impressions we gathered during our journey through regions most interesting and varied, and, as regards a certain portion of them, hitherto unvisited and unexplored.

The original motive with which these travels were undertaken lay in a suggestion that a couple of years ago created a considerable stir amongst many besides scientific people, namely, that the prehistoric Mylodon might possibly still survive hidden in the depths of the forests of the Southern Andes. In a lecture delivered on June 21, 1900, before the Zoological Society, Professor E. Ray Lancaster, the Director of the British Museum of Natural History, said: "It is quite possible—I don't want to say more than that—that he (the Mylodon) still exists in some of the mountainous regions of Patagonia." Mr. Pearson, the proprietor of the Daily Express, most generously financed the Expedition in the interests of science, and entrusted me with the task of sifting all the evidence for or against the chances of survival obtainable on the spot.

During the whole time I spent in Patagonia I came upon no single scrap of evidence of any kind which would support the idea of the survival of the Mylodon. I hoped to have found the Indian legends of some interest in this connection, and I took the utmost pains to sift most thoroughly all stories and rumours that could by any means be supposed to refer to any unknown animal. Of this part of the subject I have given a full account elsewhere.

There then remained to us but one thing more to do, and that was to examine as far as we could—I will not say the forests of the Andes, for they are primeval forests, dense and heavily grown, and, moreover, cover hundreds of square miles of unexplored country—but the nature of these forests, so as to be able to come to some conclusion on the point under discussion. This we did, with the result that I personally became convinced—and my opinion was shared by my companions—that the Mylodon does not survive in the depths of the Andean forests. For there is a singular absence of animal life in the forests. The deeper we penetrated, the less we found. It is a well-known fact that, where the larger forms of animal life exist, a number of the lesser creatures are to be found co-existing with them, the conditions favouring the life of the former equally conducing to the welfare of the latter. Our observation of the forests therefore led us to conclude that no animal such as the Mylodon is at all likely to be existing among them. This is presumptive evidence, but it is strong, being based on deductions not drawn from a single instance but from general experience.

Still I would not offer my opinion as an ultimate answer to the problem. In addition to the regions visited by our Expedition, there are, as I have said, hundreds and hundreds of square miles about, and on both sides of the Andes, still unpenetrated by man. A large portion of this country is forested, and it would be presumptuous to say that in some hidden valley far beyond the present ken of man some prehistoric animal may not still exist. Patagonia is, however, not only vast, but so full of natural difficulties, that I believe the exhaustive penetration of its recesses will be the work not of one man or of one party of men, but the result of the slow progress of human advance into these regions.

I have recorded some of my observations upon the habits of Patagonian game, and have written somewhat fully upon that most interesting race, the Tehuelche Indians, but I have abstained from very lengthy appendices, for these would be of purely scientific interest.

It is my hope to be able to return to Patagonia and to go further into the many interesting subjects to which my attention was drawn. In any book that may result from this second journey, I look forward to including lists of various zoological, palæontological, and botanical collections, all the materials for which have not at the moment of writing arrived in England.

I would very cordially acknowledge the unfailing help which Dr. F. P. Moreno has accorded to me in every way, and would specially thank him for the photographs and maps he has allowed me to use in the following pages. My thanks are also due to Dr. A. Smith Woodward, F.R.S., for his kind permission to reproduce his description of the Mylodon skin and other remains discovered at Consuelo Cove by Dr. Moreno; to Dr. Moreno for permitting me to reprint his account of that interesting discovery, and to Mr. Oldfield Thomas, F.R.S., for allowing me to make use of his description of Felis concolor pearsoni, the new sub-species of puma which we brought back. I further offer my acknowledgments to the Zoological Society, in whose "Proceedings" the two first-mentioned papers originally appeared.

My best thanks are also due to the Royal Geographical Society, who lent us instruments and gave us every aid in their power, and also to Dr. Rendle and Mr. James Britten, of the Botanical Department of the British Museum, for their kindness in preparing a botanical appendix.

I must record my indebtedness to Mr. John Guille Millais for the pains he took with his illustrations for this book. Before I started, my friend, Mr. Millais, drew me some sketches of huemul, guanaco, and other Patagonian animals. These I showed to the Tehuelches, and was once taken aback by being offered a commission to draw an Indian's dogs. He offered me a trained horse as payment. The praise of the "man who knows" is, after all, the great reward of art.

My thanks are also due to Mr. Edward Hawes, who kindly overlooked the proofs of this book to correct the spelling of the Camp-Spanish. And I would add the name of Mr. Frank A. Juckes, who saw to the outfitting of a medicine-chest.

I would not omit grateful mention of Señor Garcia Merou, the late Minister of Agriculture of the Argentine Republic, of the late Señor Rivadavia, the then Minister of Marine, to Señor Josué Moreno, to Messrs. Krabbé and Higgins; also to Mr. Ernest Cattle, Mr. Theobald, of Trelew, and to the many kind friends who live in the Argentine Republic.

I am indebted to my friend, Alfred James Jenkinson, Scholar of Hertford College, Oxford, for his kindness in preparing photographs for reproduction.

Most of all I owe a debt (a debt which runs yearly into compound interest) to my mother, who is accountable for anything that is worth while in this book, and who has collaborated in its production.

H. HESKETH PRICHARD.

THE PAMPAS (SHOWING FIRST DIVISION)

CHAPTER I

PATAGONIA

Physical features of Patagonia—The pampas—Climate—Discovery of Patagonia by Magellan—Description of the natives—Sir Francis Drake—Other travellers—Dr. Moreno—Coast-towns—Farms—Gauchos—Emptiness of interior—Route of expedition.

Patagonia forms the southern point or end of the South American continent and extends, roughly speaking, from about parallel 40° to the Straits of Magellan. Up to very recent times the geography of this southern portion of the New World has been in a nebulous condition. Vast tracts of the interior of Patagonia are as practically waste and empty to-day as they were in the long-past ages. It is certainly curious that this land should have been left so completely out of view when the great overspill of European humanity looked overseas in search of new homes where they might dwell and expand and find ample means of livelihood.

ONE OF OUR GAUCHOS

Perhaps the description of Patagonia given in the earlier part of the last century by Darwin had something to do with this omission. He spoke of it as a land having "the curse of sterility" upon it. He dwelt on its desolate appearance, its "dreary landscape," and it would seem that his undervaluing of the country of which, after all, he had but a short and curtailed experience, influenced the whole circle of the nations, with the result that only during the last thirty years or so have the peoples who desire to colonise been discovering how desirable and profitable is the great neglected land of the south.

Patagonia has grown to its present condition very rapidly. Not so long ago it was almost entirely given up to Indians and the countless herds of guanaco. Now there are farms upon the coast, and a few settlements, such as Gallegos with its 3000 inhabitants, and Sandy Point or Punta Arenas, still more populous with 11,000. Behind this narrow strip of sparsely inhabited coast-land the immense extent of the interior lies vacant.

Patagonia strikes the traveller as huge, elemental. Its natural conformation is stamped with these characteristics. From the River Negro on the north it tapers gradually to the Straits of Magellan on the south. Three great parallel divisions, running north and south, of plain, lake and mountain, each strongly marked, make up the face of the country. From the shores of the Atlantic the pampas rise in gently graduated terraces to the range of the Andes, while between them are strung a mighty network of lakes and lagoons, some connected by rivers, others by channels, many of which shift and alter under the influence of climate and other local causes. From the sea to the Sierra Nevada stretch the pampas, all tussocky grass, thorn, guanacos and mirages. On the western rim of the pampas the Cordillera stand against the sky, a tumult of mountains climbing upwards, their loftier gorges choked with glaciers, their hollows holding great lakes, ice-cold, ice-blue, and about their bases and their bastions thousands of square miles of shaggy forests, of which but the mere edges have yet been explored.

AMONG THE ANDES

Within its 300,000 square miles of surface Patagonia offers the most extreme and abrupt contrasts. Flat pampa with hardly a visible undulation, mountains almost inaccessible in their steep escarpments. Side by side they lie, crossing many degrees of latitude, the contrast descending to the smallest particulars, mountain against plain, forest as opposed to thorn-scrub, rain against sun. The wind only is common to both more or less, though it is felt to a far greater degree upon the pampa. The contrast extends to the coasts. The eastern coast is a level treeless series of downs with few bays to offer shelter to shipping; the western coast, on the contrary, is grooved and notched with fjords, and the beetling headlands loom dark with forests.

Roughly speaking, the country to the east of the Andes belongs to Argentina, that on the west to Chili: between them lies a long strip of disputed territory. From this great dividing-line rivers flow into both oceans, into the Atlantic and into the Pacific. On the eastern side of the range, where our travels took us, the rivers cut transversely across the continent to the Atlantic. Such are the Chubut, the Deseado, the southern Chico, which joins with the Santa Cruz in a wide estuary before reaching the ocean, and the Gallegos. At the mouth of each of these a settlement has sprung up.

On the western side the mountains approach more closely to the sea, some of the glaciers on the heights of the Andes actually overhanging the Pacific. The shore is there deeply indented with winding and intricate fjords, and dense dripping forests grow rankly in the humid climate, for the rainfall on the Chilian side of the Cordillera is extraordinarily heavy.

Patagonia is the home of big distances. The Boer used to boast that he could not see the smoke of his neighbour's chimney. On the Atlantic coastland of Patagonia it is often three, four or five days' ride to the nearest farm. The holdings are measured not by the acre or any analogous standard but by the square league. One farm alone in Tierra del Fuego is 400 square leagues in extent. The distances are at first appalling. A man accustomed to cities would here feel forlorn indeed. One stands face to face with the elemental. As you travel into the interior, Nature, with her large loose grasp, enfolds you. There is no possibility of being mentally propped up by one's fellow man. Empty leagues upon leagues surround you on every side, "the inverted bowl we call the sky" above.

Who, having once seen them, can forget the pampas? Evening, and the sun sloping over the edge of the plain like an angry eye, an inky-blue mirage half blotting it out, in the middle distance grass rolling like an ocean to the horizon, lean thorn, and a mighty roaring wind.

Out there in the heart of the country you seem to stand alone, with nothing nearer or more palpable than the wind, the fierce mirages and the limitless distances.

This wild land, ribbed and spined by one of the greatest mountain chains in the world, appears to have been the last habitation of the greater beasts of the older ages. It is now the last country of all to receive man, or rather its due share of human population.

It must not be forgotten that this is the nearest bulk of land to the Antarctic continent. It thrusts forth its vast mass far into southern waters, and beyond lie a covey of islands, small and large, upon the outermost of which is situated the famous Cape Horn.

On the Antarctic continent there is no life to speak of. In Patagonia, the nearest large land, the human race has been, through the centuries, represented by a few thousand nomad Indians, who in their long rovings followed certain well-known trails, from which only a very rare and venturesome individual thought of deviating. Far outside these paths dwelt, according to the native imagination, dangers and terrors unknown. You can follow the same trails to-day. Picture to yourself a dozen or twenty field-paths running side by side, obliterated by the fingers of the spring, and invisible under your feet, but strangely growing into distinctness half a mile ahead, waving onward towards the pampas. Such is the Indian trail.

People in England, one finds, are divided into two groups as to their opinions of the Patagonian climate. One group maintains that the country must be tropical, since it is included in the continent of South America; the other that it is an ice-bound region, for the good reason that it lies close to Tierra del Fuego. Oddly enough, both are in a degree justified, for the summers there are comparatively hot, but the severity of the winter, when snow lies deep on the country, and cutting winds blow down from the frozen heights during those months that bring to us our long English evenings, is undeniable.

Some day, no doubt, the land will lose its untamed aspect; it will become, as others are, moulded by the hand of man, and expectant of him. But now the great words of one whose eyes never rested on Andean loneliness marvellously describes it:

A land where no man comes nor hath come
Since the making of the world,
But ever the wind shrills.

The discovery of Patagonia dates from the early part of the year 1520, when that most intrepid of explorers, Ferdinand Magellan, forced his way doggedly down the east coast in the teeth of continuous storms. With his little fleet of five vessels he pushed on in the hope, which few if any of his companions shared, of finding a strait joining the two great oceans, the Atlantic and the Pacific. Upon what foundation he based this belief cannot now be certainly told, but the analogy of the Cape of Good Hope and rumours that obtained among the geographers and seafaring captains of the day, helped, no doubt, to confirm his own idea that some such outlet existed. As early as 1428, a map of the world, described by one Antonio Galvao as "most rare and excellent," showed the Straits of Magellan under the name of the "Dragon's Tail." This map, being carefully kept in the treasuries of Portugal, was, it may fairly be presumed, known to Magellan. Also there were two globes, made in Nuremberg shortly before he sailed, in which the channel between the great seas was clearly indicated.

For all that, the existence of a passage was far from being an established fact, but Magellan undauntedly continued his voyage down the Patagonian coast in search of it. He reached the harbour now known as San Julian on March 31, 1520, and there proposed to winter.

Almost at once the famous mutiny against his authority broke out, headed by those who desired to turn back, and who had no faith in the existence of the strait. One of the rebel captains was stabbed upon his own deck, a second executed ashore and a third marooned. The commander of the fourth ship, the Santiago, was a friend of Magellan's, who stood by his leader throughout the troubled time.

Weeks passed by, the winter settled down upon them with great severity, and yet no sign of native inhabitants had been perceived upon the shore. The Captain-General sent out an expedition to go thirty leagues into the interior, but the men returned with a disheartening account of the country, which they described as impassable, barren of the necessities of life, and, as far as their experience went, entirely devoid of inhabitants. But one day not long after, a native appeared upon the beach who cut antics and sang while he tossed sand upon his head. This man was successfully lured on board of Magellan's ship. He was dressed in skins, with clumsy boots of the same material, which last fact is supposed by some authorities to have led Magellan to call the people the Patagaos, or big feet. Pigafetta, an Italian who accompanied the exploring fleet, wrote an account of this Patagonian's appearance. "So tall was this man that we came up to the level of his waist-belt. He was well enough made, and had a broad face, painted red, with yellow circles round his eyes, and two heart-shaped spots on his cheeks." He further says the man was armed with a bow and arrows, the bow being short and thick and the arrows tipped with black and white flint heads. In another place Pigafetta asserts that the least of the Patagonians was taller than the tallest men in Castile.

A TEHUELCHECACIQUE

Magellan treated the man with kindness, and soon other natives paid the Spaniards visits. With them they appear to have brought a couple of young guanacos, leashed together and led by a cord. They stated that they kept these animals as decoys for the wild herds, who on approaching the tethered guanacos fell an easy prey to the hunters lying in ambush close at hand.

The Patagonians are said to have eaten rats, caught on the ship, whole, without even removing the skins! However, they seem to have been peaceably disposed towards the Spaniards, until Magellan, being struck with their great height, resolved to take home some specimens of the race as curiosities for the Emperor, and consequently he entrapped two of the young men while on board his vessel. Seeing, however, that one of these Patagonians grieved for his wife, Magellan sent a party ashore with a couple of the natives to fetch the woman: but on the road one of the natives was wounded, the result being that the whole tribe took to flight after a slight skirmish with the Spaniards, one of whom died almost instantly after being struck by an arrow. From this event it would seem that the Patagonians of that period used poisoned arrows, as do the Onas of Tierra del Fuego to-day. These people do not employ vegetable poison, but leave their arrows in a putrid carcase until they become infected.

The next navigator to visit the shores of Patagonia was Sir Francis Drake in 1578. He also commanded a small squadron of five vessels, and, curiously enough, had to cope with a plot against his life when in the same harbour of Port San Julian. The story is well known. Mr. Thomas Doughty, the chief mutineer, was given his choice of death, or of marooning, or to be taken home for trial. He chose death, and was accordingly executed. Drake speaks of the natives as being no taller than some Englishmen.

LAKES AND THE DISTANT CORDILLERA (SHOWING SECOND DIVISION)

During the next hundred years various expeditions touched upon the coasts, some captained by Englishmen, such as Narborough, Byron, and Wallis. The two latter differ a good deal from each other with regard to the stature of the Patagonians. Byron mentions a chief 7 ft. high, and adds that few of the others were shorter. Wallis, on the other hand, gives an average of from 5 ft. 10 in. to 6 ft., the tallest man measured by him being 6 ft. 7 in. At an earlier date than either of these a Jesuit named Falkner, being in Patagonia, mentions a cacique some inches over 7 ft.

In 1783 the traveller Viedma penetrated into the interior and discovered one link of the long chain of lakes lying under the Andes, which still bears his name. He gave the people an average of 6 ft. of stature. Some fifty years after this, H.M.S. Beagle, with Darwin on board, touched at many points of the coast, and short trips inland were undertaken. Darwin's journals give the first detailed account of the country. He agrees with Captain Fitzroy in describing the Patagonians as the tallest of all peoples.

During the years 1869-70, Captain George Chaworth Musters, of the Royal Navy, spent several months with the nomad Indians, traversing a great distance in their company, and becoming acquainted with many interesting facts concerning their habits and customs. Since the publication of his book in 1871 practically nothing exhaustive has been written about Southern Patagonia. One or two travellers have given short accounts of visits there, but the serious opening up of the country is due to the initiative and energy of Dr. Francisco P. Moreno, whose first excursion to Patagonia was made in 1873. In the following year he carried his investigations as far south as the River Santa Cruz. In 1875 he crossed from Buenos Aires to Lake Nahuel-Huapi and the Andean Cordillera, between parallels 39° 30′ and 42°. In 1876 he visited Chubut, and ascended the river Santa Cruz to its parent lake, which he proved was not that discovered by Viedma in 1782, but another lying farther south. To him is due the earliest suggestion of the great system of lakes which are situated in the longitudinal depression that runs parallel with the Cordillera.

Again, in 1879, Dr. Moreno crossed the country to the Cordillera on parallel 44°. Up to that time surveying in those regions was by no means exempt from danger, on account of the hostile attitude of the tribes. The amount of valuable work done by Dr. Moreno did not end with his personal expeditions. Each summer of late years the Argentine and Chilian Boundary Commissions have been surveying and opening up the country. First and last Dr. Moreno must always be regarded as the great geographer of Patagonia.

Among the gentlemen engaged on the boundary work I should like to mention the Norwegian Herr Hans P. Waag, who, on behalf of the Argentine Commission, penetrated from the Pacific coast up the river De las Heras to Lake Buenos Aires, and from thence overland to Trelew. It would be difficult to overpraise the work of this traveller.

Others, who as pioneers, travellers, scientific men, or surveyors, have taken a part in the good work of making the interior of Patagonia known to the world are Baron Nordenskjöld, Mr. Hatcher, and the members of the Chilian and Argentine Boundary Commissions. I think that in any such list as the above mention should be made of those who first settle in a district, and who realise in greater degree than even the pioneer explorers the difficulties and drawbacks of a new country, and undoubtedly their hardihood is of immense and enduring value. I would, therefore, include the name of the Waldron family, who have taken a large part in settling the southern districts of Patagonia and also in the colonising of Tierra del Fuego.

A PATAGONIAN ESTANCIA

With this brief reference to the more important journeys hitherto made in Southern Patagonia, it may be well to give here some description of the country as it appears to-day. There are upon the eastern coasts some settlements, as I have mentioned, and also the Welsh colonies of Trelew, Dawson, Gaimon, besides these a very small and recent one exists at Colohaupi, near Lake Musters, and another, The 16th October, far away in the Cordillera. This last is the single settlement of any size south of parallel 40° in the central interior.

A fringe of farms runs along the coast, and at the mouths of the rivers are situated little frontier towns, such as San Julian, Santa Cruz and Gallegos. Towards the south and along the shores of the Strait the fringe of farms has grown broader and the country is more generally settled, the Chilian town of Punta Arenas being an important port. The few vast straggling farms are given up chiefly to sheep-breeding, the main export being wool. But cattle and horses are also raised in large numbers, for the land has proved very suitable for pasturage. The farm buildings vary, of course, in many ways: some are large and comfortable homesteads, others mere squalid huts, but one and all are almost invariably roofed in with the universal galvanised iron.

The Welsh colonists have introduced a good strain to the growing population, and there are constant wholesome as well as vicious importations. In a country where shepherding of one sort or another is the chief industry, it is inevitable that some equivalent of the cowboy of the North must be developed. The Gaucho is the Patagonian cowboy, and he is manly and picturesque enough to be very interesting.

ARGENTINE GAUCHO

The Gauchos are picturesque both in their lives and in their appearance: a pair of moleskin trousers, long boots, and a handkerchief usually of a red pattern, a slouch hat of black felt, and a gaudy poncho serve them for apparel. The poncho, which is merely a rug with a hole in the middle for the head, makes a comfortable great-coat by day and a blanket by night.

A Gaucho may be sprung from any nation on earth. Even as the shores of Patagonia are washed by the farthest tides of ocean, so the same tides have borne to people her solitude a singular horde of massed nationalities. But it is the man born in the country of whatever stock who becomes the true Gaucho. Infancy finds him in the saddle, and he grows there. Other men can stick on a horse, but the Gaucho can ride. Living as they do, they form a class alone. On horseback they are more than men; on foot, I am half tempted to say, less, for they would rather ride fifty miles than walk two. They are farm-hands, shepherds, horse-breakers, occasionally good working vets, and when they prosper they buy waggons and go into the carrying trade; in fact, they form the foundation of Patagonian life.

The coast settlements are similar to such places all the world over: storekeepers, men who run wine-shops, traders, and the usual sort of folk who form the bulk of dwellers on the edge of civilisation.

In Patagonia it is not difficult to leave civilisation behind you, for between lat. 43° and 50° S. the interior, save for a very few pioneers and small tribes of wandering Tehuelche Indians, is at the present day unpeopled. When the line of the Cordillera is reached, you come to a region absolutely houseless, where no human inhabitant is to be found. Comparatively speaking, but little animal life flourishes under the unnumbered snow peaks, and in the unmeasured spaces of virgin forest, which cover those valleys and in many places cloak the mountains from base to shoulder. Hundreds of square miles of forest-land, gorges, open slopes, and terraced hollows lie lost in the vast embrace of the Patagonian Andes, on which the eye of man has never yet fallen.

HALF-BREED GAUCHO

Our travels took us over a great part of the country. Starting in September 1900, we zigzagged from Trelew by Bahia Camerones, to Lakes Colhué and Musters and along the River Senguerr to Lake Buenos Aires. After spending a time in the neighbourhood of that lake, we followed the Indian trail for some distance, then touching the Southern Chico we reached Santa Cruz on the east coast in January 1901. Leaving most of the expedition there, I returned with two companions by the course of the River Santa Cruz to the Cordillera, where I remained for some months, and in May I once more crossed the continent to Gallegos to take ship for Punta Arenas, the only port in Patagonia where a steamer calls regularly. I left Patagonia in June 1901. I compute that the whole distance covered by the journeyings of the expedition cannot have fallen short of 2000 miles.

Of the zoology of Patagonia little is known. Of the fauna and flora of the Cordillera of the southern central part it is not too much to say that practically nothing is known. Patagonia thus offers one of the most interesting fields in the world to the traveller and naturalist.

With these preliminary remarks, I will beg the reader to embark with me upon the Argentine National transport the Primero de Mayo, bound from the port of Buenos Aires for the south.

CHAPTER II

SOUTHWARD HO!

Leaving England—Start—Primero de Mayo—Port Belgrano—Welsh colonists—Story of Mafeking— First sight of Patagonia—Golfo Nuevo—Port Madryn—Landing—Trelew—A pocket Wales—Difficulties of early colonists—Other Welsh settlements—Older and younger generations—Welsh youths and Argentine maidens—Language difficulty will arrange itself—A plague of "lords"—Lord Reed—Trouble of following a lord—Itinerary—Travelling in Patagonia—Few men, many horses—Pack-horses—Start for Bahia Camerones—Foxes, ostriches, cavy—On the pampas—Guanaco—First guanaco—Maté— Dogs—Farms—Indians—Landscape—Mirages—Vast empty land—Cañadones—Estancia Lochiel— Seeking for puma—Killing guanacos—Many pumas killed during winter months—Gauchos.

We arrived at Buenos Aires early in September 1900, and on the 10th we embarked again on board the Primero de Mayo, one of the transports of the Argentine Government, by which my companions and myself had courteously been granted passages to Patagonia. The Primero de Mayo is a boat of 650 tons. We carried an extraordinary amount of deck cargo, for there were a good many passengers on board, as these transports offered the sole means existing at that time[1] of communication by sea with Argentine Patagonia.

We started about one o'clock. Lieutenant Jurgensen, the commandante, was good enough to invite us to dine on that night with the officers in the deck-house. He subsequently extended his invitation to cover the entire voyage. After dinner we went out upon the deck. It was starlight, and the Primero de Mayo was steaming down the brown estuary of the Plata.

First night out! What a penance it is! It is "good-bye" translated into heaviness of heart, and it knows for the time no future and no hope. You can only look back miserably and long for lost companionship and

All dear scenes to which the soul
Turns, as the lodestone seeks the pole.

It is a time when romance fades out, and nothing is left save the grey fact of recent partings and the misery of unaccustomed quarters.

First night out—when one renews acquaintance with the thin cold sheets and those extraordinary coverlets whose single habitat in the world appears to be upon the bunks of steamers. Our fellow passengers also seemed very much under the same influence of greyness. They had packed themselves round the saloon-table, and were keeping the stewards busy with orders.

There were not only a good many people, but peoples, on board; all nations in ragged ponchos with round fur caps or those pointed sombreros that one associates with pictures of elves in a wood. As wild-looking a crew were gathered for'ard as ever sailed Southward Ho! Germans, Danes, Poles, and heaven knows what other races besides; each little party formed laagers of their possessions and resented intrusion with volley-firing of oaths. There was one laager in which I found myself taking a particular interest; it was made up of two men, a woman, and her brood of children. Their only belongings appeared to consist of four ponchos, a maté pot and kettle, and a huge basket of cauliflowers. They crept in and entrenched themselves between the cauliflowers and the port bulwark in the waist of the ship. From there they did not move, but sat swaying their bodies during the entire voyage. Was Patagonia an Eldorado to which those people were journeying? On that dark night, as the ship slid groaning and creaking over the brown waters, the dark scene, lit by stray blurs of light, called up a memory of Leighton's picture, "The Sea shall give up its Dead."

Among the passengers was the Governor of Santa Cruz, Señor Don Matias McKinlay Tapiola, who speaks English very well. There were also one or two gentlemen interested in sheep-farming in Patagonia. Of these, Mr. Greenshields, whose estancia or farm we visited later, owned the credit of having broken new ground in colonising a part of the country some one hundred and fifty miles south of the Welsh settlement of Trelew. The earlier sheep-farms lay about Punta Arenas, eight degrees to the southward, and there the men of the south swore by the south, and much difference of opinion existed as to how sheep would flourish in the more northerly region chosen by Mr. Greenshields. But it seemed that his daring was likely to be richly repaid, and that many, when they heard of his success, would follow his example.

J. B. SCRIVENOR

At length it was bedtime, and we turned in with the comforting reflection that when we woke "first night out" would be over.

Next morning land had sunk from sight and there was a light ground-swell, but the Primero de Mayo was rolling heavily, a trick that Government transports possess and seem to regard in the light of a privilege all the world over. The evenings and the mornings followed each other in grey but serene regularity, till on the 12th we turned coastwards, heading for Puerto Belgrano, and ran between low, green, hummocky banks up a stretch of shallow, mud-coloured water to our anchorage. It was a reddish sunset with lightning playing continuously upon the horizon, and while we were at dinner a thunderstorm broke with heavy rain. That night we were permitted the privilege and amusement of choosing the morrow's menu. We chose a truly British repast; roast beef, jam-roll and plum-pudding figuring amongst the items. There are no employments too trifling to help one to pass the time on board a ship doing service as a coaster. As to the arrangements made for our well-being on the transport, the Minister of Marine had, I was informed, kindly given most generous orders with regard to our treatment.

In the morning we disembarked forty-two sailors for the four men-of-war lying at anchor in the bay. Then we sailed away again for the south with a warm sun upon the crowded planking and a cold wind blowing aft. It was at this time that I altered my original plans and decided on landing at Puerto Madryn, our next stopping-place, instead of at Santa Cruz, which lies some seven degrees of latitude farther to the south. Upon hearing that winter had not yet relaxed its grip on the country south, it became clear that the horses down there would be thin and in poor condition, with the spring sickness upon them, and therefore quite unfitted to start upon such a journey as lay before us. The new scheme also promised a saving of time, as the Primero de Mayo, owing to the necessity of calling at various little places on the way down to Santa Cruz, would be a good deal delayed; besides, the horses we required could probably be got together more quickly at Puerto Madryn.

We had a number of Welsh with us on the transport, who were on their way home to the Welsh settlements of Trelew, Gaiman and Rawson. In the evenings of the voyage it was their custom to forgather and sing psalms in Welsh, psalms the sound of which took one's memory back to the Scottish hills and the yearly ante-communion preachings in the open-air. The surrounding greyness aided the idea—grey sea, grey sky, grey weather.

By the way, on board we learnt a fact, or so we were assured it was, about the South African War, which is certainly not well known even among those who love the Boer. One night at table, one of the diners solemnly declared that at Mafeking the English ate the flesh of the Kaffirs and were thereby enabled to hold out for so long. He was not attempting to hoax us, he really believed the fable himself, poor fellow! I did not gather the gentleman's name.

Coming on deck on the morning of the 15th, we saw, drawn across the western sea-rim, a low brown line. Above it a sky of steel-blue gleamed coldly and below a wash of grey sea. This was our first view of Patagonia. All day we crept along the grim, quiet, solitary-looking cliff, until at last the Primero de Mayo was swallowed up in the vast embrace of the Golfo Nuevo. It was between evening and night when we approached our harbourage, Puerto Madryn. The half-lights were playing above it, and the afterglow of the sunset still shone feebly behind the land. We saw only raw cliff capped by dark verdure—the rim of the vast pampas which roll away in rising levels league upon league towards the Andes.

The sea was cold, the wind was cold, the land looked forlorn and a-cold. Presently from it a little boat put out containing a figure wrapped in a long military cloak. This was the sub-prefect, who thus welcomed us to these desolate shores, for Patagonia from the sea is a desolate prospect indeed. It would be difficult to give an adequate idea of the dismal aspect presented by Puerto Madryn upon that evening. Suffice it to say that the settlement consists of half a dozen houses and a flagstaff; the first crouch on the lip of the tide and the second shivers above on the bare pampa-rim.

There seals and divers haunt the sea, a few guanaco-herds live upon the coast-lands, and there, in inhospitable fashion, the little colony of human beings clings, as it were, upon the skirts of great primordial nature. In the evening lights the cliffs showed curiously pallid above a strip of dead sand and shingle, only the sky and the water seemed alive.

Next morning we hoped to get our baggage ashore and were moving early with that object in view. But the trend of public opinion in Puerto Madryn appears to be towards the conviction that there is no sort of reason for hurry under any circumstances. Hence the cargo disgorged itself slowly, and after interminable waiting we found our particular share of it would not be reached that night. It was, in fact, not till the afternoon of the second day that we achieved a partial recovery of our belongings from the holds and took the first consignment of it ashore. The morning had broken clear and fine, but mid-day brought a change. And by the time we had our boatload completed and rocketed away shorewards at the tail of the Primero de Mayo's steam-launch, a beam sea was flying in spray high over us.

There was an anxious moment when the launch slipped the towing-cable and the sailor in the bows flung a rope, which dropped short of the black wooden jetty, and we were swept some boat-lengths away by a big broken sea. To be swamped at the moment of landing!—the thought was too disastrous to be dwelt on; half our rifles and a box of instruments were on board. It cost us a long hour and a half of hard work before everything was safe ashore. And while we toiled a dozen seals came and stared at us with their doglike faces, and lazy, solemn eyes.

T. R. D. BURBURY

When all our property had been brought to land, luckily without mishaps of any kind, I left Scrivenor with our peones to bring up the heavy baggage and went on with Burbury to Trelew by the miniature train which plies to and fro between the Welsh colony and the coast. From Trelew a ten-days ride takes you beyond the farm of the last settler and into the waste places of the pampas.

Trelew is a new and pocket Wales, but very much Wales all the same. To prove the accuracy of this statement it is only necessary to say that the waggon which set us on the first leagues of our way belonged to a Jones, that another Jones accompanied the expedition to the Cordillera, that I negotiated with a third Jones for a supply of mutton to take with us for use on the first part of our journey, that I was introduced to several Williamses and did business with various Hugheses. And all this in a day and a half.

Trelew itself is a bare settlement of raw-looking houses and shanties, which has started up on the emptiness of the pampas. It cannot lay any claim to picturesqueness, and a pervading impression of being unfinished adds a suggestion of discomfort to the place. All round about the mud houses the pampa rolls away to the distances, harsh, stony, overgrown with little humpy bushes of thorn and dotted here and there with wheat-land. All through and over the settlement you are never out of hearing of three languages—English, Welsh and Spanish.

WELSH SETTLEMENT OF TRELEW

For thirty-five years the Welsh have lived in this little colony of their own founding. Exactly all the reasons which led them to forsake their far-off homes for Patagonia it would serve no purpose to set out in detail, but the root of the matter appears to have lain in the fact that they objected to the laws relating to the teaching of English in the schools; and, having the courage of their convictions, they came several thousand miles across the sea to escape the régime they disliked. At present, however, they seem to have slipped from the frying-pan into the fire, for they like still less the Argentine code, by which every man born in the Republic is subject to conscription and Sunday drilling.

Some time ago the colonists of Trelew appealed to England to intercede for them with the Argentine Government with a view to obtaining release from these disabilities. But as the Welsh had of their own free will deliberately placed themselves under the Government of the Republic, it was impossible for England to interfere, and this fact was notified to the suppliants, much to their disappointment and disgust. Even when I was there they remained rather sore over the matter, complaining that England had taken all the money subscribed for the expenses of the appeal and given them no redress in return.

The difficulties and hardships which must inevitably have beset the commencement of their settling in Patagonia, contrasted with their present condition, show the Welsh to be splendid people. The resolute spirit that drove them to emigrate across the seas has served to make their township there, though perhaps not particularly inviting to look at, a flourishing one in its quiet pastoral way. They have laid a railway, as has been said, to the coast at Puerto Madryn and established a telephone. Spanish and Welsh live here as neighbours. The Spaniard keeps the store while the Welshman farms, growing a certain amount of grain, but his chief business lies in breeding horses, cattle and sheep.

The Welshmen are not wanting in keen business quality. Any one who has tried to buy horses in Trelew will bear me out in this statement. The mere fact that a stranger has arrived in their colony, who wants to invest in horseflesh, awakens all their commercial instincts, and they are not at all behind the rest of the world in knowing how to form a combine for the purpose of plundering the Philistines. Quite right too. A man who can resist making a bargain over a horse whenever he gets the chance is, like "the good young man who died," over-perfect for this corrupt old world.

OUTFITTING IN A PATAGONIAN STORE

From their first settlement the Welsh have spread south through the coast-towns of Patagonia, and six weeks' journey from Trelew they have formed another settlement in the Cordilleras to the north-west which they have called the "16th October Colony." Thither waggons are always trekking, and waggon-drivers and others who return bring with them glowing and rosy descriptions of the young settlement of the interior. The adaptability of the Welsh to the peculiar needs of colonisation is very remarkable. They have certainly stepped into the "larger life" with success.

The influence of the new conditions of existence, so different from that of the Welsh peasant in his own country, is very noticeable in several ways. The older and the younger generation are unlike each other now, and will probably continue to become more so as time goes on. Physically the younger people are far better developed than their elders, red-faced, open-eyed, straight-backed boys in big felt hats, each with a bright-coloured handkerchief knotted round his neck and the guanaco-wool poncho hanging from his shoulders. They are very picturesque and look their best on horseback. In this matter of riding also there is a wide difference between the styles of the old and the young men. The latter, who are Patagonian born, seem to be part of their horses, but the elders, however excellent long practice has made them, never attain to the proficiency of their sons.

HUMPHREY JONES, JUN.

Although the colony of Trelew is to-day in a more or less flourishing condition and very Welsh, a grave danger menaces it. In fifty years time how will it be with the racial element? Will there be as many Welsh then as now? I fear not, and the result is difficult to foresee. The danger takes the form of the dark-eyed Argentine maiden, who is rather apt to "make roast meat of the heart" of the Welsh youth.

While the Welsh girls do not take very readily to Spanish-speaking husbands, the Welsh boys fall very much in love with the daughters of the South. So it is to be concluded that the language difficulty will settle itself, or, at any rate, become more easy of arrangement with each succeeding generation. If the girl you love speaks only Spanish, it is quite obvious you must learn Spanish in order to be able to talk to her, and, under the circumstances, you will not find the task a very hard one. Then children nearly always show a preference for the mother's tongue and speech in contradistinction to that of the father. Probably, if these prophecies were uttered in Trelew, the men of to-day would scoff at them. But onlookers often see most of the game. In 1865 the Welsh, in deep sorrow, left their own land to escape the tyranny of the English law, as they considered it, which sought to force upon them the English language. Their desire was to preserve their own tongue. And flying from Scylla they will fall (and to some degree have already fallen) a prey to Charybdis. But it is a very pleasant Charybdis, typified by a dark-haired, dark-eyed, lissom maiden, who will bear them sons no longer of the old pure-bred Welsh stock, but of a mixed race. And so the effort of the forefathers, who fared overseas to found a new home, shall be made null and void.

Now and again it is the fate of frontier towns to be stirred to their depths by some incursion from the old world they have left behind them. Trelew was still recovering from such an experience when we arrived there. The settlement, in short, had been suffering from a plague of lords. First appeared an aristocrat, who wished to travel in the interior, and he bought up horses with a lavish hand, and generally made preparations which, no doubt, filled the purses of the inhabitants. This gentleman's projected tour, however, fell through for some reason, and he departed whence he had come into the unknown world outside of Trelew's daily cognisance.

Presently after him followed a second "lord," who gave his name as Lord Reed, and who was received with open arms by an enthusiastic community. A run of lords appeared to be setting in, and was regarded by the Trelewians as a distinct dispensation in their favour, which it was their happy duty to work out thoroughly to their own advantage. By some mistake Lord Reed had left his ready money behind him, and, therefore, borrowed pretty extensively from the kind-hearted Welshmen. After a time Lord Reed vanished, and upon inquiry being made it was discovered that no such title as Lord Reed was to be found in the Peerage of Great Britain. When this fact became established, more than one Welshman is reported to have gone out after Lord Reed with the family gun, and, I believe, he was finally caught with a lasso! But the incident was not without its bearing on our personal affair, for the Bank of Trelew would have nothing whatever to say to my Cook's letter of credit. In vain I recited my credentials, and gave such proof of genuineness as was in my power to give. They would none of me. The bank evidently argued that it was easier to pretend that you were a bona-fide traveller than that you were a lord. Lord Reed too; it was rather a taking title. I could not at first understand where the humour of the question, put to me by several people I met in Trelew, of "Are you not Lord Prichard?" came in. In fact, it was disconcerting; but later on, when I heard the above story, I did not grudge the colonists any fun that might be got out of the situation, for certainly Lord Reed, taken all in all, had been far from a subject of pure amusement to them.

We remained six days at Trelew making those last few purchases which were necessary with the small stock of extra money that I had left myself as a margin. It was directly owing to Lord Reed that I finally set forth into the interior with but thirty dollars in Argentine notes and large drafts on Cook and Son, which were quite useless. Although the wilderness does not seem a likely field for spending money, yet, before our travels were at an end, I was glad to sell horses to supply the needs of our party.

The journey which lay before us to Lake Buenos Aires was about six hundred miles in length, and this distance might be subdivided into three stages: the first, from Trelew to Bahia Camerones, where the expedition became complete; the second, from Bahia Camerones to the Lakes Musters and Colhué; and the third, to Lake Buenos Aires itself. My instructions gave me an entirely free hand, within reasonable limits, as to the number of men I might take with me.

I had from the first been convinced that the smallest number possible would also be, in our case, the wisest. The immense extent of the country to be traversed, and the difficulties which must inevitably lie in our way to hinder and delay us, as well as the practical emptiness of the country, which requires that an expedition shall be self-supporting, were salient facts; and our plans had to be made and modified in relation to these facts. The mobility of the party was the main point to aim at. Hence it was necessary to cut down the personnel of the expedition to as low a number as possible, and it was further most important to have plenty of horses and to spare.

THE FIRST GUANACO

The difficulty of feeding several men when travelling through such a country was obvious, and therefore not to be thought of, as, besides the four horses each individual needed for riding, the extra animals for carrying provision and bedding, clothing, tents, &c. had to be taken into account. No pack-horse should be allowed to carry his load two days consecutively, and, in fact, one day's work in three is enough. If waggons are taken, each should be allowed three teams of six horses each.

With such ideas in view, those arrangements were made which, in fact, enabled us to cover the distances we achieved. Any expedition of this sort is killing work for the horses, and it stands greatly to Burbury's credit that we lost but one out of nearly sixty during the months we spent in Patagonia, and that one was a colt that died of eating poison-shrub.

There is not the slightest doubt that the policy that spells success in Patagonian travel is summed up in the words, "Cut down your men and your stores, and take enough horses to enable you to move lightly and rapidly."

On September 21 we left Trelew in the afternoon. The weather was magnificent. Our caravan at this period consisted of a couple of waggons as well as the horses. Two estancieros, Messrs. Greenshields and Haddock, accompanied us, as our way led past their farms. I sent the waggons ahead and rode on afterwards with Burbury and Humphrey Jones senior. When we came to the place fixed on for our first camp we found the men had gone on, for there was no water there. We pushed forward in the dark, and presently the fire of the encampment glimmered out in front of us; it seemed to be quite near, but it took a good while to reach. We heard an occasional fox, and as we sat round the fire a few birds passed in the dark, calling. The first night in camp is like the first night at sea, a gloomy time.

The next day we again had a bright sun with a strong west wind. We chased some pampa foxes and an ostrich (Rhea darwini) and killed two of the former. Jones and Burbury caught a cavy (Dolichotis patagonica). So we marched on over the rolling downs day after day, sometimes catching a glimpse of the sea, sometimes journeying across pampas where the far horizons met in pale blue sky and puffed white clouds above, and below grass and endless scrub. We saw Cayenne plover (Vanellus cayennensis) at an early stage of our travels.

THE START OF OUR LONG TREK

I have already mentioned the herds of guanaco that roam the interior. This animal belongs distinctively to South America, and is to be found nowhere else in the world. Darwin writes of it as follows: "The guanaco, or wild llama, is the characteristic quadruped of the plains of Patagonia.... It is an elegant animal in a state of nature, with a long slender neck and fine legs." In colour the guanaco is of a golden-brown with white underparts, the hair upon the sides being somewhat long and fleecy. Enormous herds of from three to five hundred live upon the pampas, and we were aware that we should chiefly depend for meat on those we might chance to shoot during many months to come.

One evening, when I was riding ahead with the troop of horses, I saw my first guanaco. Coming round a bend of the winding cañadon, I looked up and perceived him. The sight was highly picturesque. It was an old buck standing alone on the top of a cliff some two hundred feet high and looking down at me. He was posed against a background of pale green glinting sunset. I had hardly time to unsling my rifle before he bounded away. We saw many thousands afterwards, but somehow in the nature of things I shall never forget that first one.

On the coast-farms, which, it must be recollected, are many of them scores of square leagues in extent, the guanaco grows comparatively tame, becoming used to the passing of mounted shepherds; but in other parts of Patagonia, noticeably in the valley of the River Chico of Chubut, through which we passed later, they are very wild, allowing no human being to approach within half a mile. This is owing to the Indians, who hunt them perpetually in that district.

Once in camp in Patagonia life is very enjoyable, though perhaps the enjoyment varies with the amount of game to be seen. Up at sunrise, when the sun pokes its big bald lemon-coloured head out of the bed-clothes of the sky. Then some early camp-man stirs and rises, and waddles down to the wet grey ashes of yesternight's fire, and soon a weak trail of smoke goes rocketing away in the wind. The big pot is put on and breakfast is made and eaten. Then the cargo is packed, and the horses are rounded up by a Gaucho or two, riding bareback. We saddle up and the caravan moves off on its leagues-long march.

Marches vary from fifteen miles to forty, and when the afternoon sun waxes less strong the horses are off-saddled and turned loose, the waggons unpacked and the camp-fires lighted. Maté eternally, a roast, tea afterwards and a pipe, and then the sleeping-bags. Maté or yerba, I must explain, is the great drink of the pampas, and is most invigorating. A cup or tin is half filled with the yellow powdery leaves, to which is added a little cold water, followed by hot. It is drunk through a bombilla or tube, the maker of the decoction taking the first pull, and afterwards it passes from hand to hand, and I must add from mouth to mouth, round the circle. It is the greatest insult to refuse to partake, and when the originator of the brew happens to be an old and rather unappetising Tehuelche lady, the effort to take your turn and look pleased is often something of an ordeal.

Day after day went by in much the same manner, but few remembrances remain with me more vividly than the pampa fox and cavy hunting which we enjoyed during those early times of our expedition. Four lurchers of sorts and my big greyhound, Tom, trotted behind our horses, and when game was sighted we went after it at full gallop. In that keen air nothing can be more exhilarating than such a chase over the broken ground of the pampa, where we were often successful, but among hummocks and hills the quarry frequently made good its escape.

MR. LANGLEY'S ESTANCIA ON THE ROAD TO BAHIA CAMERONES

On the 25th we passed a farm that was quite English in appearance—wire-fences enclosing sheep and lambs on downs that descended in undulations to the sea. By evening we were in broken country patched with red rock. The horses were rather troublesome; Hughes, one of the Gauchos, rode an untamed mare and gave a good exhibition of horsemanship. Among the sheep and the hills an Indian rode down from the high ground; he wore a poncho of red and black, tinted like autumn trees. His camp consisted of a little fire of three or four sticks, by which squatted his china. He took his place beside her, and watched our line of waggons and horses wind away out of sight.

From Trelew to Camerones the country was for the most part like the bare deer-forests of the Scottish Highlands, brown bracken being replaced by espinilla (thorn, a general term) and the green shrub called by the Welshmen "poison-bush," the same blue sky above, the same occasional lochlike lagoons. For the first two days or more the pampas stretched to the rim of the horizon, empty and somewhat harsh even in the sunlight. Now and then mirages like squadrons of cavalry hovered along the edges of them. A few guanaco and ostriches, a sprinkling of cavy, and many pampa foxes seemed to eke out an existence there. It was a land of vast prospects, a scene laid forth with a sort of noble parsimony, which—as in the case of a miser so miserly that for the very exceedingness of his vice you respect him—was yet stupendous in its one or two grandly simple salient features, and drove the spectator to that admiration which verges upon fear. Picture one such characteristic vision of Patagonia. As far as eye could reach a spread of wind-weary grass, roofed by a wind-blown sky, an eagle poised far off, a dot in the upper air. Nothing more.

A man alone within this vast setting seemed puny. Lost here, without a horse, he would be the most helpless of things created. It was across this gigantic primordialism that our way led us. Three times we made our camp upon the bare pampas, three times in one or other of the many cañadones before reaching Bahia Camerones. You may be voyaging at an easy jog over the pampa, seeing the land roll apparently quite level to the horizon, when suddenly you come upon a spatter of white sand, a track leading between the shoulders of the pampa, you dive down and are lost to sight in a moment; then, perhaps, for four miles or for fourteen you are riding a couple of hundred feet below the level spread of the pampa, and as you pass the guanaco on the cliff tops watch you uneasily. To be lost in such a land is the simplest possible matter.

On the 27th we arrived at the Estancia Lochiel, where Mr. Greenshields most kindly entertained us. This estancia is situated at the head of a cañadon, which drops away to the sea eight leagues distant. It consists of a small colony of wooden houses with corrugated iron roofs. The Lochiel Sheep Farming Company, of which Mr. Greenshields is manager, have 15,000 sheep and forty square leagues of camp. "Camp," you must understand, in Patagonia means land.

The day after our arrival Scrivenor and Burbury accompanied Mr. Frederick Haddock to his farm, eight leagues away, in order to bring back the horses I had purchased by contract in Trelew. I remained behind as Mr. Greenshields' guest, for a puma was reported by the shepherd to have killed five sheep upon the edge of the farm during the previous night.

Macdonald, the Scotch shepherd, Barckhausen and I set out to see if we could find the puma. On my way to the spot I shot my first guanaco. He appeared upon the skyline doing sentinel, possibly against the very puma we were after. We rode under the hill on which the guanaco was watching, and he began to move uneasily. At the bend of the hill was a small hollow, and, as we rode through this, I told my companions to ride on and threw them my cabresto (leading-rope of a horse). I slid off the horse and crawled up the hill. Upon the bare face of it was a thicket of poison-bush, and into this I ultimately made my way. The sentinel guanaco was there above me, stretching out his long neck, and every now and then giving his high neighing laugh. When one hundred and twenty yards off he saw me, and I had to snap him quickly. Swing went his neck, and away he galloped with his swift, uneven gait. I thought I had missed him, when, to my delight, he began to slacken speed, and finally lay down in an ungainly attitude, his long neck crooked in a curve in front of him. I crawled nearer, and up he got and was off again. I ran down to my horse and mounted, and Macdonald let Tom, my hound, loose. We galloped the guanaco up. He was very sick indeed, and inside of three hundred yards Tom pulled him down again.

FREDERICK BARCKHAUSEN

The Mauser bullet had hit him two inches behind the shoulder about half way down the body. It had not come out. How he managed to get so far I cannot understand. We then went onwards, and saw by the way several herds of guanaco. I did not shoot any more, however, as they were uncommonly tame, and there was, of course, mutton at the estancia. We reached the spot on the hills above the puma's kill, low thorn bushes, vast mountain and blue sea, but no sign of the puma was to be found. These animals will often travel four or five leagues after a kill.By the way, when you fire at a guanaco they will sway their heads downwards with an odd sort of ducking motion. Not one individual but a whole herd will do this at any unaccustomed sound. The effect is most curious.

While at Bahia Camerones our party was completed. We took with us five Gauchos, who are active, handy men as a rule. The population of the country is largely composed of Gauchos; in fact, they form the foundation of Patagonian life.

They live by the horse, and the horse lives by them. They drive mobs of cattle or of horses for owners across three degrees of latitude to sell them. They have been born in the camp, live in the camp, and will very likely die there also. In Patagonia they treat their horses in a method very different to that which we employ in our crowded country. There nature gives grass, water, and the horse; man tames the animal as little as possible from his wild state, and forces an alliance with nature. At night the mares are hobbled and the horses turned loose; while the Gauchos light their camp-fire and drink maté through the bombilla.

At the first light next morning they take it in turn to bring in the troop, which they do with an astonishing swiftness. Sometimes, of course, the horses "clear," and then it is that the Gauchos in charge find them by tracking.

In a country intersected by deep cañadones, which offer a secure hiding-place in their many hollows, this is a difficult matter. The tracks perhaps run easily through a belt of soft marsh, and then are invisible upon a pampa of shingle and thorn.

A true Gaucho must be able to do a number of things—to back an untamed colt, to lassoo, to use the boleadores, which are heavy stones attached together by a hide rope, and are to the Patagonian what the boomerang is to the Australian aborigine. He must be able to cook, to make horse-gear from the pelts of beasts, to find his way without a compass from point to point, by instinct as it were.

The Gaucho shares with the poet the honour of being born, not made. This proves that Gaucho work is Art, with a big A. Take, for instance, the power of driving single-handed a big mob of wild horses and keeping them compact. No one who has not tried it can imagine what heartbreaking work it is to a beginner. One learns to do it after a fashion in time, but never like the man who has been bred to the craft.

FOOTNOTE:
[1] Since writing the above I learn that a German line has put steamers upon this route.

CHAPTER III

THE BATTLE OF THE HORSES

Leave Bahia Camerones—Horses wild—Decide on taking one waggon—Bell-mare—Names of horses—Breaking-in of horses—German peones—Horses stray—Gaucho trick—Watching troop at night—Four languages—Signalling by smokes—Searching for horses—Favourite words and phrases—Nag of the baleful eye—Cañadon of the dry river—Bad ground—Flies—Ostrich eggs—Shooting guanaco—River Chico of Chubut—Puma's visit at night—Condor—Lady killed—Singing in camp—Stormy night—Breakdown of waggon—Guanaco on stony ground—Long chase—Guanaco's death.

I will not bore my readers with all the technicalities of our preparations for the real start.

Suffice it to say that our total belongings were stowed upon a waggon and on the backs of four pack-horses. We had in all sixty horses, and eight men. About forty of these horses had been running wild upon the pampa for eight months previous to our acquiring them. During that time they had been lost and had only been recaptured shortly before our arrival in Trelew. The purchase of them was, however, the best speculation I could make under the circumstances, since all the animals were good and sound. Had I bought by small instalments in Trelew, not only would every man within journeying distance have very naturally attempted to palm off upon me the worst and most vicious animals he possessed, but the horses, not being used to one another's company, would have been impossible to keep together at night upon the pampas, as the various sections composing such a tropilla would inevitably have scattered to the four points of the compass.

Patagonian horses, which are descended from those brought over by the Spaniards in the sixteenth century, are never stabled, but are turned out rain and snow in their troops. These troops or tropillas consist of any number from six animals to thirty, and to each is assigned a madrina, or bell-mare, which is never ridden, and which is trained to be caught easily. At night she is hobbled, and her troop remain round about her. Naturally a well-trained madrina is one affair, while a badly-trained one is quite another. In my mob of horses I had four troops, two good madrinas and one bad one, while the fourth was a rosada, whose sole object in life seemed to be to get away from her own troop and to kick any one who came within ten feet of her.

A PAMPA ROUND-UP

When you desire to put a strange horse or colt into a troop, it is necessary to couple him to the madrina for some days, after which he will remain with the troop. The madrina should never be driven in hobbles, a mistake that is often made when bringing in the horses of a morning. A horse used to hobbles can travel in them four or five leagues in a single night, so the reason why the mares should not be allowed ever to become used to travelling in hobbles is obvious. The madrina has a bell attached to her neck, and the last sound heard before you sleep is the soft tinkle of these bells and the comfortable sound of feeding horses, unless the troop happens to take it into their head to make off, in which case you will have a long ride upon their tracks in the morning.

The horses throughout the Argentine Republic are known by their colours (for which the Spanish language supplies an extraordinary variety of terms signifying every tint and shade), and to these names they answer. Some of the names are melodious and pretty—alazan, which means chestnut, cruzado, the name given to a horse that possesses alternate white feet, the off fore and the near hind foot, or the other way round. There is a theory among the Gauchos that a cruzado will never tire. I cannot do better than give a list of the names of the horses of my own tropilla, though, of course, there are many others:

Alazan, chestnut.
Asulejo, bluish-grey and white in patches.
Bayo, fawn.
Blanco, white.
Cruzado, with crossed white feet.
Gateado, yellow with black stripe down back.
Horqueta, slit-eared.
Moro, grey.
Oscuro, black.
Overo, piebald or skewbald.
Pangaré, brown or bay with fawn muzzle.
Picaso, black with white blaze and white legs.
Rosado, red and white in patches, roan.
Rosillo, strawberry.
Tordillo, grey.
Tostado, toast-coloured.
Zaino, brown or dark bay.

The taming of these horses is a business of which an account may not be uninteresting. The methods used are of a very rough description. The colt is caught from the manada, or troop of mares in which he was born, with a lasso, a head-stall is put on him and he is tied up to the palenque, or centre-post of the corral. Here he is left for twelve hours or so, during which he generally expends his energies in trying to pull the palenque out of the ground. He is then saddled up, generally with an accompaniment of bucking, and the Gaucho who is to tame him climbs upon his back. Another mounted Gaucho is near by to "ride off," which he does by galloping between the colt and any dangerous ground or object. Probably the colt will begin by bucking, but if he does not do so during his first gallop it by no means follows that he will turn out to be free from the fault. Indeed it is quite probable that he may be soft and fat after his easy youth upon the pampas, and not till about the fifth or sixth gallop will he show such vices as are in him. At first he is ridden on the bocado, which is a soft strip of hide tied round the lower jaw. This answers to the heavy snaffle which is the first bit a colt has to submit to in England.

The Gauchos of Patagonia are not nearly patient enough with the mouths of their mounts, spoiling many by harsh treatment. Different colours in horses are supposed to indicate different temperaments; thus they say a Moro colt is generally docile, while a Picaso has the reputation of being very much the reverse.

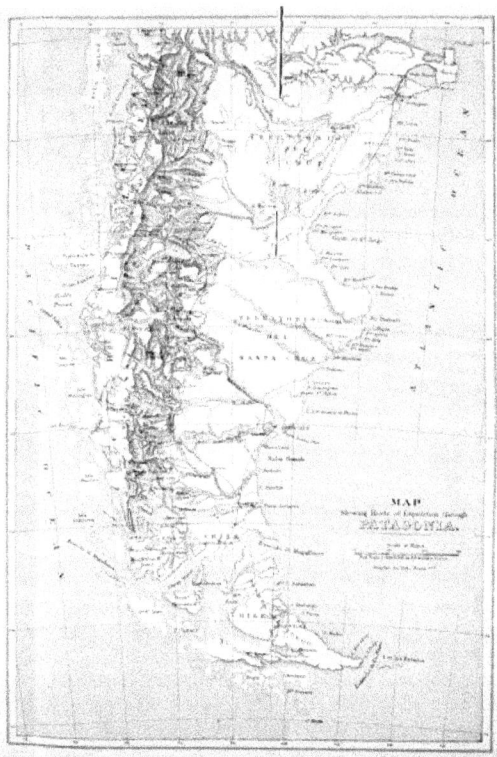

MAP SHOWING ROUTE OF EXPEDITION THROUGH PATAGONIA

The horses of Northern Patagonia—such as were ours, for they came from the banks of the Rio Negro—are reputed to be more spirited than those bred in the south. But this theory is possibly owing to the fact that the average Gaucho of the north is a better rider than his brother of the south. The horses are, I fancy, much the same.

Many Patagonian horses are what may be called "quick to mount," starting at a canter as soon as their rider's foot touches the stirrup. This also is the fault of the breakers-in. There are few tricks more annoying or, upon a hillside, more dangerous.

After this short description my readers will be able to understand more fully the happenings which I am about to describe.

On October 3 we set out from Mr. Greenshields', and at the moment of starting Fritz Gleditzsch, a German from Dresden, whom I had brought with me from Buenos Aires, and whom I had engaged on the best recommendations, came to me and told me that he could not go farther because he had had no meat to eat upon the previous night. As the meat-shed was situated about two hundred yards from where my men were encamped, and as he had free access to it, I began to understand that Fritz was something of an old soldier. Had I been able to get another man to replace him on the spot I should have done so, but with my large troop of horses I was more or less in the hands of my peones, a not uncommon difficulty to overtake the traveller in Patagonia, and one upon which many peones count.

The real reason for Fritz's recalcitrance turned out to be the arrival in my camp of a compatriot and erstwhile companion, Hans Hollesen, who had applied to join the expedition. I took them both along, for, having paid Master Fritz's way from Buenos Aires, I did not relish the notion of obtaining no return for the outlay, and I knew that, once we passed Colohuapi, I should be master of the situation.

I heard months afterwards from a New Zealander, who had been on board the Primero de Mayo with Fritz, that that gentleman was looking forward to a soft job, and had boasted that he would certainly desert us if we marched more than ten miles a day.

Our first march was about three leagues, and we made our camp beside a small shallow lagoon upon which a couple of ashy-headed geese (Bernicla poliocephala) were swimming. I shot them both for the pot.

It was about six o'clock when we camped, and Burbury, who was in charge of the horses, took every possible precaution to prevent their straying, a very likely contingency upon their first night in the open pampa. In spite of the fact that the horses were watched all night, morning found us with but thirty-seven out of the whole number. Soon after daylight Burbury, with some of the men, rode out to recover them. They returned unsuccessful. During the morning a wandering Gaucho came into camp and said he had seen some horses in a cañadon near by. The Welshmen rode out there but came back disappointed, as the horses were not ours. At eleven o'clock next morning I sent three of the men back to Mr. Haddock's, from whose estancia the lost troop had been acquired, the probabilities being that they had headed back for home. But shortly after Burbury and the Germans returned with the horses, which had travelled about nine miles, and were discovered calmly feeding in a cañadon. It was Burbury who discovered them by a smart piece of Gaucho work.

Next night, October 6, we watched the horses in turns. It was a cold night lit by a moon. We had some reason to believe that our Gaucho friend of the day before had not been altogether innocent in connection with the straying of the horses. Such a man will ride quietly through the scattered horses feeding in the gloom and stampede them. He will follow a small mob and drive them into some fold of the hills, such as, no doubt, he knows a dozen of, and hide them there until, after several days, a reward is offered by the owner. The Gaucho will then ride casually into the camp, drink a maté, hear the story, and remark that he is well acquainted with the country round. If asked whether he can give any opinion as to the whereabouts of the lost horses, he says, "Quien sabe?" but suggests they may be in a "cañadon muy limpio," to which horses often stray. In reply to any question as to where the cañadon may lie, he replies, "Over there," and waves his hand half round the compass. He may add that he is looking for seven mares of his own that strayed away last Friday week or he would himself undertake the office of guide. If any hint of payment be given, he goes on to say that, since his mares have been lost so long they may remain lost a little longer, while he guides and aids the travellers in their search, not, of course, for the money's worth, that will not recompense him for the mares, which may wander away altogether out of the province because of his delay in looking for them, but because he would do a kindness to persons for whom he has conceived a liking. So he acts as guide, and, after a decent interval, finds the horses and pouches his reward. It is an excellent trade, as there is no risk and plenty of emolument to recommend it, and, in fact, it is a common enough trick in Patagonia.

I sat most of the night by the fire—except when my turn came to ride round the horses, which we had placed in a small hollow—writing up my diary by the light of the fire, and watching the men ride in and out of the moonlight and the shadows. As the night advanced the cold increased. The moon left us about 3.30 A.M. and it became very dark. As I circled on my beat I passed by a wild cat. Morning found the horses all right. We had, however, to delay a little to allow of our men returning from Haddock's.

On October 7 we fared forth once more upon our way, and the ill-luck that had attended us at this first camp was with us up to the last moment of the three days we spent there, for as the waggon began to move off an alazan fell beneath the front wheel, which passed clean over his near fore leg. Strangely enough, owing to some inequality of the ground, the waggon, although very heavily laden, did not hurt the animal. He was not even cut, and when we got him up he resumed his journey as if nothing had happened, and eventually turned out one of our best horses.

J. B. SCRIVENOR (GEOLOGIST) AND MULA

We now made two or three good marches in succession, but on October 10, in spite of all precautions, the horses belonging to the black mare's troop deserted her.[2] Upon this, finding that until the horses of the different troops became more used to each other, it would be almost impossible to keep them together on the open pampas, where, as a further disadvantage, the grass was poor and sparse, and the horses had to scatter a great deal to feed, I decided to cut across to the Rio Chico of Chubut and march along the river valley, the tall cliffs of which would serve as a barrier to prevent the tropilla straying. Never was such an awful place as these pampas in which to lose anything, or, worse still, to get lost yourself. You ride a hundred yards or so and you are in some deep-mouthed cañadon, lying flush with the pampa, and out of sight of your companions in an instant.

On the expedition we spoke four languages—Spanish, English, German and Welsh, but English was more used than the others.

On one occasion we had to light a couple of fires to signal some of the men who were out looking for horses; one of these spread rather much, but was easily put out with a spade. It is strange how small an area burns in that part of the country, even with a high wind to help the flames. The weather was windy and bitterly cold.

I extract the following from my diary:

"October 10, evening.—I write this by the camp-fire. The men take it in turns to cook. Two armadillos (Dasypus minutus) have been caught by the Germans. They are strong little beasts; you can hardly pull one, which has half buried itself in the ground, out with both hands. We roast them whole with hot stones and they taste like chicken. Fritz and Hollesen went for the horses this morning and found three of the Trelew troop gone, the Tordillo, the Zaino, and the Blanco, and this although one was maneado and the other two tied together. This is a great hindrance. We got the waggon ready on the interminable pampa and decided to strike down at once for the Rio Chico by way of a large cañadon four and a half leagues long. This will add some days to our journey to Colohuapi. But if we continue losing and searching for horses, shall we ever get there? One day we cover twenty-one miles, the next nothing, because of strayed horses. Nor can you soga them up, for the grass is poor and they must have a large range. Here we are in this huge country looking for horses upon and about a pampa intersected by many cañadones, each of which would take an entire week to explore thoroughly. At breakfast I decided to march, sending Jones, who is a good tracker, off to see if he could find the horses where he found them yesterday.

"We have a big buck-jumper, a piebald, which is a strong horse suited to the waggon. It took an hour and a half to get him harnessed, and we started on the back track, for the cañadon we must strike lies a league behind us. Barckhausen was to ride an untamed black horse with the strangest light blue glimmering eyes, which for some reason makes me repeat over and over to myself the lines of Q.:

"His glittering eyes are the salt seas' prize,
And his fingers clutch the sand.

"Rather far fetched, but so it always is. One notices how much in camp-life a man gets into the habit of a 'Punch, brothers, punch'—a haunting phrase which he applies to everything. In one case it is some grim and grotesque oath that he mentally lives on, sometimes it is a line of a hymn, sometimes it is a bit of an advertisement. There are few books in the camp, and mine not out yet from the tin box. The Welshmen have a Bible in their own language; Hollesen has a paper of short stories about missing heirs and such like; Scrivenor has 'Pickwick.'

THE BIG OVERO, A BUCKJUMPER

"But to return to Barckhausen. The nag of the baleful eye would not be caught, and had to be chased about the pampa by Hughes and myself. Finally, Jones got a lasso on him, and he danced at the edge of the lagoon with four men at the other end of the lasso. We tied his legs in slip-knots and pulled him over, and when quieter saddled him. He bucked around with the saddle. At length Barckhausen got up and rode him the whole afternoon. It was a terrible job driving the horses, and that even though we were in the cañadon.

"On each side of us were bare, bald grass hills, rolling in hummocks and their sides sprinkled with thorn-scrub. In the centre, winding in sharp bends, a dry river bed. Towards evening, after travelling all the afternoon down the cañadon since one o'clock, I rode on and found the bed of the river held water in four places. Near the third of these we camped. Saw an ostrich and a few sentinel guanaco. Caught an armadillo. The scenery here consists of alternations of pampa and cañadon, cañadon and pampa, and over all the tearing wind, which seldom drops.

"I have given out two tins of jam and one of Swiss milk, one of coffee and milk and some vegetables. Sometimes we soak our biscuit and bake it. It is very good treated so. I am writing this by the fire at seven o'clock. Coldish.

"Jones has not turned up yet, and must have had to sleep out in nothing save a blanket, poor chap! He was to have cut our tracks and followed them up.

"October 11.—All our tropillas right this morning, and at 8.30 I rode out of the camp and met Jones, who had found the three strayed horses about a league from the old camp.

"We started and made our way down the empty river-bed, which now broadened and was pebbly, like a Scotch trout-stream. Before we left Mal Espina estancia the foreman told us the road down the cañadon was very clear—'muy limpio,' and only four and a half leagues in length, but we have been in it two days and are in it still. About 5, as I was riding ahead with the troop of horses, I came upon the track of wheels in deep scrub. I went back to the waggon and found it on the left bank of the river-bed. Upon one side were thorn-bush and sand, and upon the other a swampy vega of wet grass. Through this the track led, and into this the waggon lumbered, then two of the horses foundered in the black mud and the waggon sank. Of course that put an end to our day's journey, and I sent on Jones to bring back Burbury and the troop. We were in a land of many flies, chiefly sand-flies, which buzzed and stung horribly. Jones had tied up the horses on the Rio Chico and we could not reach them to-night. Fritz found sixteen eggs in an ostrich's nest and Hollesen found one. The one was fine but the sixteen were chickenny.

"We all turned to, unloaded the waggon and pulled it out with some toil from the marsh, and before dinner loaded it up again.

"By evening we reached the cañadon of the Rio Chico and camped upon the banks.

"October 12.—With an effort got away by nine o'clock. I rode on down the cañadon, as we had no meat and some was wanted. We appear to be now entering a good game country. Saw five ostriches. I rode the big Tostado. He loped lazily across stony ridges, which crawl to the foot of the purple hills that are on the other side of the Chico. Two herds of guanaco fled while I was on the horizon. I cantered a long way, it seemed very far, over the rolling ridges of pebble and thorn-bush. Mirages smoked and danced on the horizon. I came at length to the waggon-track which runs through the wild gorge of the Chico, and is only used about once or twice a year. I rode down this track, and at the side found a single ostrich egg. Shortly after I sighted the horses, which Jones had tied up here and there. I left my belt and the egg, and went back into the scrub to seek for that game which I could not find. Saw one guanaco, but it had seen me first, and would not let me approach within a quarter of a mile. Sighted the horses and waggon far away on the high ground and rode to meet them. Put them in a new troop and got away again at one o'clock. Found that if I could not shoot a guanaco we must open our reserve of tinned meat, and I did not wish to begin upon it so soon. Rode on ahead of the troop revolving these matters. My horse was extra lazy. I was thinking of the ostriches I had observed when I saw over a ridge to the left the ears of a guanaco. There was a dry nullah-bed which curved in beneath the ridge. It was pebbly and sparsely set with thorn. I lay down and crawled until I came to some water, and then I looked again. I could see the first guanaco, an old buck, peering with his long neck swaying, and looking at the Tostado which I had tied up. To tie up your horse in view is the most successful thing you can do in this country of long-necked game, and of game which is so often pursued with dogs and on horseback. Sometimes the most ordinary game takes, from the circumstances surrounding its pursuit, a reflected interest not its own. So it was in this case; nor, indeed, is the guanaco always an easy quarry, in fact it is a shy animal in the districts where it is hunted by Indians.[3] I crawled along, just a thorn-bush, and that a lean one, between me and detection. I had set my hopes on a low green belt of poison-scrub, and this I attained at last. From it I saw a foot of the big buck's neck and the heads and ears of six more. I had made up my mind to take a fine bead shot, but he gave me no chance of doing so. I had only time to snap him as he saw me. The bullet smashed his neck. As the others ran away I put two shots out of four into one, and killed it as it entered the scrub of thick, thorny, califate bushes that lived hardily there in the valley. I went on after shooting the guanaco and left Fritz and Hughes to cut up the meat. We made a league and a half through the gorge of the Chico when up came Fritz and said the waggon was broken down by, so he explained, a "horse falling on the pole" within a hundred yards of where I had shot the guanaco. This was a disaster indeed. Here were we just doing a good march when this wretched breakdown occurred. We turned the troop and went back only to find the waggon, a league away, coming merrily towards us. They said it could go no farther, but after repairs it achieved a league and a half more.

THE HUNTER'S RETURN

"Passing along we agreed it was a good country for lions (F. c. puma, locally called lions). We encamped beneath a high cliff, sixty feet of moss-grown basaltic rock beside the muddy river, where it winds through the marshes. In the night the dogs began to bark, for a lion came into camp. We could hear it moving by the dead camp-fire among the pots and pans. Burbury fired his revolver in its direction; he was sleeping on the outside of the tent. This morning we have found the lion's lair, twenty yards up in the rock above our camp. Fritz said last night, 'And if you hear me cry out, it is the lion, he zomp on me.'

FELIS CONCOLOR PUMA

"Fritz is very jocular sometimes: 'Aha, my little horse, he zomp!' and 'Mine little bitch, you go and catch a guanaco.' To-night he was roasting an ostrich egg and it exploded and shot him all over with yellow yolk. He remarked, 'He is goot, this egg, but he smell a bit of skunk.'

"October 13.—Mending waggon, no wood. At ten o'clock waggon mended but needed a rest in the sun till the hide of guanaco we had bound it with should dry. So I decided to take to-day as our Sunday and march to-morrow. Burbury is making a plum-duff. Served out tobacco this morning.

"Mock Sunday and at rest, a time for dreaming. Away at home the trees are browning. How one's heart turns to them and dreams of them! The men born out here wonder how we can look forward to the happiness of going home, perhaps for the sight of some village church hidden in English lanes and fields. Half the charm of this life we are living out here lies in thinking of our return to the land that gives us all comfort and a silent welcome of green springs. Went out to-day after the lion and found tracks, but the ground was too hard for following them up. He lives in a valley of grey dead bush. As we went away from the dead guanaco yesterday, a condor (Sarcorhamphus gryphus) appeared and dropped on the carcase almost before we left it.

GUANACO HOUNDS. (FATHER AND MOTHER OF THE AUTHOR'S HOUND, TOM

"October 14, Sunday.—We got away at nine o'clock and came fast. The muddy narrow Chico flowing through a land which looks as if it led over the edge of the world. It reminds one of a flowering wilderness. Last night we tied up the dogs, and dear old Tom howled till I had to get up and correct him. When up I let poor little Lady loose, the last service I was ever destined to do for her, for to-day the waggon went over her belly, and she lies dead on the track a few leagues back. She was six months old, always cheerful, and wagging her whip of a tail, always up to the march. Half an hour before she died I saw her hunting a young fox, her first. She had brown eyes and I had got fonder of her than I knew. Tom used to drive her from her food, biting her, and from the softest bed, and I am now glad to think I sometimes made him give way to her. Just before Lady's death, I shot a cavy (Dolichotis patagonica) with the Mauser. He gave me a nice shot sitting up on his haunches, near the track on the skyline of a low bare ridge. Yesterday we had a very fine puchero or stew, pickled eggs given me by Pedro at

Camerones and two plum-duffs made with waggon-grease by Burbury, who is quite a chef at plum-duff. After our meal we had out the concertina and found that Burbury knew 'The Church's One Foundation,' and Jones a melancholy Welsh hymn.

"The two best of my horses have sore backs.

"We spent an hour trying to get the waggon up a steep ridge 100 feet high, and had to unload and all work at it. Made a long seven leagues and encamped at the foot of a ridge with 200 yards of dead bush between us and the yellow Chico. Going very pebbly, the ground here and there burnt up and arid. It is always in such places that the mirages are most common.

"October 15.—Got off 8.40. At 11 unloaded waggon, which was in great danger of turning over. Scrivenor photoed it. At 2.20 waggon horses unfit to go farther. Camped by the Chico; shot a yellow-billed teal.

"October 16.—Out of humour all day, first, because, I found one of the cameras put unprotected into the waggon among the tins of potted meat, &c. Wearily, wearily we wend our way towards the blue distant hills of our desires. Even as in life we wend towards distant ambitions, and, coming up to them, find new ones arise upon the horizon beyond, and so we travel all our days, looking longingly ahead. This valley of the Chico is a wild place, conical hillocks of sand have now taken the place of the bush-covered ones. The Chico remains yellow and winds greatly. Purple hills crown the distance. It is all high-coloured and clear-shaded as in a picture.

"To-day, coming round a bend of the Chico glen, I saw seven guanaco feeding in the valley. They had seen me and begun to move, so I galloped round the ridge, and as I jumped off my horse one passed and halted within seventy yards. The herd made a pretty picture standing on the bare, desert-brown hillside in the tearing wind. I clean missed the buck with the first shot, and only killed him as he ran off, hitting him low behind the shoulder. The wind was blowing hard to-day and full in our faces.

"A windy night, the sand of the river-bed driving and filling everything. Presently we shall crawl into our sleeping-bags and, with our feet to the wind, bid any weather defiance. A pipe is a mighty ally. Here am I in the little 4 ft. tent which Burbury and Scrivenor have pitched to sleep in, wrapped in a poncho a-reek with the smoke of Indian camp-fires, enjoying a pipe and writing this, and as it grows too dark to write and the wind roars and bellows louder down the river-bed, I shall sit here watching the red glow of my pipe and dreaming.

"October 17, 9 o'clock.—A month hence from to-day will be my birthday. Where shall we be? At the Lake Buenos Aires, I hope. Several horses this morning have sore backs, and Burbury, excellent fellow, has been doctoring them.

"How the face of this country changes with the weather! Bleak and windy even in warm sunlight, though fine and bracing; in evil weather it wears an aspect of forlornness. The farther you penetrate into Patagonia the more its vast emptiness weighs on you and overwhelms you.

"Eleven o'clock.—Where shall we be a month hence? Where, indeed? To-day we had a great disappointment, and I hardly know how to write of it. The natural difficulties of the country are very great, but with care, in spite of boulders and hard-going, it seemed as if I could get my waggon up to the foothills, and I looked forward to bringing back many specimens in it. But after 300 and odd miles of travel a particularly hummocky valley proved too much for its endurance. When the horses tried to move it this morning it broke up altogether, and here it lies!

"Total day's march, 200 yards. Burbury and Jones have ridden on towards Colohuapi, where there are some pioneers' huts, to try and get wood and bolts. What is to be done? I do not know. Take to cargueros? We could bring back no specimens to speak of in that case. One must wait and see what Burbury can get from the people at Colohuapi. The camp is in a valley and is surrounded by bare mud cones 100 feet in height, a few bushes shiver in the throat of the upper end of the gorge. In the gorge and round our camp-fire spreads a growth of rank lean weed, full of yellow flowers, and a few small wind-polished stones lie at the base of one of the ant-heaplike hills.

"'Oh, the dreary, dreary moorland! Oh, the weary, weary shore' (of the Chico)! I took my gun down to the river and shot five widgeon (Mareca sibilatrix) and six martinetas (Calodromas elegans).

"Late in the evening Scrivenor and I went up over the ridge of bare hills rather with the idea of shooting, if possible, a condor we had seen poised high up. Sight at back came off Scrivenor's Mauser.[4] We went on and saw a herd of guanaco, one much nearer than the rest, and we crawled towards him. The stones were a penance. The only cover was thorn, and little of that up there on the high pampa above the valley where our camp is. At two hundred yards I shot and hit him, but he went on, and presently swayed his neck and lay down. I crawled up and had a shot at his neck. Thereafter followed periods of cantering in a rickety way, followed by periods of lying down, and at last we went round over a rise and crawled down on him. I thought he was dead but for the shadow of his neck, and I crawled on with but one cartridge left in my gun. As I neared him, up he got and I fired again and hit him. He was growing very weak. Scrivenor shouted that he had no revolver, and so here were we with only our knives. I followed the guanaco and Scrivenor went round. I was upon him first but my knife was weak. Scrivenor, startled from his usual calm, and with a shout, leaped at the guanaco and caught him round the neck. So we bore him to earth and slew him. I examined him for wounds and found four. Two of the shots were vital, yet he had led us a chase of two and a half miles, and we had to carry the meat back to camp. Arrived there, and preparing a meal by the fire, in came Burbury and Jones. They had met a Gaucho trekking to Colohuapi, who told them that Colohuapi was yet twenty-five leagues away and that there were no bolts or wood to be had there. I went to bed and smoked, feeling pretty sad. There is but one thing to do. We must jettison some of the cargo and sew up the rest in the skins of guanacos, and go forward with pack-horses."

FOOTNOTES:

[2] When a mare is in foal—as was the case with the black mare—her troop will often desert her and wander away, but when the foal is born the horses become very much attached to it.

[3] Darwin describes the guanaco as "generally wild and extremely wary."

[4] This happened in the case of two Mausers I had with me. One came off at the third shot from the mere recoil—a serious business.

CHAPTER IV

THE BATTLE OF THE HORSES—(continued)

First march with pack-horses—Difficulties—Friendship among horses—The melancholy Zaino—Revolt of an old philosopher—Shifting cargoes—Reach River Chico—Guanaco-shooting—A glimpse of a puma—Pumas and sheep—Arrival at Colohuapi—Hospitality of pioneers—The value of horse-brands.

Morning (19th) came to us very grey with a pallid sun, and ushered in the first day of the new system. We found it necessary to use sixteen horses as cargueros or pack-horses. In the early dawn we caught the chosen animals, and tied them up to the smashed waggon. It is one of the inconveniences of pampa travel that bushes strong enough to hold a horse which is at all restive are few and far between. In that particular spot there was absolutely nothing in the way of a bush, however small, which could by any chance have borne the strain.

READY TO BE CARGOED

So we tied them up to the waggon and they immediately proceeded to tie themselves and their headropes into still more complicated knots: they made cats' cradles, reef-knots, sliding nooses, a dozen knots one knew and a dozen one had never dreamed of. Of the sixteen horses, half had never had a cargo on their backs until that day; we had meant to break them in, but the waggon succumbed too soon to the hardships of the way, and before we had had time to carry out our intentions.

During the three days we remained in camp among the strong-scented yellow flowers where the waggon lay, all hands had been hard at work sewing up stores into the skins of guanacos, which I had killed for food on the march. The proper arranging of packs for horses is a very difficult matter; shape, size and weight have all to be considered. Each cargo should be divided into three portions, the balance of the two sides being carefully adjusted, and the centre piece, that which surmounts the pack-saddle, should not be more than twelve inches high. There should be at least two rugs and a sheepskin underneath the saddle. As we had not enough sheepskins, the pelts of guanaco were in some cases made to serve our purpose. Several different forms of pack-saddle have each of them points to recommend them, but to my mind the form used on the cattle-plains of North America is preferable to any other, and is more easily loaded, as the horse can be led between the two side-packs, which are hung along upon hooks attached to the wooden frame of the saddle. The whole cargo is best kept in place by means of a couple of cinches or girths. This form of pack is, however, but little used in the Argentine Republic. With such pack-saddles Hähansen and I, at a later date, travelled one hundred and fifty miles, during which it was not necessary to stop more than once or twice to readjust the cargoes.

During the whole of our subsequent wanderings, the horses entered so much into our lives that some descriptive remarks having regard to the peculiarities of each will perhaps not be out of place. Any one who has been thrown very much into a close association with horses can hardly have failed to notice the extraordinary friendships which these animals not infrequently form between themselves.

Among our troop there was a pale bronze-coloured horse to which the Spanish language assigns the term Gateado. This creature's whole life was spent in close attendance upon the largest horse in the tropilla, a piebald, called by us the Big Overo. The Big Overo was a buck-jumper, and when we wanted to catch him, he and the Gateado, his intimate, were wont to evade us together. If we could catch the Big Overo by craft, the Gateado was as good as captured also; but if, unluckily, our first attempt upon the Big Overo failed, both animals made a point of charging about the camp and frightening all the other horses. On one occasion, when it was judged well to give the Big Overo a lesson, Hughes bolassed him and after a gallop of a couple of hundred yards he came to the ground in an inextricable tangle.[5] The Gateado remained by his side and allowed himself to be caught without any struggle. After a time the intimacy between these horses grew to such a pitch that we gradually dispensed with a rope for the Gateado, knowing that if the Big Overo was once tied up his friend would stand beside him and allow us to put on his cargo quietly. This odd friendship finally reached such an extreme that when the Big Overo was sogaed out for the night, the Gateado was in the habit of giving up his hours of feeding in order to satisfy the claims of friendship. The feeling was mutual, for the Big Overo manifested almost as many proofs of his preference.

MRS TRELEW

Another case of friendship was struck up between two of the madrinas, but this was an essentially feminine affection, all upon one side. The Rosada would follow the Trelew mare, who was in foal, and would hardly allow her to feed in peace. Mrs. Trelew, as the men nicknamed the round-barrelled old black mare, objected very strongly to the advances of her admirer, and once they had a regular quarrel owing to Mrs. Trelew kicking the Rosada with such force as to nearly break her ribs, which the latter rather resented. The Rosada was a vicious unbacked brute within five yards of whose heels it was unsafe to approach, and she, in common with the long-maned Little Zaino, acquired the execrable habit of attempting to kick any one who on horseback ventured to come near. This is a trick that is very rare even among the most untamable and vicious horses, which, although they will kick a man on foot, will seldom do so when he is mounted.

YEGUA ROSADA

Then there was the Old Zaino, a melancholy animal of the sardonic school. He was the worst of all the horses. I remember once Burbury making me laugh very much by saying in a moment of indignation: "You haven't been a colt these thirty years, you evergreen son of a buckjumper!" This horse had a way of coming to standstill in the very centre of the troop on the march, and, after regarding us with a patient but baleful eye, he would solemnly buck all his cargo off and attempt to kick it to pieces. At one time he was used as a riding-horse, having, indeed, a turn for speed, but his paces were so rough and his trick of rearing as one was mounting so uncomfortable that we were compelled to make him one of the cargueros.

But perhaps the horse that caused us the most amusement was the Asulejo. He was a sort of uncertain dapple-grey in colour, and to look at him you would say that a more quiet, lazy, say-nothing-to-anybody little bit of old age did not crop the grass in Patagonia. Often and often did we feel sorry for that little animal and lighten his load. One afternoon, as we came along with the waggon, he seemed to be thinking more and more of the past, of the time when he had the power to make his riders sit tight and used to be a creature of some truculence. He had upon his back a light cargo of cooking-pots, and it took the undivided attention of one man to keep him at a walk. We fixed our camp upon an open plateau of coarse grass and thorn beside a lagoon in a shallow hollow. The cargoes were pulled off and the cook of the night made a grateful smoke ascend. I took a shot-gun and went after some geese for the morrow's breakfast. It was, perhaps, an hour and a half later, and a good league from camp, that I heard the neighing of horses, and was surprised to see seventeen of our troop hurrying off, as it were, upon some unknown errand. And well in front of them—could I believe my eyes?—was the horse we knew as the Asulejo, but his eye was brighter and he neighed in the joy of his heart as he trotted friskily along! He was the obvious leader of the revolt. No sooner did he see me than he fell behind, trying to look as though one of the younger animals had lured him from the path of duty, but that pretence did not serve, and after driving him back into camp we put maneas on him, upon which he recognised with the philosophy of age that he could not fight against the inevitable, and so retired into the lee of a thorn-bush, where he lay down to dream, no doubt, of the days when things were different and he had been a scampering three-year-old on the banks of the River Negro.

THE ASULEJO

However, to return to our journey, and our earliest attempt at marching without a waggon. It was first and last one of the most trying days that we experienced. To begin with, the eight fairly well-behaved horses were cargoed up, and then the wild ones were taken in hand. The first of these happened to be the Gateado. His load was flour and tinned beef. He allowed himself to be saddled up with no more than the usual accompaniment of blowing and snorting. He even suffered his cargo to be slung and the noose to be slipped along the cinch until it was in place.

Every horse needs two men to put on his cargo. One ties the knot and hauls while the other takes in the slack. The latter has to hold up his side of the cargo with his shoulder, and to do this must get pretty nearly under the animal.

In our case, although we jettisoned a portion of our belongings—including, I am sorry to say, a number of birds which I had spent my evenings in skinning, and which I truly grieved to leave behind—some of the packs were of necessity rather unwieldy. This, indeed, is almost always the case during the earlier stages of any expedition.

The behaviour of the Gateado was similar to that of many of the cargueros. He waited until his man was well under, and then he came into action with a series of diabolically well-aimed, one-legged kicks. Having after a little got rid of us by this means, he went on to buck all his cargo off, and then stood with his saddle cork-screwed round under his belly. Jones held on to the head-rope, or no doubt the Gateado would have completed his performance by clearing off into the low hills or hummocks which surrounded the place.

Most of the others were, in their separate ways, as bad as the Gateado. Some bucked, some reared, some would not be approached, but all agreed in one thing—all, when cargoed up and ready for the start, solemnly lay down and rolled on their cargoes. If they got them loose, the wretched animals rose again and bucked them within reach of their heels, after which they extricated themselves by kicking.

That morning was, indeed, a study of shifting cargoes. They came off all ways, bucked off, kicked off, rolled on. Some stuck out to port of the horse and some to starboard, a few hung disconsolately beneath the carguero's body. Again and again we did our part, and again and again the horses defeated us by their horrible tricks of lying down and rolling. Meantime the sun had risen, and heat and flies were added to the long tally of the day's disagreeable items. A very heavy wind was also blowing, which made it exceedingly difficult to place the saddle-cloths upon the horses' backs. I have often noticed that, when saddling up a colt or wild horse, it is well to make use each day of the same saddle-cloths, as he grows used to these, and does not fear them, especially if you allow him to bite and smell them.

At length, however, shortly after midday the horses began to get worn out. The cargoed ones ceased to struggle and lay still, tongues out, fat-barrelled, like a troop on a battle-field, humped with cargo and grotesquely dead. In the fighting-line, I remember, remained only a horse named Horqueta (the slit-eared), and the indefatigable Gateado. Horqueta's cargo consisted of a pair of tin boxes, for, bucking apart, he was a fairly steady pack-horse. He and the Gateado were the last to be finished, the others having yielded after the long struggle of the forenoon.

All would now have gone well had it not been for the fact that the handles of one of the tin boxes upon Horqueta were loose. The moment we let him go he began to buck and the unlucky handles to beat a devil's tattoo upon the body of the tin box. He made off into the troop of cargoed horses, and the noise he brought with him proved too much for their nerves. They scrambled up to their feet and four of them broke away in different directions. Five minutes later we surveyed once more a scene of scattered cartridges, flour, oatmeal, sacks of beans, clothes, skins bumped out with tinned provisions, and I don't know what else. They lay in confusion among the grass and bushes in the valley, and up and down the slopes of the conical mud hills. The Germans were reduced to inarticulate oaths, and the Welshmen looked out of heart.

But to camp upon a failure is the worst of business and of policy, and so the men were laughed into a good humour, and we all went at it once more, the ammunition and our other goods were collected and the cargoes were fixed up yet again.

It was ten minutes past three o'clock by my watch when we rode slowly up the cliff that lay between Waggon Camp and the River Chico of Chubut. We reached the top without mishap, chiefly, I think, because the horses were now fairly exhausted with their exertions. At the top of the rise we stopped and looked back; our broken waggon lay dark and low among the coarse yellow weeds, the afternoon sun, still warm, beat upon the bald hills, and that was the last we saw of our unlucky camp.

The procession moved slowly on, and we did not rest until twilight, by which time we had travelled between twelve and thirteen miles. Our march now lay along the banks of the Chico. The going was soft, and more bushes began to appear on the landscape. That night we celebrated our first carguero journey by serving out cocoa for all hands.

The night we struck the River Chico was a very cold one, the temperature falling 12° below freezing-point. These figures, however, give no idea of the cold, as one of the characteristics of Patagonia is the prevalence of tremendous winds. And when these blow from the direction of the Cordillera, they bring with them chilly memories of the snows over which they have passed. Wind, of course, increased the rigours of the cold, and I remember that during the night on which we felt the cold most severely the temperature did not fall below 35°.

The next morning we got off about 10.30, having less trouble with the cargueros. I went on in front to choose our way, which here passed over very bad ground.

THE AUTHOR'S TWO BEST HORSES, THE CRUZADO AND ALAZAN

At the midday halt it was found that only part of a haunch of guanaco had been brought on from the last camp. I therefore galloped on ahead with a shot-gun and shot thirteen ducks, of which only six came to hand, as several fell among the reeds in the marshes which fringe the river. Of these six ducks, four were brown pintails (Dafila spinicauda) and two were Chiloe widgeon (Mareca sibilatrix). In the afternoon I exchanged the shot-gun for the rifle, as a few more guanaco-skins would be very handy for various purposes and meat was wanted. About four o'clock, when riding behind the troop, I saw a guanaco among the hills to the east. I was fortunately mounted upon the Cruzado, who had by this time learned to stand to shot and to remain standing when his reins were dropped over his head. He was infinitely the best shooting-horse in the troop, and I used always to ride him when game was wanted, although, owing to his being a large horse, his canter was not suited to riding behind the tropilla. He had come to us with a very bad name for throwing himself back, which is one of the nastiest tricks a horse can possess. But this he soon gave up, and except that he always remained rather hard to catch in the mornings, was what an advertiser would call "a thoroughly confidential horse." I am glad to think that when I left Patagonia he became the property of Burbury.

The Cruzado seemed to enter into the spirit of the chase, and in the present instance went off at a fast canter towards the hills. The guanaco had moved from his point of vantage upon the top of a conical hill of mud, and had probably, according to the custom of these animals, sought another eminence. I thought he had seen me, in which case he would at once have made for the highest point within reach, but, as I came into the throat of the gorge where there were some mud hills, I saw him again upon the side of a large hummock one hundred feet or so in height. I immediately tied up my horse.

The guanacos of the valley of the Chico were very wild owing to the fact that the Tehuelche Indians hunt them there during the months of October and November. This valley was once celebrated for the abundance of its game, but of recent years the herds seem to have moved westwards and northwards. This guanaco was the first we had seen that day.

I crawled up the hill, sinking to my knees at every step into the dry mud. When half-way up I saw the ears of the guanaco appear against the sky-line. I lay down, and he remained still and utterly unconscious of my presence for some minutes. He was watching my companions, who, with the horses, were moving off into dimness down the valley. Presently he ran forward one or two steps and gave out his high-pitched neighing laugh in a sort of strange defiance at our retreating troop. He was a very old buck with dark markings on his face. He was about fifty yards away, and when I fired he reared and fell backwards. I threw out the cartridge, and at the same instant seven guanacos, startled by the report, dashed across the valley and galloped along parallel to me on the other side of the cañadon at about one hundred yards distance. I fired at the second one because it looked fat, and brought it to the ground. The guanacos now turned in great affright and raced past me again, when I dropped two more. This brought them to a standstill, as they had not yet made out where the shots were coming from, and no doubt I might have been able to shoot the entire herd, but we had now enough skins. When I rose the remaining four sprang down into the valley and disappeared up the opposite barranca.

I now went to the top of the hill, where I had fired at the old buck, and found that the bullet had broken his neck. He was, as I had surmised, a very old animal, and bore upon him traces of an encounter with a puma. The skin of his neck was immensely thick and his teeth were worn down. One of the other guanacos, which had fallen upon the far side of the valley, proved to be a year-old doe, so it was unnecessary to take any of the meat of the buck. I now signalled, and Burbury soon joined me to help in cutting up.

When we overtook the horses we found that the hounds, Tom and Bian had killed a cavy (Dolichotis patagonica), so that we had a good stock of meat. The cavy is excellent eating, resembling English hare. I was told that Tom had not covered himself with glory, for, although he proved himself very fast, and turned the hare, it was Bian that killed it. Bian was a rough, yellow lurcher, who stood the rough ground and hard experiences of our journey very much better than Tom, although the latter was a well-bred hound with a pedigree to back his pretensions. Bian belonged to young Jones.

During the day we observed enormous flocks of Chilian widgeon (Mareca sibilatrix) as well as some grey teal (Querquedula versicolor).

On October 22, as we had expected, we arrived at Colohuapi, the farthest settlement in the heart of Patagonia. Near by lie twin lakes Colhué and Musters. About one o'clock, coming over a rise, we saw the Lake. As the sun was shining it was very blue, and upon the far side rose the hills. The mournful whistle of waterfowl in countless flocks was to be heard. A breeze from the north-west was blowing across the lake, and there was that peculiar wet smell in the wind which can only be derived from a passage across wide waters.

This day the Gateado bucked off his cargo of tinned meats and was unfortunate enough to give himself a deep wound in the pastern. Jones tied it up with his handkerchief, and the horse was so lame that we thought it would be necessary to leave him behind at Colohuapi. As it turned out, however, being of a very strong constitution, he improved rapidly, and was with us to the very end of our journeyings.

Our march on this occasion was upwards of twenty-seven miles, and at the end of it I rode ahead to choose a place for a camp. Earlier in the day Burbury, who was riding the Colorado, a half-broken colt that had had only a few gallops, got into difficulties, and I relieved him of a bag which he was carrying. I had tied this bag to my saddle, but just before we camped it came loose, and, thinking I was not going to have any other chance of shooting, I slung it over my rifle, which I was carrying across my shoulder as usual in a sling. I had chosen a valley to camp in and turned round to jog quietly back to meet the troop, when with the tail of my eye I caught sight of an animal which I thought was Tom, but it looked too large, and I turned my head to see it more fully. There, fifteen yards behind my horse, staring at me, switching its tail slowly from side to side, and standing full up, was a fine male puma (F. concolor). I rolled off my horse, which, fortunately, had neither seen nor winded the puma, and began to unsling my rifle. In the middle of the operation, when I already had the hindering bag upon the ground, the puma, which up to that moment had continued to lash its tail and stare at me, turned round and loped off at the cumbrous and uncouth canter habitual to these animals. At one hundred and fifty yards it stopped for an instant, but was off again at once. I attempted to mount my horse with the idea of galloping down the puma, an easy thing to do, as these animals never run far, and are readily blown, but the horse, which happened to be a mule-footed oscuro, known as Mula, became quite unmanageable. I at once coo-ed and was joined by young Humphrey Jones, who in eighteen years' residence in Patagonia had never seen a puma, and as he had strong sporting instincts, was extremely anxious to encounter one. We followed the track of the lion—as the puma is locally called—but after topping the hill it led along a bare slope and was lost in a clump of high dry bush, where it was quite hopeless to find the creature. We rode back into camp very disappointed.

Just as Mr. Selous remarks that hunters sometimes spend years in Africa before they come upon their first lion, so many a man is as long in Patagonia before he comes across his first puma. The puma is a very furtive and cowardly animal, and though we saw so few during our months of travel, I have no doubt that many a puma watched our troop passing across the pampa from the safe cover of rocks and bushes. Seeing or not seeing pumas is purely a matter of luck, and the tales concerning pumas having attacked men, which abound in the country, are generally fabrications. A puma with young will attack man if he stumbles upon her and her family, and my friend Mr. Waag told me that on one occasion a puma in the Cordillera had shown evident signs of attack. In the majority of cases, even when wounded, the puma will only snarl and spit, and the Indians, as well as the Gauchos, despatch it with the bolas.

The puma is a terrible foe to the sheep-farmer, levying heavy toll upon flocks, and often enjoys a long career of sheep-killing before strychnine or the bullet puts an end to its existence.

The snow is directly responsible for the death of a great many pumas, for when it is lying on the ground the animals can easily be tracked. At this season the shepherds of the estancias near the coast attempt to clear the ground of their very unwelcome visitors, the weapon most commonly used being the .450 revolver, and the shot is often taken at a distance of less than ten paces. The puma is very easy to kill, especially if the first shot is well placed. It is the first shock which tells in the case of these animals.

Great sport could, no doubt, be had with the puma were he hunted with a pack of dogs that would bay him and distract his attention. The average hound of the country is, however, far too wise to pit himself against such an animal, and will often even refuse to acknowledge the scent.

That night the lake, as seen from the camp, was wonderfully beautiful. The waters were leaden-grey bounded by faint blue hills, with soft mists of an unearthly green clinging about them. The only sounds to be heard were the wash of the ripple on the shore and plashing of wildfowl.

On October 23 we made as early a start as possible, and pursued our way over very level pampa, which had not yet been hardened by the sun of spring. We put up an ostrich (Rhea darwini) from his nest, and found three eggs. Presently there appeared in the centre of the pampa, ahead of us, three little huts of earth and three black cattle. Save for one gorge through which the River Senguerr flows, and through which we afterwards took our way, a perfect circle of hills of greatly varying heights surrounded the small settlement. The huts belonged to a Welshman named William Jones, who, with his wife and six children, had trekked out here some six or eight months previously.

One of the three huts, which was untenanted, Mr. Jones put at our disposal, and after taking off the cargoes, Burbury and Scrivenor accompanied me across to William Jones' home. Mrs. Jones received us with hospitality and treated us to maté with milk, tea and scones, and we got a sight of ourselves in the looking-glass. The wind of the pampas had removed all the skin from our faces, and we were a good deal unlike the individuals who had started from Trelew some four or five weeks before.

SETTLEMENT OF COLOHUAPI

That night the men slept inside the hut, but it was too warm for my sleeping-bag, so I took up my bed and went out, passing the night on the lee side of the hut. Perhaps what delighted us most was the fact that in the shelter of the hut we were able to smoke our pipes in peace, safe from the buffeting of the wind.

At dawn Mrs. Jones kindly sent her children over with a pail of milk. It would be impossible to imagine any more healthy specimens of the Welsh race than these sun-kissed, clear-eyed youngsters. Ruddy and brown and strong, the air of the wilderness had need of no better proof of its splendid health-giving qualities. I gave the children chocolate from our store, a luxury to which they were not accustomed, and which they enjoyed immensely.

William Jones had brought his wife and family to Colohuapi in a waggon, following the banks of the River Chico from Trelew. His journey had, however, been made late in the year, when the marshes were dry, and his waggon had been more suited to the hardships of the way than was ours.

Two other Welshmen with their wives lived higher up the valley, and the full strength of the colony was made up by a Swede named Oscar, who acted as comisario, and an Argentine who had settled on the other side of the river. To the last-named gentleman Burbury paid a visit on the following day.

Now set in another era of preparation. We purchased sheepskins and laid in a stock of mutton, and on the 25th once more made a start. Before taking leave of Colohuapi I should like to record my appreciation of the great kindness which the settlers there extended to us especially Mr. and Mrs. William Jones, the latter of whom was thoughtful enough to bake us a large loaf to speed us on our way. On the eve of our departure we gave a small dinner, at which the menu was as follows: Mutton puchero, made with desiccated potatoes and cabbage; stewed apple-rings and milk; lime-juice tablets; chocolate food; and two tins of sardines. I was very sorry not to be able to add a bowl of punch to the feast, but the fact was I had with me but three bottles of brandy, and those for purely medicinal purposes.

The country round about Colohuapi is very suited for cattle-breeding, but, of course, the chief difficulty encountered by the colonists are those connected with transporting their produce to the market, as the district is not yet in any way opened up. But I hope and believe that a prosperous future lies before the young settlement, and much of the good to come should certainly fall to the lot of the Welshmen William and Walter Jones, whose pioneer efforts deserve great reward. At present it is a hard life that the colonists are obliged to lead, divided as they are by more than a couple of hundred miles from their nearest white neighbours. One could not help being struck by the solitary aspect of the two or three small huts, set as they are at present on the edge of the hill-encircled empty plain.

Just as we were off from Colohuapi, the comisario rode up and proceeded to make the necessary examination of our horses. In this connection very strict laws obtain throughout the northern provinces of the Argentine Republic. In a country where horse-breeding is carried on upon so extensive a scale, and where, besides, the animals are allowed to wander freely upon the wide spaces of the pampas, a strong check must be placed upon any infringement of the law of property. A strict system of registration and surveillance as to brands upon horses must be kept in force, and is, in fact, one of the first steps towards security.

The brand, which I had registered in Trelew, and which was invented by Burbury, represented the rising sun. It was an excellent brand, as it had not much "fire" about it, and was very different to any other mark we came across. Another point to be considered in choosing it was that it would be a difficult one to fake. Our branding took place at Bahia Camerones, Mr. Greenshields being good enough to allow us to use his corral for the purpose. Our half-wild horses did not permit us to operate upon them without a struggle. A few days after the operation the burns caused by the iron had quite healed.

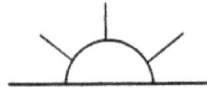

OUR BRAND

FOOTNOTE:
[5] *Except in very rare cases the boleadores should not be used to catch horses. For a kicking animal they are, however, a good corrective.*

CHAPTER V

THE RIVER VALLEYS

Arbitrary distribution of animals in Patagonia—Trouble with Gauchos—Indian guide—Germans turned back—Cañadon of River Senguerr—Bad weather—Old

Zaino again causes damage—Loss of clothes, ammunition, &c., in the river—Shooting upland geese— River Mayo—Hailstorm—A day's sport in Patagonia—Shooting a wild cow—Was it a wild cow?— Musters' account of wild cattle—First meeting with Tehuelche Indians.

In consequence of the visit of the comisario we were somewhat late in starting from Colohuapi, but nevertheless made a good march of about fifteen miles, and camped in the valley, after driving the two horses past a bend of the river that would prevent them from attempting to break back towards their pasture at Colohuapi. The day was very warm indeed and the night rather cold, the thermometer at midday and at night being respectively 74° F. and 37° F.

We were now upon the banks of the River Senguerr, the Senguel of Captain Musters.

The extraordinary tameness of the upland geese in the neighbourhood of Colohuapi was very remarkable; they allowed one to approach within eighty yards before bestirring themselves. After the first day's march beyond Colohuapi we never saw again any specimen of the Patagonian cavy (Dolichotis patagonica), although round the shores of the lakes Musters and Colhué these animals abound. It is strange that the habitat of the cavy should be so sharply defined, considering that there appears to be no apparent reason, such as alteration of the nature of the ground or vegetation, to account for the fact. The armadillo (Dasypus minutus), which is found in numbers on the north bank of the River Santa Cruz, is entirely absent from the south bank, nor, to my knowledge, has a single specimen ever been secured there. This instance of the distribution of the armadillo agrees with other facts of the same kind which are common to Patagonia. The rivers running from west to east across the continent mark the limit of the distribution of some of the mammals. Thus I am assured the jaguar (Felis onca) is not to-day found south of the River Negro. And the puma does not exist in Tierra del Fuego, the dividing water in this latter instance being the Straits of Magellan. The guanaco, however, is distributed throughout the whole of Patagonia and also in Tierra del Fuego. I met with this animal deep inside the Cordillera, and indeed once, with consecutive shots, I killed a huemul and a guanaco.

About this time it became apparent that neither Fritz nor Hollesen, the German Gauchos, were very much in love with the hard work and hardships which they conceived lay before them. It was a favourite trick of theirs to fall out of the troop on the plea of fixing a cargo, and then, as soon as we were lost to sight, to sit down and smoke their pipes; in fact, they had determined to take things easy. On the evening of our leaving Colohuapi Hollesen asked me for some cartridges for his revolver, saying that when working under the Argentine Boundary Commission he had had a quarrel with an Indian concerning the Indian's wife, and that he feared meeting him, for the man had sworn to be revenged.

During the night the dogs ate about ten kilos of mutton which we had brought with us from Colohuapi, although it was wrapped up in a tent, so the next morning we were forced to breakfast upon an old gander, that made a very tough and tasteless puchero. Our next march was about six leagues, and that evening an Indian rode into our camp and offered to guide us across the pampa to Lake Buenos Aires. He was a Tehuelche, and he told us that some of his tribe were encamped in the valley of the River Mayo at its junction with the River Chalia. All the following day, leaving the river and guided by the Indian, we rode across bare stony pampa devoid of game, and in the evening, after passing three lagoons, we made our camp round a spring of water. As, owing to the depredations of the dogs, we had no fresh food, I took the gun and attempted to stalk a couple of upland geese.

THE GERMANS

As I was returning unsuccessful, Burbury met me and told me that the Germans had again been giving him trouble. I was prepared for the news, as I had noticed they were inclined to shirk work of late, constantly lingering behind and in every way making themselves objectionable. On an expedition where there is naturally plenty of work for every one, it is useless to have men who growl at doing their fair proportion of it. They were also trying to influence the other Gauchos, for this trick of deserting at a critical time, when their services cannot be replaced, is a very old one with peones, who on such occasions can sometimes force their employers into giving them disproportionately high wages. I was, of course, resolved not to yield to their demands but to push forward, even if they left us. I consulted with

Burbury, who agreed that we could manage without their help, though it would leave us awkwardly short-handed.

On arriving at the camp I asked the Germans the reason of their late behaviour, but they could give me no satisfactory answer, but burst into a tirade about an inoffensive companion, Barckhausen, which was obviously only an excuse to cover their real designs. I told them they must in future behave properly or else leave my camp next morning. After a certain amount of talk and bluster Fritz said that not only Hollesen and he but the Welsh peones would in that case turn back.

During the course of the evening I spoke to Jones, who informed me that Fritz had persuaded him to desert, but on my pointing out that this would not be a very wise proceeding, he at once threw in his lot with us.

In the morning, finding I was of the same mind, the Germans again informed me of their wish to turn back. I therefore gave them food to last them upon their journey to civilisation, as well as the worst buck-jumper of the troop, and told them to leave the camp as soon as possible. Fritz, after some further talk and after remarking to Hollesen in German that they had better have stayed after all, climbed on to the horse and rode away.

The Germans at the outset had been admirable workers, apart from their cunning, which tinged most of their conduct. Yet perhaps, if they had gone on with us, we might have paid for Hollesen's misdoings with the Indians, by getting into trouble with the tribe who had saved his life and whom he had so scurvily requited. As it happened, a few days later we came upon the very tribe with whom he had had to do.

I will now take some extracts from my diary:

"October 28.—The Germans left us this morning. I think we shall be all the better without them. Immediately on their departure I determined to march to the cañadon or valley of the River Senguerr, giving up the route suggested by the Indian, as it was likely that the horses would stray upon the pampa. It was necessary to decrease the weight of some of our cargo, which we at once set about doing. The reason for this was that, having so few men, each pair of us would have to look after six cargueros, or pack-horses, and we were consequently obliged to lessen their number.

"While we were getting ready a thin rain and a yelling wind came down the cañadon as we started to catch the horses. The salt marsh over which the Germans had gone lay behind us, and ahead were shallow lagoons around which the tussocks whistled in the wind. But I think we none of us noticed the inclemency of the weather, we were soaked to the skin as we worked, and in an hour and a half—a record as to time in cargoing up even with the aid of the men who had gone—we had loaded the last carguero of the twelve, and with extra ropes hanging to the saddles, a brandy bottle protruding from each of the pockets of Barckhausen and with Jones perched high and stirrupless upon a sack of beans, we set off."

Providentially, not a single cargo shifted, although we covered something like fourteen miles. I should have mentioned that one of the reasons which weighed with me in again seeking the cañadon of the River Senguerr was the fact that four of the horses had strayed in the night. It was our intention to camp as soon as we reached a suitable place in the valley and to scour the country for the lost horses. This, however, turned out not to be necessary, as we came right upon the truants grazing in the mouth of a small rift in the cliff of the cañadon. One of them cantered out with a neigh to meet the troop upon the hillside.

It rained so heavily in the night that we put up the tent and were glad of its warm shelter. Morning came with pearl-grey mists in the valley. We worked like slaves, and our hands became very sore with the new cargo-ropes.

RIVER SENGUERR, WHERE DISASTER OVERTOOK US

The next day, had I but known it, marked the last of our misfortunes, for after that we enjoyed as good luck as we had hitherto experienced the reverse.

We spent most of the morning in slowly marching a couple of leagues, and then Scrivenor, who was leading, came back to say that our way was barred by a sheer cliff, close under which the river ran. Burbury, however, was of the opinion that it would be easier to proceed than to attempt to scale the tall barranca, which was our only alternative choice. We straggled across the half-dry marshy grass that fringed the river-bed, which here winds greatly.

Presently we climbed on to a steep slope on the cliffs, where directly below us the river ran with a current of about three knots. The passage along this slope was very difficult, and we were driving the horses with infinite care. The face of the cliff was scarred with the traces of a landslip. One of the horses, the Old Zaino, so called not because of any weight of years, but on account of the gravity of his demeanour, climbed up and up, in spite of all our efforts, among the shifting earth and loose stones until he was some hundred feet above the main body of the troop. He was a tall, ewe-necked animal, and always bore an exasperating expression of insulted dignity. He was carrying a cargo of flour.

When he had, in his own opinion, managed to get sufficiently ahead of his companions, he stopped dead and looked down upon us with a baleful eye as we toiled beneath him. Then suddenly, but methodically, he began to descend towards us in a succession of devastating bucks. No cargo, tied with ropes, could withstand such treatment. The cinch gave way, and he and his pack arrived simultaneously in the middle of the troop.

THE OLD ZAINO

He cannoned against a black horse carrying ammunition and oatmeal, and it began to slide down the cliff towards the river on its haunches. The remainder of the horses stampeded, some fell, some got into impossible positions.... For several minutes the big black horse hung within measurable distance of violent death upon the rocks below, but Barckhausen made a great effort to save him, and succeeded, though the cargo was kicked off in a most perilous place. Only a guanaco track led along the steep hillside, and over the edge of the slope our belongings dropped into the river a hundred feet below. Each lifted a small cloud of spray as it fell and floated serenely away on the current or sank from sight. The water was dotted with the various packages. All Burbury's clothes, some of mine, flour, oatmeal, a case of corned beef, six hundred rounds of ammunition, and the concertina—these were among our losses.

THE GUANACO (AN INTIMATE OF THE OLD ZAINO'S)

A salvage-party was at once despatched to attempt the rescue of such of our goods as were still swimming, while the rest of us collected the horses and returned with a sufficiency of ropes to enable us to get down the cliff, for upon the ragged edge left by the landslip and overhanging the river some of our things had lodged. We felt that we were for the time being out of luck. We had not long lost the waggon, and now followed the losing of important stores and the yet more important ammunition. We knotted together eight of the cargo-ropes, and while Scrivenor and I were doing this, Barckhausen retrieved one of the boxes of ammunition, and told us that there were a couple more farther down, and out of reach, he feared, which had stuck in the soft earth of the landslip. However, with the aid of the rope I managed to bring both up to safe ground.

"During this time we could see Burbury and Jones far away in the valley, where the river narrowed and the current swinging near the bank offered a hopeful chance of catching the floating articles. They succeeded in dragging ashore most of the packages, but Burbury's clothes, which were in a brown waterproof bag, sank, the bag, I fancy, having filled with water. Our total losses thus amounted to 200 12-bore cartridges, a tin of Mauser ammunition, a 25-kilo bag of oatmeal, and the clothes. On the whole we could not help thinking things might have been very much worse.

"The horses had meantime come to a standstill in a patch of high grass farther along beneath the barranca, and there we rounded them up and re-cargoed.

"When this was done it was found that we had another place, almost as difficult as that upon which we had come to grief, to surmount. This time, however, Burbury led a horse in front, and the others followed meekly in his track. We had wasted several hours in negotiating the first barranca, and it was soon time to camp. As we had no meat, I went to see if I could not kill some geese (Chloephaga magellanica), which I had observed upon a neck of land, that stretched out into the river. There were five geese, and I was lucky enough to kill two, both females, which are very much more tender than the males. On one side of the camp was a chain of small lagoons, evidently formed by the overflow of the river, and in one of these I saw a flock of brown pintails. These were easily stalked behind the rushes, and the discharge of two barrels of the 12-bore left five upon the water. At dark a storm of rain blew up.

THE ALAZAN COLT (NEARLY KILLED ON THE SENGUERR)

"October 30.—This cargoing work is very wearisome, and has got upon our nerves. Even in one's sleep one sees the reeling, writhing mass of kicking and struggling cargueros on the white and ragged-sided barranca.[6] Got off at 10.30 and reached the River Mayo, a very small stream here, flowing through a wide valley lined by bare steep cliffs 200 feet or so in height. We are all becoming quite expert with the cargoes; Burbury and Barckhausen, and Jones and I work in pairs. The newness has now worn off the ropes, and hauling on them does not any longer cut our hands. Still an occasional cargo shifts, and the horse, wildly refusing to be caught, gallops away kicking at his cargo. Thus did the Alazan to-day, scattering Mauser ammunition among the bushes, and kicking the spout from our last kettle, so that we can only fill it half full.

"There is comparatively little game in this bit of country, few guanaco, and those very wild because of the Indians, whose beat we are now approaching. When there is rain, which fortunately is not often, we have to carry our change of clothing upon our saddles to dry them. To-day Jones was very much loaded up with his extra breeches and top boots, that were wet, a gun-cover, fifty rounds of ammunition dropped by the Alazan, two ducks, a telescope, and a water-bottle!

"October 31.—Soon after we started a big cloud blew out of the south and brought with it a heavy hailstorm, which whistled before a driving wind. The horses would not face it, but huddled together in the centre of the valley. We encamped early as we needed meat. Jones and I left the camp here among the sand-dunes in the valley and went a-hunting. We rode up a cañadon, in the centre of which our horses foundered in some very bad ground. Getting out of this we struck a stretch of desolate pampa, across which we cut towards the big cañadon of the Mayo in order to explore the route which we must follow upon the morrow. To my surprise we presently came to a clear stream, flowing through another wide cañadon, which joined the Mayo from a south-westerly direction. Can this be the River Genguel? The Indian guide told us that it would take us a month to get from here to Lake Buenos Aires. If it is the Genguel, however, we should arrive at the lake in ten marches—a very different matter. It would be as well to halt to-morrow for the day, so that an observation may be taken to determine this point, and also to enable us to go hunting, as we have but one duck in the camp, and, since our losses at the Senguerr barranca, it is more than ever necessary to save our stock of tinned provisions.

"To-day the Old Zaino, this time fortunately not carrying a cargo, again attempted to repeat his trick of the Senguerr barranca, but was circumvented by Burbury and Barckhausen.

"November 1.—To-day Scrivenor shot the sun 70° 56′ W. long, and 45° 39′ S. lat. So the river we saw yesterday is the Genguel, which is excellent. Jones and I went out to shoot for the pot. As there were no guanaco in the neighbourhood, he took the Paradox and I my 12-bore, and we confined ourselves to following some flocks of upland geese which we had observed in the valley. I will describe the day's sport at length, as it was very typical of Patagonian wild-fowl shooting in a fairly good district.

"We rode our horses, of course, I taking the Cruzado and Jones 'J.V.E.' a small brown animal, so called because he bears that brand upon his flank. The first geese we came upon were a party of five standing upon an island in the Mayo. As it was impossible to stalk these birds we tried driving, and I sent Humphrey Jones, who, by the way, was a very keen sportsman, to attempt to drive them over me, where I had taken up my quarters in some bushes upstream above them on the bank. Jones meantime made a large circle and galloped up towards them. When he was within about 200 yards they rose, and honking indignantly made straight up in my direction, flying, however, a little too wide. They went down again about a quarter of a mile away, and we repeated our tactics, I remaining where I was. I could not help thinking how much time was saved by Jones being on horseback. Had he been on foot it would have taken him a long time in that bare valley to fetch a circle big enough. As it was, in five minutes the birds were again on the wing, and this time they gave me a chance and I brought down two; one, however, falling on the other side of the river, had to be abandoned."

Any one who travels through Patagonia cannot fail to be struck by the enormous quantities of upland geese (Chloephaga magellanica) which abound in the vicinity of the rivers and lagoons. At this time a great many of the birds are paired, but at a latter date in the valley of the Coyly we once made a camp round which the country in all directions was covered by thousands of these geese. After our shot Jones rejoined me and we proceeded to the edge of a small lagoon, where he told me he had seen some ducks. On approaching it I examined the birds through my telescope and discovered them to be brown pintails (Dafila spinicauda). I held the horses while Jones enjoyed the stalk, which ended in his killing two of the birds, to retrieve which it was necessary to wade into pretty deep water.

We now rode towards the valley of the Genguel, and there flushed innumerable snipe, at which we did not shoot, as we could not afford to waste ammunition on so small a bird. We next descried a flock of nineteen geese, which were peculiarly wideawake and would not allow us to approach for a long time, and presently we deserted their pursuit in favour of that of a single old gander that was standing upon the shingle beside the river. I got up quite close to this bird and had a rising shot at him as he flew across the stream. I killed him quite dead, but it seemed impossible to retrieve him, and we were rather disconsolately watching his body drift away when it struck us that Jones, who was very clever with the lasso, might manage to recover it at a point where the current brought it within reach of our side. We therefore galloped parallel to the bird along the bank, and after one or two ineffectual efforts, Jones succeeded in getting the lasso round him, and so dragged him in.

WILDGOOSE CAMP

"We next had lunch which consisted of maté. As we sat waiting for the kettle to boil, several blue-winged teal (Querquedula cyanoptera) passed over us and went down in a small marsh towards the Genguel. After these Jones had another stalk, and killed two. As he was returning a couple of geese flew over at about thirty-five yards distance, and he dropped the female quite dead. It is extraordinary what an amount of shot these geese will in a general way carry off with them. For all my shooting in Patagonia I used No. 4 shot and 26 gr. of ballistite. The gun which I used most was a 12-bore moderately choked in both barrels, and this I found answered every purpose of wild-fowl shooting in Patagonia excellently.

BAD STALKING (CALIFATE-BUSH ON PAMPA)

"At reasonable ranges a number of black-necked swans (Cygnus nigricollis) fell to this weapon.

"After picking up the goose, we again turned our attention to the nineteen that I have mentioned earlier. They then went on a good distance downstream, and here, under cover of the rushes, we stalked up within twenty yards of them, and shot three as they rose. One of the flock swung back, and both of us fired at him, bringing him down. Thinking we had enough geese, we decided to follow the ducks, which we did in a rather desultory manner. We bagged two more, both pintails, before we returned to camp in the evening, having had a very pleasant day's sport."

Although I never attempted to make a big bag upon any day during the time I spent in Patagonia, yet, no doubt, an enormous quantity of geese could be shot in a single day. Quite close to the settlements a couple of hundred might be secured by two guns in a day, and during the migration a far greater number.

The whole of the valley of the River Chico is excellent for wild-fowling, and I expected the numbers of birds to increase as we drew nearer to Lake Buenos Aires. And certainly in the cañadon of the River Deseado I was not disappointed, but of that I will write in its due place.

On November 2 we resumed our march, still following the valley of the Mayo, past the scenes of our sport of the previous day. A little after midday Jones saw a whitish object among some bushes at the edge of the river and asked my leave to go and see what it was. Presently he came riding back to say it was a wild cow and that he had observed her through the glasses. She was nearly a mile distant, and, taking my rifle, I rode off with Jones and we stalked her to about 200 yards. We again examined her carefully through the telescope, and seeing that she was five or six years old and unbranded, the fact of her belonging to a wild herd rather than being a truant escaped from the settlements two hundred miles away appeared to be certain. It was with considerable keenness that we crawled up nearer, as wild cattle afford the best sport of all Patagonian animals.

These wild cattle have some of them been wild for many generations, their remote ancestors probably being the herds which the Spaniards originally possessed in the Valdez Peninsula on the east coast during the earlier occupation of Patagonia. Since then from time to time numbers of cattle escape from the coast-farms and run wild, and, joining the older free herds, breed wild. Such herds are still to be found in considerable numbers among the foot-hills of the Cordillera. Musters in his book gives an account of meeting with a wild bull. "We had expected before reaching this point to have found cattle in considerable numbers, but the warmth of the day had probably driven them into the thickets to seek shelter..... Presently ... after riding about a mile, I espied two bulls. Two men were sent round to endeavour to drive the animals to a clearing where it would be possible to use the lassoo.... At the end of five minutes ... a yell from the other side put us anxiously on the alert, and we had the gratification to see one of the animals coming straight towards our cover. Alas! just as we were preparing to dash out, he turned on the edge of the plain, and after charging furiously at his pursuer dashed into a thicket, where he stood at bay. We immediately closed round him, and dismounting, I advanced on foot to try and bring him down with a revolver. Just as I got within half a dozen paces of him, and behind a bush was quietly taking aim at his shoulder, the Indians, eager for beef, and safe on their horses at a considerable distance off, shouted, 'Nearer, nearer!' I accordingly slipped from my cover, but had hardly moved a pace forward when my spur caught in a root, and at the same moment el Toro charged. Entangled with the root, I could not jump on one side as he came on; so, when within a yard I fired a shot in his face, hoping to turn him, and wheeled my body at the same instant to prevent his horns from catching me, as the sailors say, 'broadside on.' The shot did not stop him, so I was knocked down, and, galloping over me, he passed on with my handkerchief, which fell from my head, triumphantly borne on his horns, and stopped a few yards off under another bush. Having picked myself up and found my legs and arms all right, I gave him another shot, which, as my hand was rather unsteady, only took effect in the flank. My cartridges being exhausted, I returned to my horse and found that, besides being considerably shaken, two of my ribs had been broken by the encounter.

"The Indians closed round me, and evinced great anxiety to know whether I was much hurt. One, more courageous than the rest, despite the warning of the cacique, swore he would try and lasso the brute, and, accordingly, approached the infuriated animal, who for a moment or two showed no signs of stirring; just, however, as the Indian was about to throw his lasso, it caught in a branch, and before he could extricate it the bull was upon him. We saw the horse give two or three vicious kicks as the bull gored him. At length he was lifted clean up, the fore-legs alone remaining on the ground, and overthrown, the rider alighting on his head in a bush. We closed up and attracted the bull in another direction, then went to look for the corpse of our comrade, who, however, to our surprise, issued safe from the bush, where he had lain quiet and unhurt, though the horse was killed. This little incident cast a gloom over our day's pleasure, and lost us our Christmas dinner, as Orkeke ordered a retreat to the spot where we had left our mantles, although we tried to persuade him to attack the beast again, or, at any rate, remain and eat some of the dead horse, and try our luck next day, but he was inflexible.... On our way across the plain previously described, wild cattle were seen, and one chased; but he, although balled by Orkeke, contrived to slip the bolas, and escaping to cover, stood to bay, where he was left master of the field."

A DAUGHTER OF THE TOLDOS

In the present instance, however, nothing at all exciting was in store for us. My first bullet struck the cow behind the shoulder a little high, she went down upon her knees, and a second shot brought her to the ground. On our approaching she staggered to her feet, whereupon Jones gave her a shot in the brain. We then set about grallocking and skinning our quarry, and were delighted to find that she carried a good deal of fat. We were at the time running very short of this essential article of diet, for, as has been said, the guanacos supply none at this season of the year, when they are still in poor condition after the hardships of the winter.

When we had finished cutting up the meat, we packed it as well as we could upon our saddles and rode away. The amount of meat with which we had laden our saddles made them extremely uncomfortable; this was very much so in my own case, as I was riding a little black horse whose temper was not of the sweetest, and which had been but seldom ridden since our start, and was consequently very fresh and skittish. We had spent a long time over our task of cutting up the cow, and the troop had gone far ahead. After riding about an hour we saw a white bull upon the hillside above us, but on using the telescope perceived it carried a brand upon its flank. We therefore left it in peace.

A little later, as we were riding under the western barranca of the cañadon of the River Mayo, we came upon some fairly fresh tracks of sheep. This fact, taken in conjunction with the appearance of the white bull, made me begin to wonder whether it was possible that the cow I had shot might not prove to be a tame one. We pushed on more rapidly, the tracks growing sharper and more distinct. Presently the tracks began to run into beaten lines, and such always mean in Patagonia that man is not far off. As we rode we discussed the chances as to who the owners of the sheep would turn out to be, and this we found sufficiently exciting, as we had beheld no strange face for many a day.

Very soon, as we rode round a curve of the cliff, we came in sight of five armadillo-shaped tents lying snugly in the valley. We had not expected to come upon the Indians, who, so our guide had told us, were in the valley of the River Mayo, until some time later, but this was undoubtedly the encampment to which he had alluded. A number of sheep and of horses, together with a small herd of cattle, proved them to be an unusually rich tribe.

The remainder of our party, on sighting the huts of the Tehuelches, had halted and were waiting for my arrival. We now rode together in the direction of the tents, and, while we were yet afar off, the hounds about the squat tents broke into a chorus of barking. As we drew nearer we could see that the tall figures, wrapped in guanaco-skins, were standing in the openings of the toldos, on the look-out for the arrival whose presence had been heralded by the dogs. The sun was setting by this time over the high cliffs of the cañadon, and the toldos threw lengthened shadows upon the ground.

WATI! WATI! (TEHUELCHE EXCLAMATION OF SURPRISE)

When we came within a short distance, the Indians stepped forward, finely developed men, of a swarthy brown, with high cheek-bones, their coarse black hair falling round their faces, and tied about the brows with a red band. The tents seemed to be full to overflowing of old women and lean hounds, all huddled together upon the ground, and a crowd of curious faces peeped forth. The toldos were made of guanaco-skins, sewn loosely at their edges, and supported squarely on awkward-looking props or posts, forked at the top to admit the ridge-poles. The skins were fastened to the earth outside with wooden pegs. These dwellings appeared to be anything but weather-proof, for at the seams and lower edges were gaping slits, through which the sky or the ground was visible. As to the shape of the toldos, if you can imagine a very squat, deep-draught boat, cut off at rather beyond the half of her length, and turned upside down, you will have some idea of their appearance. On the roof, and about the wooden props, pieces of guanaco-meat had been hung out to dry in the sun. Within, as I have said, upon the skins which strewed the floor the dogs and grandmothers of the tribe were mingled.

It was our first experience of a Tehuelche encampment, and perhaps the most remarkable feature of it was the presence, in one form or another, of the guanaco. Some of his flesh was cooking at a fire outside the tents, the toldos themselves were composed of his pelts, the ponchos which some of the women were weaving were made from his wool, the boots were formed of his neck-skin, some of the horse-gear of his hide, the men's capas of his skin, while dogs, men, and women alike were fattened upon the food he provided. As I stood there, examining all these things, my mind kept running upon the cow which I had killed, and which I was now more than half afraid might have belonged to the Indians. If such proved to be the case, I knew that they would resent it very bitterly, and even perhaps attempt to make some sort of reprisals upon our horses. The idea of saying nothing about it, were my surmise as to the chance of its having been their property correct, struck me as being the least troublesome course to pursue; but nothing is more abhorrent than dealing in this way with aboriginal tribes. Personally, I should look upon picking the pocket of a civilised person as, in comparison, almost a meritorious action. I may as well say at once that I told them of the matter of the cow through the vaqueano or guide whom I hired from their tents, and offered to pay for it if it happened to be their property. The vaqueano, however, said that no cow of that colour belonged to their herd, and, taking into consideration that she was six years old and unmarked, I made my mind easy on this point.

I shall now break off from the thread of my narrative and give a description of the Tehuelches, detailing the facts which I gathered about them during my residence in Patagonia. I will only preface it by saying that few peoples are more interesting to study than the Tehuelches, of whom various travellers have given such widely differing accounts.

FOOTNOTE:
[6] Any traveller, settler or cattleman who is acquainted with the vagaries of cargueros will understand our position. Some of the horses which we used as cargueros had never before had a saddle upon their backs.

CHAPTER VI

MANNERS AND CUSTOMS OF THE TEHUELCHES

Indian method of curing measles—Driving out the devil—Magellan—Patagon—Long boots—Reports of travellers—One of the finest races in the world—Nomadic—Hunters—Decreasing in numbers—Introduction of horses—Bolas—No history—Keen bargainers but not progressive—Features—Good teeth—Women—Morality—Young and old women—Half-bloods—Paisanos—Reserved in character—Habits—Infants' heads bandaged—Dance—Wives bought—Price of a wife—Marriage ceremony—White man in toldos—Bad influence—Connections of white men and Tehuelche women—Dress and adornment of women—Work—Lazy race—High wages—Ceremonies and customs—Religion—Gualicho—Fear of Cordillera—Fat hunger—Tehuelche lives on horseback—Esquimaux and Tehuelche—Primitive peoples and their habits—Food—Tobacco—Pipes—Language—Tribal government—Physical strength—Decreasing numbers—Men of silence and men of uproar—Courtesy of a Tehuelche.

Snow lay in the hollows so deep that only the lean crests of the higher bushes could thrust themselves through its surface. The wind, which had driven the snowstorm of the morning away to the east, swept drearily down out of an evening sky where neither sun nor sunset hues were to be seen, nothing but a spread of cold and misty grey, growing slowly overshadowed by the looming promise of more snow.

In the middle of the level white pampa two figures upon galloping horses were visible. As we came nearer we saw that one was that of a man clothed in a chiripa and a capa in which brown was the predominating colour. He was mounted on a heavy-necked powerful cebruno horse, his stirrups were of silver, and his gear of raw-hide seemed smart and good. As he rode he yelled with all his strength, producing a series of the most horrible and piercing shrieks.

But strange as was this wild figure, his companion, victim or quarry, was stranger and more striking still. For on an ancient zaino sat perched a little brown maiden, whose aspect was forlorn and pathetic to the last degree. She rode absolutely naked in the teeth of the bitter cold, her breast, face and limbs blotched and smeared with the rash of some eruptive disease, and her heavy-lidded eyes, strained and open, staring ahead across the leagues of empty snow-patched plain.

Presently the man redoubled his howls, and bearing down upon the zaino flogged and frightened it into yet greater speed. The whole scene might have been mistaken for some ancient barbaric and revolting form of punishment; whereas, in real truth, it was an anxious Indian father trying, according to his lights, to cure his daughter of the measles!

It appeared that the girl had taken the disease in an extremely acute form, and Indian belief and reasoning run something on these lines:

First fact—The child was possessed by a devil of great power and ferocity, who set up such a trouble inside her body that it came forth through her skin in blotches and spots.

Second fact—A devil is known to dislike noise and cold. All devils do. Hence the ride of the unlucky patient without a shred to protect her from the strong west wind snow-fed with bitter cold, and the almost incredible uproar made by the old gentleman upon the dark brown horse.

If one concedes the premises, it must be admitted there was method in his madness.

A NEW CURE FOR THE MEASLES

The above account was given me by Mr. Ernest Cattle, an accurate observer, whose knowledge of the wild districts of Patagonia is unique.

Such is the Tehuelche Indian of Patagonia to-day, and facts tend to show that he has in very few particulars departed from the customs, manner of living and modes of thought which distinguished his forefathers in the dawn of authentic Tehuelchian history. The earliest mention of the natives of Patagonia occurs on the occasion of the discovery of the country by Magellan in 1520. They were described as men of huge stature, giants in fact, and the very name Patagonia is said to be derived from the epithet "patagon," or "large feet," which the Spaniards bestowed upon them on account of the enormous tracks their footsteps left upon the sand of the seashore. The Tehuelches are not, as it happens, a large-footed though they are a tall race, but, considering the curious persistency of habit, which is one of their chief characteristics, the idea taken up by the Spanish is easily explained. The Tehuelches wear boots of potro (colt-skin) or guanaco-skin, which project in a narrow point some inches beyond the toes. There can be little doubt, judging by all else we know of them, that their ancestors of Magellan's day wore the same shape of foot-gear. The impressions left by such boots would very naturally, on being observed by voyagers, take their place as indications of a race of giants. In connection with this idea I may mention that several early writers united in giving a very bad name to the Tehuelches. No reputation could be more totally unmerited. From reading such accounts one would be left with the conviction that the Tehuelches are blood-thirsty and barbarous savages. This is certainly not the case now, and I do not believe, judging from all I saw of them under various circumstances, that such accusations could ever have been deserved. Some travellers appear to have fallen into the error of confounding them with other Indian races of South America, whose characteristics and history differ absolutely from the people of whom I am writing.

We see here how easy it is for travellers to make mistakes. More than one writer has charged them with the habit of eating raw flesh; whereas they cook the meat for food, but on occasion they will eat raw fat and drink the warm blood of the ostrich, which facts, no doubt, have given rise to the above misstatement.

Although not giants, the Tehuelches are certainly one of the finest races in the world. Most of them average 6 ft., some attain to 6 ft. 4 in. or even more, and in all cases they are well built and well developed. Physically, the men are splendid fellows, who look yet more nobly formed and proportioned because of the ample folds of the skin capas and ponchos in which they wrap themselves. Their way of life tends to muscular excellence, but even taking that into consideration the development of the arms, chest, and, in fact, the whole body above the loins is extraordinary. But the lower limbs are sometimes disappointing, being, in fact, the lower limbs of a race of riders.[7]

The Tehuelche Indians of Patagonia are essentially nomads, living chiefly upon the proceeds of their hunting, and, in a less degree, maintaining themselves upon sale or barter connected with their limited holding of domestic animals. Agriculture or tillage is absolutely unknown among them. The hunting-ground is farm enough for them, and they pitch their tents of skin where they will, or change their quarters at the dictates of necessity or whim. They always break camp if a death occurs among the tribe, for the spot is then considered accursed. And they are, of course, also largely influenced in their movements by the wanderings of the guanaco herds, which form their principal quarry.

There are five existing camps of Indians to be found in Patagonia. I visited two of them and a third small outlying group. Their numbers have sadly decreased since the days of the opening 'seventies, when George Chaworth Musters made his abode in the tribal toldos and followed with them in their wanderings. He speaks of two tribes of Tehuelches, the northern and the southern, only distinguishable by a slight difference of dialect, and who met and intermarried, although they did not object to espousing opposite sides in a quarrel. Other tribes whom he mentions did not inhabit the part of the country of which I am writing.

The Tehuelches proper appear to have been fairly prosperous and numerous in his day, but even then he says, speaking of them: "Supplies of rum procured in trade at the settlements ... and disease, small-pox especially, are rapidly diminishing their numbers." Things have undoubtedly gone from bad to worse in this unhappy direction, and I am inclined to think that the number of Tehuelche Indians surviving at this period can be little over a few hundreds in number. Rum is undoubtedly their chief foe. Drink to the uncivilised man is a danger against which he is provided with no defence, either social or moral. Having once tasted its fatal pleasures, he has no reason for forbidding himself an indulgence his animal nature craves.

ARROWHEADS AND KNIFE, FOUND NEAR COLOHUAPI, CHUBUT

Since the day on which the Spanish adventurers first sighted the Patagonian coast, perhaps the one "event" in the history of the Indians may truly be said to be the introduction of horses into their land. Otherwise they seem to have altered little in their way of life. Magellan says they came down to the ship clad and shod in guanaco-skins; they are clad and shod in guanaco-skins to-day. Their tools and knives were sharp-edged flints; I have seen the Indians skin their quarry with precisely the same weapons.

Bows and arrows were indeed in use among the tribes when the Spaniards visited the coast; these have now been superseded by the boleadores, an innovation which in its present form came into fashion after the Indians began to know the value of the horse. The bolas is the weapon of the Tehuelche. With it he kills his game, and with it also he catches wild colts, and finds it useful in his simple process of training. The bolas is made up of three thongs of raw hide fastened together at one end, the other free ends having attached to them stones or bits of pot-iron sewn up in skin. The Indian throws his weapon with marvellous accuracy at any animal he may be pursuing, and the thongs coiling instantly round the legs or neck of the creature, bring it to the ground, or, at any rate, entangle it hopelessly.

It may well be judged that this race have no history. They remain in touch with the methods and customs according to which their forefathers were wont to live centuries ago, and who in their turn had derived them from still older generations. Though most of the men now possess cheap store knives of steel, I have seen, as I said before, many a quarry skinned with the prehistoric flint knife. They are an intelligent people, indeed keen where bargaining is concerned, as long as they are sober; yet they seem to be entirely lacking in that quality which would enable them to forget the past with its traditional usages and methods, and to follow even remotely the sweeping onward rush that, like a tornado, carries with it the lagging races of mankind. Although the men possess unusual strength, they do not in the least know how to apply it. Their faces are somewhat flat, although the features are more or less cast in the aquiline mould, and fairly regular. The hair is coarse and lustreless, its blackness relieved by a fillet or handkerchief of scarlet. Their teeth are excellent, toothache being almost unknown in their tents. Although they bathe, I have never observed among them any article that would in any way correspond to the tooth-stick of other nomadic peoples. Their beautiful teeth are perhaps due to their habit of chewing a gummy substance that exudes from the incensio bush. Musters, in his book, says they use this as a dentifrice.

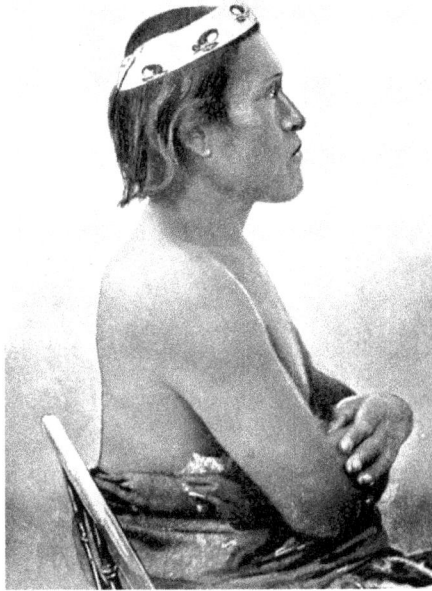

A TEHUELCHE CACIQUE

The women are not, according to our European ideas, beautiful, and such comeliness as they may sometimes possess in youth blossoms and fades quickly. They are, however, strong, and much of the camp work falls to their share. The older women can boast of a brand of ugliness all their own. Age to these ladies brings several vices in its train. Most noticeable is a craving for strong waters, a weakness from which the younger women are entirely free.

The morality of the Tehuelches is, on the whole, admirable. Unfaithfulness in the wife is rare, and not often bitterly revenged. A point as regards the morality of the women is to my mind rather luminous. While the younger chinas are unexceptionable in their moral virtues, the older women cannot be so highly commended. They are rather apt to wander from the stricter paths of decorum. When the husband of one of these elderly houris dies, as soon as the due period of mourning is past, the bereaved one will take up with any male in her tribe for either a longer or a shorter period. For ugliness sheer and unrivalled these grandmothers of the tribes stand alone. Also, as they get on in years, these ladies often run to fat. I remember one immense woman in the toldos on the pampas between Lake Argentino and Gallegos, who had put on flesh in a manner and to an extent almost unbelievable.

The younger women, while the flush of girlhood is still upon them, possess a certain comeliness which I can only describe by the adjectives "savage" and "stolid." Yet the abundant coarse black hair hanging round the heavily quiet faces, in which the features, though flattened, are still slightly aquiline, the wide-open, patient eyes, the healthful colour, and the strong, white, even teeth, which their slow smiles disclose to you, make them, on the whole, a personable race.

The half-bloods, as is usual, often possess real beauty, the alien strain giving them that vivacity which the pure race seems to lack.

Some of the pictures show an unsightly slit of the lip in the case of a few paisanos.[8] This hare-lip is by no means universal, but is an hereditary peculiarity that appears in many of the members of one special household. The arrival of a stranger in the camp makes the women retire shyly within themselves, and it is only by chance—as it is in the case of wild animals—that the new-comer ever sees the unaffected and natural character shine out. When in contact with whites the Tehuelche man also becomes reserved, the whole expression of his countenance changes, and he is very suspicious of being laughed at, a point on which he is very susceptible, and which he deeply resents.

I cannot but think that the constant accusations of uncleanliness that have been brought against the Tehuelche Indians are due to the single fact that their dogs are allowed to live in the toldos. The result in a country where scab is common may be left to the imagination. But, apart from the crawling things which inhabit his toldos, the Indian is fairly cleanly, bathing each day and swimming in the lakes and lagoons. The women make excellent mothers, and the father is inordinately proud of his offspring, especially of his sons. Of how many races can so many good things be truthfully said?

They have a singular custom of bandaging the heads of infants in such a manner as to produce a flattening of the back of the skull. It might be worth the while of physiologists to go deeper into the matter, with a view to discovering how far this alteration in the brain-space determines the character of the individual operated upon. Interesting results might thus be obtained and some vexed problems solved.

A certain stage in the life of each girl is celebrated by a festivity in the camp. An ornamented toldo is put up temporarily for the girl's occupation, and the young men of the tribe march round it singing while the women howl, probably with a view to exorcising any evil spirit who may be lingering about the camp.[9] The ceremony is followed by a feast, and the evening winds up with a dance. The men alone take part in this, and it consists in circling round the fire, pacing sometimes slowly and sometimes quickly. A few dance at a time, accompanying their movements with a constant bowing or nodding of the head, which is adorned with tufts of ostrich feathers. When one party is tired out another takes its place.

Wives, of course, are bought and sold, but when a lady is purchased by a suitor whom she happens to dislike, there is trouble for the bridegroom, and conjugal obedience is only enforced after struggles, of which the not infrequent result is that the mark of the lady's teeth remains permanently upon her lord.

The price of a wife varies, as must be expected in the natural course of things. Strangely enough, a girl's value often depends upon the number of her brethren, who must receive two horses apiece. To buy a bride with means or rather animals of her own, an heiress in fact, who comes of well-to-do people, as much as a hundred mares have been given—or shall I say paid.[10]

When desirous of carrying on matrimonial negotiations the would-be bridegroom must always employ a go-between. To omit this ceremonial method of approach would be an outrage on etiquette. I conclude, though I do not know it for a fact as regards Patagonia, that the go-between in that country gets his pickings from both sides as his congener does elsewhere.

The marriage ceremony is delightfully simple. After the preliminary bargaining has been successfully brought to a close, the happy bridegroom mounts his horse and rides to the toldo of his intended and hands over his appointed gifts, receiving those of the parents in return. He then carries back his bride amid the cheers and cries of his friends, and in the evening there is a feast. Musters remarks that on these occasions the dogs are not permitted to touch the meat or offal of the animals killed, as it is considered unlucky if they do so.

The gifts which are exchanged between the parties form in a more or less degree a marriage settlement, for in case of divorce her parents' gifts accrue to the wife. Polygamy is allowed but not much practised among the tribes.

Few phenomena are to my mind more unaccountable than the action of the white man who "goes fantee."

"Went fantee, joined the people of the land,
Turned three parts Mussulman and one Hindoo,
And lived among the Gauri villages,
Who gave him shelter and a wife or twain."

TEHUELCHE MATRON, SHOWING HARE-LIP

This singular mental or moral warp which results in a man "going fantee" is by no means uncommon in Patagonia. Of course, as may be imagined, a certain proportion of such men fall to this condition at the end of the career variegated. Others prefer ruling in Cathay to serving in any other community more dignified; others again take daughters of the land to wife because their trade lies with the Indians.

There is, however, one very strong objection to this latter course of marrying, Tehuelche fashion, a china of the toldos, and that is that all the relatives of the lady in question are apt to quarter themselves upon the bridegroom. Occasionally the white man objects, but I imagine that the cases of those who object successfully are rare. But there is one estanciero in Patagonia who is the father of two buxom daughters by a Tehuelche wife. These girls are now grown up, and their tribe was encamped during the winter of 1900 not two hours' ride from the dwelling-place of their father. Yet I am assured the father never aided the tribe or his own offspring in any way, although that winter was so severe that starvation visited the toldos of the tribe. A man of this mettle is, however, not frequently to be heard of, and cases of a quite laudable affection having existed between a white man and a china are on record.

But, at the same time, it must be repeated that the influence of the white who goes to live among the Indians as one of themselves, almost without exception, makes for evil. I have already spoken of the offspring of the mixed unions. The Tehuelche blood gives to the faces of the half-breed women an expression of sad patience, while the Spanish connection adds certainly to their gift of beauty. The women have very simple ideas of adornment. They generally take the form of silver necklets and the red fillet bound in their hair.[11] Their dress is composed of the picturesque guanaco-skin capa, or mantle, worn with the wool inside. Woman, to tell the truth, holds no such bad position among the Patagonian Indians. She does the cooking, but little else that can be called hard work, except the taking down and pitching of the toldos when the tribe break camp. They carry on a slack industry in the form of weaving ponchos from guanaco wool. Some species of earth is used for dyeing the wool, but the resulting colours are dull. In this particular the Tehuelches differ from the Indians of the northern pampas, whose dyeing materials are derived from herbs, and give brighter tints. These ponchos and saddle-rugs made by the chinas are much prized and sought after as curiosities, hence the makers demand very high prices for them—even up to thirty or forty dollars each.

The women also spend some of their time in sewing together the skins of guanaco or ostriches into rugs, using sinews for thread. Rugs of this kind and bunches of ostrich feathers form the staple commodities which they offer at the settlements for sale.

The hair of the adult animal, being harsh and coarse, is of less value in the market than that of the young guanaco; therefore the hunters endeavour to secure chiefly the pelts of the young guanaco, some of the rugs being even made from the skin of the unborn, which is cut out of the mother a few days previous to the date when they would naturally be dropped. At certain seasons enormous numbers of these pelts are to be seen drying, pegged out, beside the Indian toldos.

The time of year during which the hunting of guanaco chicos, or little ones, is carried on includes the latter half of October and the month of November.

I am afraid it must be confessed that the Tehuelches are a very lazy race. Nearly everything which makes any demand upon their energies—with the exception of hunting—seems too much trouble for them to do. Few individuals become even comparatively rich, and even then live none the better for it. One could never guess whether a man were rich or poor by his dress; he carries no sign of improved circumstances in his person or bearing. The owner of two thousand beasts will come into camp and sit by your fire, putting in a plea with the humblest for a cupful of maté. Occasionally an Indian will act as a guide across the empty distances of the pampas. They have an excellent idea of the value of their services and of the paper peso of the Argentine Republic. They set a high price upon themselves—a vaqueano, or guide, demanding five dollars a day or seventy dollars a month.

But however this quality may seem to approximate to civilisation, the customs with which he still surrounds the events of birth, sickness, and death are the old cruel forms that have been perpetuated through the ages, and they stamp him as remaining even to this day the very slightly diluted savage.

In some cases when a child is born, a cow or mare is killed, the stomach taken out and cut open, and into this receptacle while still warm the child is laid. Upon the remainder of the animal the tribe feast, and when they feast they carry out the notion thoroughly. After eating their fill, they lie about gorged and half insensible and let the world spin on. This is a quiet festivity, and only takes place in this modified form when the tribe happen to be out of fire-water.

But should there be liquor at hand, the younger women, who never drink on such occasions, go round beforehand and gather up every knife, hatchet, or, in fact, all and any weapon they can find, and bury them in some hidden spot about the camp.[12] This custom, which is in its own way pathetic, speaks for itself. Under the influence of liquor the nature of the peaceable Indian becomes completely changed. It maddens him, and the dance round the fires often ends in a free fight.

A variation of the foregoing birth-ceremony is yet more savage. If a boy is born, his tribe catch a mare or a colt—if the father be rich and a great man among his people, the former; if not, the latter—a lasso is placed round each leg, a couple round the neck, and a couple round the body. The tribe distribute themselves at the various ends of these lassos and take hold. The animal being thus supported cannot fall. The father of the child now advances and cuts the mare or colt open from the neck downwards, the heart, &c., is torn out, and the baby placed in the cavity. The desire is to keep the animal quivering until the child is put inside. By this means they believe that they ensure the child's becoming a fine horseman in the future.[13]

If an Indian dies the place becomes accursed. The camp is immediately removed to a fresh locality. When the dead man or woman is buried, certain ceremonies are observed about the grave, evidently with a view to enabling the departed to start in another life with an adequate outfit. Horses and dogs are slaughtered, so that he may have the means to pursue and kill the guanaco in the land of ghosts. Food and dead game are also placed in the grave to supply his needs at the outset of the new existence. Should the dead happen to be a child or a person of tender years, fillies and colts are slaughtered at the burial.

In former times, and in fact until quite recent years, it used to be the custom to place beside the corpse the silver-mounted horse-gear of the dead man, and to close the grave upon it. In a land where life depends not infrequently upon the strength of your raw-hide head-stall, for instance, the value of sound gear is properly appreciated; therefore this particular precaution for the welfare of the dead shows a very practical solicitude on the part of the survivors. To-day the Tehuelches still bury these possessions in the grave, but the custom is only continued with a reservation. Instead of leaving the valuable gear under the earth for all time, they now at the end of a twelvemonth dig it up again. How they reconcile this economical arrangement with the comfort of their lost friend I do not know, but it may be suggested that they imagine the inhabitant of another world has had full time in the course of a year to make suitable new gear for himself.

The religion of the Indians is interesting. It consists, of course, in the old simple beliefs in good spirits and devils, but chiefly devils, which, with variations dependent on climate and physical environment, represent all over the world the spiritual creeds of uncivilised races. The dominant Spirit of Evil, as feared by the Tehuelches, is called the Gualicho. And he abides as an ever-present terror behind their strange, free, and superstitious lives. They spend no small portion of their time in either fleeing from his wrath or in propitiating it. You may wake in the dawn to see a band of Indians suddenly rise and leap upon their horses, and gallop away across the pampa, howling and gesticulating. They are merely scaring the Gualicho away from their tents back to his haunts in the Cordillera—the wild and unpenetrated mountains, where he and his subordinate demons groan in chosen spots the long nights through.

The expedition under my command happened to encamp near one such place upon the southern shore of Lake Rica. It was a moonlight night, and loud rushing noises broke the peace of every hour of it. There happened to be a huge glacier on the opposite side of the lake, from which great pieces became detached at frequent intervals (for the mass of the glacier overhung the cliff), and these plunged with strange, loud explosions, I might almost call them, into the water. Such are the noises that terrify the Indian; he cannot explain them, and it is small wonder they excite his fears in the highest degree. For it must be remembered that in all practical ways the Tehuelche is a very brave man. Yet no pay can tempt him within the region of the Cordilleras, where to his superstitious mind the near presence of the Gualicho is manifested by those awful groanings and sounds which no human agency known to him could by any possibility produce.

CHILDREN OF THE TOLDOS

In common with other savage peoples, the Tehuelches believe the Good Spirit to be of a far more quiescent habit than the spirits of evil. Long ago, at the epoch of Creation perhaps, the Good Spirit made one effort for the benefit of mankind,[14] but since then he has been otherwise occupied, and shown himself little interested with earthly matters. Like Baal, he is perchance upon a journey, or perchance he is sleeping. The result is the same; his worshippers must take care of themselves as well as they can, and the best method which offers is to ward off by all means in their power the attacks of the maleficent influence. For the Gualicho is of a very active disposition, and shows no scorn of small things. On the contrary, he is quite capable of descending upon a single Indian to punish him for an offence and to work him harm.

It is a humiliating reflection that the great mass of peoples have always been, and will always be, far more ready and fervent in propitiating an evil spirit, or endeavouring to avert the action of any punishing power, than in seeking the favour of the Good Spirit or returning him thanks for benefits received. Human nature under the frock-coat of civilisation is much the same as under the capa of the Tehuelche.

By inference one can see that the Patagonian believes in a future life—a life much on the lines of his earthly one, but abounding in those things which he most desires, and which here he finds in short measure. I only know that the land he is going to after death is a land flowing, not with milk and honey, but with grease. On the pampas of life here below the guanaco is lean and seldom yields an ounce of fat, and as I have myself experienced the craving for fat, or fat-hunger, I know it to be a very real and uncomfortable demand of the human system. But in the Patagonian Beyond the guanaco herds will be plump and well provided with supplies of suet, and the califate-bushes always laden with ripe and purple berries.

The traditions of the tribes go back to the epoch when they hunted on foot and used bows and arrows, as well as the bolas, armed with a large single ball of stone. That period may be one hundred, or possibly a hundred and fifty, years ago. Then a tribe of Pampa Indians rode down out of the north and brought to the Tehuelches the inestimable boon of horses.

At the present day no worse evil can happen to an Indian than to be left without a horse and dependent on his own legs. He rides perpetually, and in consequence has almost lost the walking capabilities of other men.[15] He lives upon horseback, and there earns his living, so to speak. With his dogs he rides down his game, but he has no skill in tracking any more than the dogs. But, for all that, his sight is keen; the quality of extraordinary long-sightedness, which distinguishes men used to scanning vast levels of sea or land, is essentially his.

The Tehuelche, although in many ways offering a complete contrast, yet in some points forms a strange parallel to the Esquimaux. The Esquimaux has never seen a horse, the Tehuelche never uses a boat, although his land abounds in sheets of water. Both races are eminently sluggish and peaceable. Both fear evil spirits, which they fancy live in particular localities. It is indeed a far cry from Greenland to Patagonia, but if you substitute the horse for the kayak and the seal for the guanaco, you will find that, although separated by space and race and circumstance, a certain resemblance between the people of the Far South and of the Far North exists. And of both races little evil can be said.

These primitive peoples, living close to nature, divided from man's original state only by the thinnest and filmiest of partitions, attain in a wonderful degree the art of doing without things. The Esquimaux starts upon a long day's hunting, with the thermometer marking many degrees below zero, upon nothing save a drink of water! A luxury such as coffee is said to enervate him.[16] The Patagonian Indian rides out of a morning having taken nothing at all in the way of sustenance. But he puts a pinch of salt in his belt, and when his dogs pull down their first guanaco or ostrich, he draws off the blood and swallows it mixed with salt.

The tribes live to a considerable extent on guanaco, and it is practically their life-work to follow the wanderings of the herds through the changing seasons. But the flesh of the ostrich is more palatable, and is, consequently, preferred when it can be procured. They drink maté in large quantities, which, as has been shown, is the universal habit on the pampas, where it is, in fact, indispensable, supplying, as it does, to a certain extent, the place of vegetables, besides having the valuable quality of refreshing and invigorating in a quite extraordinary degree.

They rarely smoke pure tobacco; it is too precious. They mix it with about 80 per cent. of califate-wood shavings. Once, when short of tobacco, I tried their mixture, and in truth there are many worse smokes upon the English and American markets. The califate is certainly a little acrid, but burns with a very blue smoke. I fancy one could get on tolerably well with this faked tobacco, aided by a bit of imagination and a strong throat.

TEHUELCHE MATRONS

For the most part the tribes use stone pipes of a very singular coffin-like shape. One Indian, however, possessed a silver pipe, the stem of which had begun life as a bombilla, or silver tube for drinking maté through. Musters mentions frequently seeing the men become insensible after smoking, which would lead to the supposition that they use some drug corresponding in its effects to opium. I never observed a single instance of this sort, although I smoked the camp-fire pipe on many occasions with Tehuelches. In fact, of those I met, two out of three were not smokers at all.

The language of these people is very guttural, and one word is used to signify a number of different things, which proves its elementary and simple character. In most of their camps Spanish is understood more or less, and with even a slight knowledge of this tongue one can get on very well.

Practically the Patagonian is governed by no tribal laws. He does not need their restraint, for, save when drunk, he seldom commits crimes of greater or less magnitude. In politics he is democratic apparently, for though it is true that a cacique is at the head of each camp, his authority seems limited to ordering the plan of the hunt. If any individual objects he can leave the community, an alternative extremely distasteful to so gregarious a people. Quarrels and fights are of very rare occurrence, except when there is drink in the tents. The natural peacefulness of the Indian is certainly commendable, for his muscular development is enormous. He can tear the skin from a guanaco after merely raising enough with his knife to give him a hand-grip.

Once it was a free and a happy life that they lived, with fortunes ruled by the changing of the seasons. In those days, five-and-twenty years ago, they were scattered throughout the country, moving along the Indian trail. Now, in the whole of my long travel through Patagonia, I came upon only three encampments of them, and I have reason to believe I visited nearly every one that exists at the present day. It is probable that I may be their last chronicler; they will be brushed off the face of the earth by the sweeping besom that deals so hardly with aboriginal races, and is known as "civilisation."

The cause of their disappearance is not far to seek. You may dust a savage people with Martinis and increase their manhood, if the punishment be not severe and too prolonged, but as sure as the whisky bottle—the raw, cheap, rot-gut country spirit—is introduced among them, a primitive people is doomed. In all sorts of places in the world I have seen this baleful influence at work.

The Indians, as I knew them, are a kind-hearted, docile and lazy race. In all the dealings I had with them I found them invariably most courteous. Treat them as you desire they should treat you, and not in the odious "poor-devil-of-a-heathen, beast-of-a-savage" sort of style, which obtains with some of our own countrymen abroad, I am sorry to say, and you will receive a grave and quiet consideration, and they will call you buen hombre, a good man.

Progress, the white man's shibboleth, has no meaning for the Patagonian. He is losing ground day by day in the wild onward rush of mankind. Our ideas do not appeal to him. He has neither part nor lot in the feverish desires and ambitions that move us so strongly. As his forefathers were, so is he—content to live and die a human item with a moving home, passing hither and thither upon the waste and open spaces of his native land. He is far too single-minded and too dignified to stoop to a cheap imitation. He does not shout aloud that he is the equal of the white man, as more vulgar races do. It has often struck me that the primitive races of the world might be put under two heads—the men of silence and the men of uproar. Among the men of silence we have the Zulu, the North American Indian, the Tehuelche, and some others. These silent peoples cannot exist, like the negroes, as the camp followers of civilisation. They have not the ya-hoop imitative faculty of the negro race. They are hunters, men of silence and of a great reserve. When they meet with the white man, they do not rush open-mouthed to swallow his customs.

The men of silence will, in the savage state, take a hint as quickly as an English gentleman; the men of uproar will only accept a hint when it is backed by a command. The Tehuelche will not remain at a camp-fire where he is not wanted. He lacks passion, perhaps, but appreciation pleases him. His dignified courtesy can best be exemplified by a story.

A TEHUELCHE BEAUTY

At one time, while we were travelling across the pampas and had camped for the night, an Indian rode in upon us in the twilight. The Indian did not talk Spanish, nor could we speak Tehuelchian. In silence he joined us at our evening meal and stopped afterwards to smoke a pipe of tobacco, then he got to horse and rode away.

The next morning our horses were missing; they had evidently strayed during the night. I went out to look for them, and after a time saw them far away across the pampa advancing towards me in a compact mob. A rider was driving them up. As soon as he saw me, and I had recognised our guest of the preceding evening, he sent forward the horses at a gallop in my direction, and, wheeling round, was off and out of sight in a moment. He did not wait to be thanked, and yet it was obvious, from the condition of the horses, that he must have found them a long way off and driven them for a considerable distance. It is in courtesies of this kind that the silent peoples excel.

I am no wild admirer of the noble savage. He is, generally speaking, a highly objectionable person. But to see a race—so kindly, picturesque, and gifted with fine qualities of body and mind—such as the Tehuelches, absolutely at hand-grips with extinction, seems to me one of the saddest results of the growing domination of the white man and his methods of civilisation.

CHAPTER VII

TEHUELCHE METHODS OF HUNTING

Hunting season—Surefooted horses—Description of big hunt—Ring round game—Splendid riding of Tehuelches—Horses dislike jumping—Game killed and spared by Tehuelches—Difference of their hunting methods from those of the Onas of Tierra del Fuego—Artistic perception of Onas—Ill-faith of early settlers—Indian trail—"No place for us"—Deterioration of horses—They prize piebalds—Method of breaking in—Perfect riders—Helpless on foot—Staying powers of horses—Dogs—Evil of liquor trade—National sin of permitting this traffic—Picture of trader—Drinking bout of Tehuelches—Gambling for horses—Fatal weakness of Tehuelches—Another instance.

During the latter half of October and during November, which is the Patagonian spring, the Tehuelches hunt the guanaco chicos, or young guanaco.

At this period the young have not all been dropped, and the most prized pelts are those of the unborn young, which are obtained by killing the mother. These pelts, being very soft and fine in texture, are used to make the most valuable capas or robes, and if sold out of the tribes at the settlements, bring in the highest prices.

At this season the Indians move to their favourite hunting-grounds; it is, in fact, to them the most important period of the year. Two requisites are necessary to make their hunting a success: the first is plenty of game, and in this there is rarely any disappointment; the second is good ground on which to hunt it. As long, however, as the guanaco do not take absolutely to the crags, the Indians, with the help of their sure-footed unshod horses, are able to levy a heavy toll on the herds.

The method of hunting adopted by the Tehuelches is interesting enough to call for description at length. On the morning of the hunt, the Indians saddle up a good long-journey horse apiece, they also catch each man his fastest mount, upon which he puts a bozal and cabresto, as well as a bit in his mouth. The hunter rides the former horse, and leads the latter for use later on.

BOLEADORES
FOR OSTRICH   FOR GUANACO   FOR HORSES
(IN THE COLLECTION OF THE AUTHOR)]

The big herds of guanaco have meantime been located, and the plan of the day's hunt arranged by the cacique. All the hunters start forth in couples, riding in different directions, and so form an immense circle, into the centre of which they systematically drive the game. They then signal their whereabouts to one another by means of smokes until the ring round the guanaco is complete. Each hunter is accompanied by his dogs, of which he possesses probably a score. Six or eight gaunt hounds of no particular breed, but whose characteristic points run chiefly to legs and teeth, follow their master. As the circle narrows the terrified game huddle together in the centre of it, and there may be seen hundreds of guanaco, many ostriches, and possibly a puma or two. The guanaco bucks pace upon the edge of the herd, and give out their neighing, half-defiant call as their human enemies approach.

The positions assumed by guanaco when under the influence of curiosity and fear are most singular. They will stand staring at the Indians for many seconds, and will then dash off at a wild gallop with the strange leaping run peculiar to them. The necks, too, swing and sway at all conceivable angles, and whenever their ears are assailed by a sudden sound, I have seen a whole herd, upwards of one hundred strong, sway their necks to within a couple of inches of the ground almost in unison.

In the meanwhile the Indians draw remorselessly nearer, dismount from their saddle-horses, leap on their led animals, and precipitate themselves from all sides upon the frantic herds. The horses that are left have generally been carefully schooled to stand when their reins are dropped forward to the ground over their heads. The Indians howl and roar as they dash down upon the guanaco, whirling their boleadores round their heads. This bolas, with which they hunt the guanaco, is very heavy, and the three balls are generally made of stone, but they use a lighter form for the capture of the ostrich. In the case of guanaco chicos, clubs are often employed.

Holding his weapon by the shortest of the three sogas, or thongs, and while going at full gallop, the Indian launches it at the long neck of the guanaco; a doe is always selected if possible. Extremely expert in its use, the rider's weapon probably reaches its mark, and the quarry, maddened by the tightening of the sogas, bucks and rears, until she becomes hopelessly entangled.

I have mentioned that the Tehuelches hunt in pairs. The companion of the Indian who has thrown the bolas then leaps to the ground and despatches the guanaco. Meantime his comrade has dashed forward at the tail of the herd, and has probably secured another animal. The dogs, too, do their part, and as the storm of the chase sweeps across the pampa, it leaves the ground in its path dotted with the yellow-brown forms of the slain.

The chase tails itself out for many miles, and may be followed over desolate leagues marked by lines of dead guanacos and dropped boleadores which have failed to carry home. I should be afraid to say how many animals are killed at one of these singular battues. To see the Indian hunt the guanaco is to see the art of rough-riding exemplified. How they gallop! Down one sheer barranca, or cliff, and up another. The roar of loosened stone behind them. The guanaco jink and dodge and break back, always making for the highest ground in the vicinity.

The dexterity with which the horses of the hunters keep their feet is truly wonderful. They will go at full gallop anywhere, and hardly ever fall or miss their footing. There is, however, one thing which they universally dislike, and that is jumping in any of its forms. Here and there in some parts of Patagonia the pampa is cut and scored with fissures a few feet in width. To have your horse stop dead, both feet together, on the edge of one of these and violently shy away at an acute angle is no uncommon experience. Generally, however, a certain amount of inducement and coercion at length takes them over in a complicated buck.

When the chase has run itself out, the lean dogs are fed upon the grosser parts, the pelts of the young are pulled off, and the meat, such of it as is wanted, is cargoed or packed upon the horses, and the hunting-party jogs back to the shelter of the wigwams, made from the skins their fathers and their grandfathers slew before the white men began to move southward and to overrun the land.

The Indians kill no bird save the ostrich, and this is a curious fact, because the lagoons and pools literally swarm with great flocks of upland geese (Chloephaga magellanica), which are very fair eating. Perhaps the reason why they spare the geese arises from the fact that they have no weapons suitable for killing them. On one occasion when I shot a brace of geese, the Indians seized upon them and pronounced them "good." Also, they kill few animals but the guanaco and the puma. Had the guanaco a reasonable amount of fat upon it, the life of the Indians would be idyllic, but in this the guanaco fails. Of lean meat he supplies plenty, for he is a large beast, but though he lives in a land where sheep grow fat and well-liking, the long-necked Patagonian llama retains his leanness and his running condition.

BEAUTIES OF TIERRA DEL FUEGO

Although it may be slightly outside the province of this book, I cannot help contrasting the very different methods employed by the Onas of Tierra del Fuego, who are after all only separated from the Tehuelches of Patagonia by the narrow Straits of Magellan, in hunting the same animal. The Onas do not use horses, and kill the guanaco with bows and arrows. When they perceive a herd, they surround it as the Tehuelches do, but, of course, the circle is on a much smaller scale. It is their aim to remain invisible to their quarry, for which purpose, during their stalk, they are in the habit of wrapping themselves in the skins of the animals which they have formerly killed. Once the herd is surrounded, it is with the same accompaniment of screams and shouts that the hunters rush in to secure their prey.

The dissimilarities between the Tehuelches and the Onas are numerous.[17] While the Tehuelches are peaceful, the Onas are warlike. There is a story current that the only white man who has ever lived in the very primitive dwelling of boughs, which are all the Onas have to shelter them from a bitter climate, was a Scotchman whom the Indians had captured. He was with them three weeks, and his face was adorned by a singularly luxuriant crop of orange whiskers. The Onas are reported to have amused themselves by pulling these out in instalments by the roots. Might not some anthropologist base a treatise upon "The Artistic Perceptions of the Onas of Tierra del Fuego" upon this occurrence?The Onas are also a tall people, although not equalling in height my friends the Tehuelches, and their physical development is less conspicuously remarkable. The Ona woman does not, as does the Tehuelche china, form an attachment to a white suitor, appearing to have no desires outside her own race and people, but under certain circumstances the women have shared the hearthstone of the foreigner. Polygamy is allowed and practised among them. There is something of the spirit which characterises the Gipsy of Europe about this people; they are quite ready to take all they can get from the alien, while they at the same time maintain a bitter rancour against the hand that gives. But this is not, as it is in the case of the Gipsies, the continuance of an original dislike and implacability, but rather the result of the infamous ill-faith which leavened the dealings of the very earliest visitors to the coasts of Tierra del Fuego.

I must confess that all my sympathies are on the side of the primitive races, who on coming into contact with the white man suffer those outrages on their best feelings which, I am sorry to say, are only too common. You must understand, however, that I in no way refer to the settlers of this generation. My remarks must be taken to refer to the first pioneers. At the present day—so Burbury, who has had a great experience of Tierra del Fuego, informed me—the Indians there are treacherous and absolutely implacable, and do endless harm in their periodical raids upon the "white guanaco," as they call the sheep. They do this not only when hunger presses them, but at all times out of a spirit of revenge. Sometimes they drown the sheep and leave them in the ice, where they keep good for weeks, during which time the Onas feast on them.

Patagonia bears upon its length the clear-cut and long-drawn initial of the Tehuelche race. By this I mean the Indian trail, which can be followed from water to water, from good camp to good camp, stretching from Punta Arenas in the south to Lake Buenos Aires in the north and beyond it. Up and down this trail and along others, less extended, generations of Indians have wandered with their wives and children, their tents and horses. We struck it when travelling south from Lake Buenos Aires, in the early January of 1901. It was hard to distinguish the Indian road from any parallel series of guanaco-tracks, which here line the country in numbers, and, indeed, it was only by keeping a sharp look-out for the hoof-prints of horses that we were able to follow the trail at all. It runs along under the Cordillera at a varying distance of about twenty or thirty miles from their bases. It was a sad remark that an Indian made to us while talking about the ancient wanderings of his people. "Once," he said, "we had the sea upon the one side of us, and upon the other the Cordillera. But this is not so now. The white man is ever advancing upon one side and the Cordillera remains ever unchanging upon the other. Soon there will be no place for us; yet once the land was ours."

One would imagine that a people so dependent on their horses for the very necessities of life would give attention and care to the breeding and improvement of the stock. But this is far from being the case. The Tehuelches appear to be, like other far less intelligent races of uncivilised peoples, incapable of much forethought. They live for to-day and make little provision for to-morrow. As a case in point, they are allowing their horses to become very deteriorated. The animals are, almost without exception, to use a Spanish term, mañero, which means of a spoiled temper. In some localities they have been crossed with the horses of the settlers which have a strain of English blood, and the result is animals of spirit and of character, but muy mañero. The Tehuelches prize white horses, and overos, or piebalds, exceedingly. The backs of their horses are generally badly galled, but this is no matter for surprise, as they often ride upon a sheepskin flung anyhow across the beast. The method of breaking-in or taming is simple and severe in the extreme. It consists of leaping on a raw colt and galloping him to exhaustion. One reason why their horses are falling below level certainly is that the Indians have a foolish trick of riding two- and three-year-olds both hard and far. A colt of this age once fairly "cooked" by an over-long ride will never be of very much use afterwards.

And yet these people are peculiarly dependent upon their horses. They will not walk ten yards if they can ride them. And they have undoubtedly carried the art of riding to the last perfection. I never knew what riding really meant until I went to Patagonia and saw the Indians on horseback. We once asked an Indian what he could do if he were left on the pampa without his horses. "Sit down," he said. This man, however, was not a Tehuelche but a Pampa Indian.

SONS OF THE PAMPA

The horses are far from large, the average running to about thirteen hands, but they are wiry, untiring beasts, and some show extraordinary speed. The manner in which they carry the heavy well-developed Indians is wonderful. They are entirely fed on grass. When the camp is made, they are simply turned out to graze upon the pampa, where frequently the grass is sparse and poor enough, though near many of the Indian camping-grounds good vegas of rich grass exist. In winter, of course, the tropillas become very thin and in poor condition, but at that season they have infinitely less work to do, as there is hardly any hunting, and the camp is usually stationary for the coldest months.

The hounds of the Indians are something like our lurcher breed. In the tents they lie about among the rugs and bedding. They are irreclaimable thieves and very cowardly. A good guanaco hound is, however, of very great value, for a pair of accomplished hounds, skilled in the chase, represent a capital upon which an entire family can live.

One of the strongest feelings which I brought away with me from Patagonia was a hatred of the trader who battens upon the failings of the Tehuelches. If he hears of a festival or any tribal ceremony, he arrives upon the spot with drink. He sells liquor in exchange for horses, and when his customers are well steeped in the poison he brings, he makes some magnificent bargains. His influence is far-reaching and fatal as far-reaching to the picturesque and harmless race out of whose degradation and death he makes his living. Savage races may survive war and internecine struggles, and the decimation not infrequently caused by a cruel rule such as was T'Chaka among the Zulus, but they never survive the Civilisation of the Bottle. The horrors of the wars of history would pale beside the cold-blooded slaughter, the gradual, malignant, poisoning processes which the most self-satisfied and religious nations of the world allow to continue year after year, I should say century after century, among the aboriginal tribes, who live nominally under their protection. The pioneer trader with his stores of cheap maddening liquor is free to sell as much as he pleases, although it is a well-known fact that such trading means ruin and extermination to the unhappy ignorant folk who buy. The sin after all is national rather than personal, for the trader has his living to earn, whereas the nation which is responsible for allowing him liberty to traffic puts out no hand to stay the evil. I do not in the least bring any charge against the Argentine Government; we British are guilty of the same crime or carelessness, and in some of our dependencies terrible object-lessons of precisely the same kind can be observed.

Let me draw a picture of one of these traders for you. A lean stooping man of Paraguayan extraction, dressed out in store clothes which he but half filled. A plump face of the caste peculiar to the lowest type of the Latin peoples, with a full greasy-lipped animalism stamped upon it, after the manner of his kind. The lean body and fat face formed a contrast that struck you with repulsion as an actual deformity. This fellow played a very old trick upon a batch of Indians and considerably enriched himself thereby.

The Indians had come in upon the outskirts of a coast-town, rich with the sale of a six-months harvest of ostrich feathers, guanaco-skins and other such merchandise as they gather from the pampas. After some drinking and a variety of games of chance, our friend the trader started an argument as to which of the Indians owned the swiftest horse. A race was soon decided upon, the trader most liberally offering a prize in the shape of a bottle of drink. The race was to be ridden bare-back, as is usual in contests of this description among the Indians. The trader further suggested that the race should be run off in heats. A horse with a white blaze and a very fine head won, and his proprietor, a tall Indian in a black poncho, received the prize, which he, with help, soon disposed of. After this the talk fell naturally upon the merits of the respective horses.

"Your picaso is a good horse," said the trader to the tall Indian, "but I have a horse in my troop that could leave him far behind."

At first the Indian laughed, but the trader's boasting and insistence presently stung him to resent the aspersion on his mount, and he said he should like to see the thing done.

The trader jumped at the opportunity. The Indians had had sufficient drink to destroy their ordinary cautiousness, and were ready to take up any challenge.

"The loser to forfeit his horse to the winner," continued the trader, who had laid his plans beforehand. He then called a Chileno lad, who soon appeared leading a big lean alazan. It was easy for any seeing eye to recognise that the animal had been tied up the night before and was in quite fair racing trim; besides which, the Indian's picaso was already tired with the previous races. The Chileno boy swung up and the two horses came thundering along their course. The Indian's weight also told as compared with the lightness of the Chileno boy, and the result was altogether a foregone conclusion.

TEHUELCHES VISIT GALLEGOS

But this by no means ended the business. The Indians were excited and ripe for any amount of gambling, and being skilfully handled by the trader they did not leave the settlement until he had stripped them of all their possessions. The tall Indian, who had come in with eighty dollars and five horses, returned to his camp with a two-kilo bag of yerba and on a horse which he had been forced to buy for the return journey from the trader at, of course, the trader's own price.

There are many Indians who avoid the coast-towns, but although these do not go to the trader, the trader, as I have mentioned in another chapter, comes to them.

Throughout Patagonia, upon the rim of civilisation, are scattered boliches, or frontier drink-shops, whose liquor sales consist chiefly of "champagne cognac," whatever that potion may be. These establishments hold out a perpetual temptation to the passing Indians. The frequent presence of silver gear, such as the Tehuelches possess when fortune smiles upon them, that is almost always hanging from the ceiling of the neighbouring store, tells its own tale. An Indian has rarely enough money to "look upon the wine when it is red," or rather upon the unwholesome jaundice tinge of "champagne cognac," so he pays in kind; and when once the craving for drink grips him he will gamble away everything to satisfy it. This infatuation appears to lay a fatally strong hand upon the uncivilised peoples. They have no principles to stay them, no scruples to overcome, they have found a short cut to a wild species of happiness, and one cannot wonder that they seek its extraordinary pleasures as often as possible. So it is that liquor has destroyed whole races, wiped them clean off the face of the earth. Some one has written:

Oppression and the sword slay fast,
Thy breath kills slowly but at last,

and it is certainly a terrible truth in this connection.

I can call to mind two Indians, whom I saw ride up to a boliche near Santa Cruz. They offered a contrast to one another which it is not easy to forget. The first was an Indian with a close-shut mouth and the dark and ponderous dignity of the big Tehuelche. His gear was richly studded with silver, and his saddle covered with embroidered cloths. His head was bare, save that his brows were bound with a band of red finery. He made a picturesque and imposing figure as he cantered up on his white horse with its glinting eyes. Followed the second. He, too, was an Indian, but his gear was guiltless of silver, his bozal was worn and blackened with age. The best thing he possessed was his horse. He wore an ancient tail-coat, once black but now green, this in conjunction with a chiripa, or Indian loin-cloth, gave him an appearance sufficiently incongruous. Instead of the quiet dignity of the first man, his face expressed little save vacuity. He was a pitiful object in the strong pampa sunshine, his health evidently broken by frequent orgies. And no doubt he had been a self-respecting Indian enough—before the trader came within the province of his knowledge.

THE TEHUELCHE TOLDOS

FOOTNOTE:
[17] The Tehuelches are enormously above the Onas of Tierra del Fuego in the scale of civilisation. A Fuegian woman has been known to live in the Tehuelchian tents, but how she came there I am unable to

say. On the other hand, I have never heard of any Tehuelche living with the Tierra del Fuegians, and cannot conceive such a state of things to be possible. But the Tehuelches will mix occasionally with the Araucanian tribes of Northern Patagonia, and intermarriages are common.

CHAPTER VIII

THE KINGDOM OF THE WINDS

Como No—Wind and driven sand—Laguna La Cancha—Como No's dogs—Cold winds—Lake Buenos Aires and Sierra Nevada—Cross River Fenix—Stony ground—Skeletons of guanaco—Fine scenery— Short rest—Colt killed—Base camp made—Boyish dreams—Sunday—Routine at Horsham Camp— Driftwood round lake—Constant wind—My tent-home—Scorpions—Guanacos—Engineers' camp— Cooking-pots—First huemul.

We now set forth upon the last stage of our journey to Lake Buenos Aires. I had hired one of the Indians to guide us across the high pampa. He was, although dwelling in the tents of the Tehuelches, not a Tehuelche. He called himself a Patagonero, and belonged to one of the tribes of Pampa Indians of the north. His tribe, he told me, were Christians. Before we left the Indian encampment, one of the older ladies belonging to it began to paint her face in horizontal lines of black, whether with a view to capturing our hearts or not I cannot say.

We left on November 3, and accomplished a very long march in the face of somewhat trying conditions. The Indian rode ahead with his dogs on the look-out for ostriches. A mighty wind from the west, cold with the snow of the Cordillera, blew in our faces, bringing with it showers of sand that stung us sharply. We could hardly persuade the horses to meet the wind, and their hoofs kicked up still more sand for our benefit. We were off shortly after nine o'clock, and about noon I would have given much to say "Camp." When fighting with the elements one goes through three distinct stages. First, there is the stage exultant, during which you feel the joy of battle, and struggle rejoicingly. The second comes when the irresistible tires you down, however strong you are, and forces the sense of your puniness so plainly upon you that you feel a sort of hurt despair, and a half impulse to give in before a force so far beyond you. Last of all, you go on enduring until you become, as it were, acclimatised, and inclined to laugh at the despair you experienced a while previously. So it was on this day's march. About noon I said to myself as we were crossing the high pampa above the barranca of the River Chalia—a desolate spot, rough and tussocky, and gambolled over by Titanic winds—"We will camp at four sharp." The decision at the moment was a comfort, but in the end we did not camp until close upon seven o'clock, blind with sand, and our hands bleeding from the cold and the harsh friction of the cargo ropes.

It was as we approached this camp that I saw beside a lagoon of snow-water two American oyster-catchers (Hæmatopus palliatus) which, no doubt, had nested in the vicinity, as, on my going closer, they rose and circled with their darting flight above my head, but I failed to find the nest. There were many guanacos about, and I was not surprised to hear that this lagoon, Laguna La Cancha, was a very favourite encampment of the Indians. The scenery surrounding the pool is peculiarly inhospitable. Some one remarked that it reminded him of Doré's illustrations to the Inferno, adding, "If you were to put heat to it, it would be Hell." Huge rolling downs, bare hills, and no vegetation save a few tussocks and scattered meagre shrubs. The Indian said the winter hits this land very hard, and the whole district is buried under snow, only the high, bald tops of the hills being visible.

The next day was Sunday, but not on this occasion a day of rest. One thought of the bells ringing far away at home and the concourse of people moving along the winter roads. Here was wind, cold, and a march, cargo to be fixed and refixed to the day's end, then a windy camp-fire, and after a short sleep till dawn. Hitherto the toil had been hard, but we were nearing the lake, and looked forward to a time of rest and hunting.

We were rich in meat with the cow, sheep, a Darwin's rhea caught by the Indian's dogs, and three geese. The hounds of the Indian proved themselves to be troublesome thieves. Burbury and I were obliged to sleep beside the meat. Besides being cunning thieves the dogs were cowards. They were to all intents and purposes wild as regarded their habits. Yet good guanaco-hounds represent very sterling value to their owners, whose livelihood they procure. The best at the work I met with in Patagonia were those which belonged to this Indian guide. We called the man Como No because, whatever question was put to him, his invariable reply took the form of "Como no?" or "Why not?" You said perhaps, "It is not far to the next camping-ground, is it?" "Como no?" he would answer. After some three hours at an amble, you would repeat your inquiry. "Is it much farther?" "Como no?" The most impossible queries met with precisely the same response.

ON AHEAD

However indeterminate Como No may have been in his mental attitude, his dogs were definitely good ones. He owned a big brindled dog, a small black one and a couple of yellow pups. Como No had a habit of riding far ahead of the general troop of men and horses, his figure making a far-off outline etched in black against the cold blue horizon of the pampa. Sometimes, when he lost sight of us for any length of time, he would burn a bush to give us our direction by the smoke, and we would follow on, driving the pack-horses and those free ones which were not being used either for riding or cargo at the time. Presently, perhaps, when rounding a low thicket, we would come suddenly upon him, squatted on his haunches beside a dead ostrich, from which he had stripped the feathers. These feathers, though far inferior to those of the African ostrich, or of Rhea americana, are worth anything from two to four dollars.

As he rode forward again, his dogs would range on either side of him. By-and-by they would again start an ostrich or a guanaco, and pull it down within 500 or 600 yards. Whereupon Como No would ride up, drive them off, kill and cut up the quarry, giving the hounds the liver, strip the feathers if it happened to be an ostrich, and then mount and ride on once more. This performance would be repeated over and over again during the course of the march, until, before we saw the last of him, his saddle had become an enormous bunch of feathers, from out of which his body and shoulders protruded in a quaint manner.

At night these dogs, however, were a terrible nuisance. They would forage about the camp for food, and pull down the meat we had placed on bushes and devour it. Such was eventually the fate of the last remnants of the mutton we had with us, and the loss was all the harder as we knew that the stolen mutton was the last we were destined to taste for months. After that we lived on lean guanaco.

By this date we had gradually climbed to some 1200 feet above the sea-level, and the temperature was extremely cold. Our reindeer-beds became a great comfort.

The 5th began with an hour of welcome sun, but it passed only too soon, and the wind rose more piercingly cold than ever. It penetrated to one's very bones. We, however, made seven leagues, and reached the River Genguel, which here makes a great curve. We camped in a narrow shute, strewn with big stones and giving upon the river, the cañadon being very wide and devoid of shelter. The water was broken into small sharp waves by the wind, and we were glad to collect what firewood was obtainable— bushes being scarce at that spot—and make a fire. The Indian burned a bush and warmed himself. His dogs had, unaided by him, killed a small guanaco and a fox (Canis griseus). We lay by the fire and the wind came down bitterly chill from the Sierra Nevada, while Jones cooked, and we learnt the delights which, in a cold climate, are to be found in mutton fat! After food to bed, and then a cold sleet set in. It was a nasty night, but in our reindeer bags we were, of course, untouched by the cold.

Next day nine leagues were achieved. Very long marches these, but we were pressing on to reach Lake Buenos Aires. Cañadon and pampa and high ground succeeded each other as we rode along, sometimes bare, sometimes sandy, sometimes thorn-covered, often stony and strewn with fragments of basalt. Generally overhead a pallid blue sky, and below wind, wind, perpetual wind. So we toiled on past little chill lagoons, ruffled with the keen breeze, until in the afternoon I came up with Burbury and the Indian on a rise, and there lay our goal before us—a great stretch of water wonderfully blue and cold-looking beneath the Sierra Nevada, whose summits were crowned with snow above their dusky purple.

The Tostado kicked off his cargo during the day, and among the scattered contents of Jones' kit I picked up a broken looking-glass. I had not seen myself since leaving Colohuapi, and confess I found no cause for vanity in the sight of a distinctly dirty-looking pirate with smoke-reddened eyes, a peeling face and nose, and with enough beard to put a finishing-touch to the horrid spectacle.

ONAS STALKING GUANACO

On the 3rd I discovered a scorpion in my bed in spite of the cold. By the 6th we reached the River Fenix, and, crossing to an island, camped in the sleet, the temperature reading that night being 30° F. From there we pushed on to the farther bank, and marched to the camping-ground of the Indians, which, though the nearest of their old camps to Lake Buenos Aires, was still a good distance from it. The Azulejo had been lost, but was brought in quite spent, by Barckhausen. Poor little beast! He lay down more dead than alive under a bush, a pathetic little figure enough. After reaching camp, Jones and I had to turn out again, pretty tired as we were, to look for food. We rode for hours, and saw only a herd of guanaco. At this season the country round about here is rather devoid of game, the ground is stony, with thorn and dry, blackened bushes. We were disappointed in our hunt again on the second day, seeing only two guanaco, lion-tracks, and a couple of pigeons, but we did not shoot them, and I am unable to speak with any certainty of the species to which they belonged. I have never seen a district so bare of life. We had come, as it were, to the world's end.

I sat in my tent-door and wrote my diary. Far away I could see the Cordillera, splendid giants, with the sun shining upon them; below, the lake that reminded me strongly of the picture in which Hiawatha sailed into "the kingdom of Ponemah, the Land of the Hereafter." That scene was just so wild, and so remote, with a great red sunset burning over it, and round about it rock and sand and marsh, with a pale wide rim of dead-wood, swept down by floods from the neighbouring forests.

On our way to the shores of the lake we had passed through a stretch of extraordinary aridity, a white and yellow spread of mud and stones that filled a valley between two scrub-covered hills. From far off it looked level, but in reality we found it to be intersected and veined with mighty gashes, which formed winding gorges. There the wind blew, and at times the sun beat down; very cold it was, and very hot by turns, but never temperate.

We had expected to find plenty of game in the vicinity of the lake, but in this, as I have said, we were disappointed, the consequence being that our supply of meat ran short. There was nothing for it but to kill the eighteen-months old colt of one of the madrinas. But before we did this we hunted for three days, during which time I shot a couple of upland geese, which made the sum total of our bag. In a new country one has always to buy experience. We were buying ours at this period. Owing to the wildness of our horses the journey from Trelew had been an especially trying one, although, under other circumstances, the difficulties need not be great.[18] The breakdown of the waggon at so early a stage had entailed a large amount of extra labour, and by the time we reached Lake Buenos Aires we were, both men and horses, pretty well done up.

On the third day of our hunting I took Barckhausen instead of Jones, who had been out with me on the two previous days. We passed along through the stony thorn-lean gorges towards the east. Here nothing lived save the strong birds of prey, and lions, whose tracks we observed leading to the rocks. Death lay nakedly there in all directions, skull and backbone, with rain-polish and snow-polish upon them, picked clean years ago by now-dead caranchos and chimangos.

During our ride we saw two monster owls, two condors, many caranchos, and so pushed on over hill rising behind hill, stony, dark, with wind-lifted wisps of sand turning and twisting upon them.

In the early afternoon we came upon a more pleasant land, and to a little marshy pool in a hollow of the hills, crowded round with forest-bushes, and upon this pool from far away I spied two upland geese. I dismounted, took my gun, and began a stalk. While I was still well out of range a bough broke under my foot, and the geese were away. We lay up for a time, but the birds did not return, so we took a turn westwards in the hope of getting some coots I had observed the day before upon another lagoon, close to Lake Buenos Aires. Upon the shore of the lake a smart shower of sleet, hail, and rain overtook us, and we had to lie down in the lee of a thorn-bush. I saw one golden guanaco racing along a hill-top against the sunset. Some coots were on the lake; I shot four, but contrary winds drove them out into the water too deep to venture after them, and we turned campwards empty-handed.

HORSHAM BASE CAMP

As we galloped over the hills the clouds broke on the western side of the lake, and made a scene ominously beautiful. The rifted dusky blue, the long pale gleam of water shining like an angel's sword, the white snow-peaks, the purple-black belly of the rain-storm, all cast together formed a picture that affected the senses strongly.

As we neared camp, I saw something gleam white behind a bush. An upland goose! I crawled up and found two. With what care I managed that stalk! I killed the female with one barrel on the ground and pulled over the male as he swung upwards. After riding seven leagues, we got our small results of the day's seeking within a mile of the camp! One or other of us had seen far-off guanaco flying out of sight, and I decided to start next day for the River Fenix to try for some, camping there the night and returning next day to begin our long-needed rest.

Yet the next day (November 9) none of us went a-hunting after all. We were fairly played out. Personally I had had not one day's rest since starting two months before, as upon me principally fell the duty of providing for the pot, so that upon coming in of an evening on the close of a long march it was usually necessary to saddle a fresh horse and ride a further distance from five to fifteen miles in search of game.

So we killed the colt to provide for our wants while men and horses enjoyed well-earned repose. I had formed a base-camp about five miles from the shores of the lake, intending to make short expeditions, lightly equipped, round and about the vicinity. As for the camp, three large thorn-bushes were Nature's contribution towards it, and what a relief even the shelter of a thorn-bush can be in the Kingdom of the Winds, you could only learn by an experience such as was ours. Below the camp, which stood on a ridge, the ground fell away in a three-mile slope to the usually angry water; eastwards was a pantano or swamp of yellow reeds, which ran a long way below the scrub-grown ridge. The tents huddled back-to-wind, as much under the lee of the bushes as possible. We made an oven, but it turned out a failure, the earth being too soft for our purpose. Round the fire was a hedge of thorn hung with horse-blankets, red, yellow and black, which gave a rather festive air to the camp. The only sounds were the neigh of a horse, the hooting of night-birds, and the never-silent wind.

STORE-CLAD INDIANS

During the night of the 10th, half a gale of wind blew up with an extraordinary rancour of coldness. I lay in my tent and heard the sides of it flapping like some great wounded bird. Sleep was put off till far into the small hours. Through the open tent-door I could look at the bushes writhing in the gale, the long black back of the ridge and the glint of stars. How often one sees in half-sleep the scenes of home and of the past! I seemed again to be watching the boats coming in and the tides rising with the well-known ripple and pouring rush of water on a shallow beach, tides that in boyish days held so infinite a romance. Where did the storms that broke there come from? whither went the dark hulls after they sank below the blue edge of sea? Or where did the fishermen sail their boats to—lonely rocks from which they brought back parrot-beaked, jelly-armed pieuvres? And yet, having drifted into some long wanderings, and now into that wilderness, no scene that I have ever looked upon, however wild or lonely, has touched me in any way that could compare with the thrill of those early dreams. Romance lies always a little too far away; only in childhood is the gate of that wonderful garden open to us, and we gaze and long for the fruit we are never to handle.

Our tents at Horsham Camp—so we named it—were the only green things in the landscape. They happened to be of a pale green. Riding out from the camp in most directions you found yourself amongst a bare and wind-swept series of ridges two or three hundred feet in height, which appeared to roll away across the wide continent. Sunday was welcome. It was noticeable how Sunday abroad always affected men, some of whom at home spared small attention for the day. Life went evenly. The others took it in turn to cook. I generally rode out early. The troop were rounded up and our first meal came about 7 o'clock. After that I used to go to my tent and write while the men busied themselves with any job on hand. Cocoa at two on Sundays, and about six a meal of meat and beans. And so to bed. The day before the colt was killed, Tom, my hound, stole a dumpling from the plate of one of the party as he sat eating. The loser at once pursued the thief, retrieved the dumpling and ate it, so you will understand that there was no wastefulness among us!

By November 12 I was tired of inaction, tired of the tent, tired of the camp. The wind continued. Surely in all his writings R. L. Stevenson never made a more perfect phrase than the "incommunicable thrill of things." A wood-scent in the morning, the sound of the wind at night, the clear cinders of the fire or a whiff of burning wood—one receives the spark that fires the train of thought and leads us far away. No indolence of the soul this, but the fulfilling of some beautiful law at the junction of the spiritual and the natural, infused through a thousand tissues and welded by a thousand heredities.... One writes much of this kind of thing, for, afar from all books or chance of interchanging ideas, one falls back upon oneself, and one's pen is a safe outlet for superfluous imaginings.

LAKE BUENOS AIRES

On that afternoon I caught a horse and went down to the long point that stretches out into the lake. Although this was a ride of upwards of twenty miles, I saw no living thing upon the land, and on the water only a couple of grebes and three upland geese. My way lay through dense thickets of low growth, the going very sandy and treacherous. The high-water mark, or, as I should rather say, the flood-mark of the lake was outlined by piles and piles of driftwood of milk-toothlike whiteness. Some of the trunks were as large in girth as my body. All this comes down from the mountain forests, carried by torrents from the melting snows. The vegetation on that side of the lake was the most florid and sizeable that I had so far seen in Patagonia. High flowering grass, thorn-bush thickets almost impenetrable, and between these and the margin of the water a wide strewing of rotten trunks of antarctic beech and poles of an arborescent grass-like bamboo. On my way back I made a short cut through the edge of the lake, of which the bed was shingly.

November 13.—I went to the River Fenix and shot a guanaco. Afterwards I took a six-mile walk and shot two snipe. Lake Buenos Aires was certainly the very heart of the wind's domain. While we were there the wind never died down, it blew all the time, often lifting sand and gravel, and sometimes a great piece of our camp-fire, sheltered as that was. It raged on most days, blowing so hard that some people in England would not have cared to venture out of doors.

I have so far given no description of our tents, which were probably the nearest approach to comfort within many hundred miles of Horsham Camp. Mine was small, seven feet by a short six, and four feet high, sustained by four ropes and a pole, the place of the second pole—which we lost—being taken by a bow-legged slip of califate-wood. The tent contained two beds made up of skins and ponchos laid on the green canvas floor, a soldered tin of plug tobacco served by way of a candlestick and upheld a candle-end. Round and about the tent and on its excrescent flooring were heaped our boxes, otherwise the wind would have blown it over. It was a mere bag of a place, with an exit like an animal's hole; but at night, when the storm howled without, our dim light looked homely, the tobacco-scented air was grateful, and a bit of camphor lent its aroma to the place. And there one could lie at ease and read or think at pleasure.

On the 14th I shot another guanaco; it was curious that we were always rich in meat or else in absolute want of it. I had gone out on Jones' black horse for a little exercise towards the River Deseado, and there I surprised the guanaco. He was an old buck and solitary. He gave me a nice shot, then walked a step or two and fell dead. At Horsham Camp we lived in some dread of scorpions; Jones found one on his saddle, Burbury another in the flour or the cooking-pot, and some roosted in our bedding. By the way, our kitchen arrangements were becoming very scanty at that period; we had but two cooking-pots left and one kettle, thanks to the energetic treatment they had received at the heels of the cargueros. It was fervently hoped by all the party that nothing would go wrong with any of these, or we should have been most uncomfortably situated.

On the 15th I started with Burbury and Scrivenor to make an expedition towards Mount Pyramide. Upon our way we were astonished to see three herds of guanaco—fourteen, and ten, and then twenty-one— at different times. Although I was well within shot I did not try to kill any, as we had meat enough.

SEÑOR HANS P. WAAG, OF THE ARGENTINE BOUNDARY COMMISSION

On this day the first huemul seen on our expedition was observed by Burbury. First he saw a buck, afterwards two does, but, owing to the nature of the ground, he was unable to get a shot. We were naturally very anxious to secure a specimen of this very interesting and little known deer, but it was not until we made our trip round the south side of the lake that we were successful.

We made our way across an abomination of desolation, a grey old desert; then crossing a marsh, we descended by a white cliff to the margin of a deep brown lagoon. Of many colours were these lagoons. Burbury said that region was more dismal than Tierra del Fuego—old deserts, varied by marshes and califate-bush, stone and boulder, thorn and sand. After a rest in the afternoon we rode on, and presently struck a deserted camp of the Argentine Boundary Commission, near which the steam-launch, which had been brought across the pampas for the exploration of Lake Buenos Aires, was secreted.

Nothing in the world looks more forlorn than a deserted camp. But we were far from being depressed on this occasion, for in this old camp of Mr. Hans Waag's we made a find which we looked upon as a great slice of luck.

On November 2nd I find in my diary: "More accidents to the cooking-pots, this time at the hoofs of Horqueta. The flat-bottomed pot still survives, but the round one and the kettle are more damaged than whole. One more such accident will mean that the corned-beef tins must be called into requisition."

In this camp we found sundry boxes, old iron-bound packing-cases, and while I was engaged in lighting the fire I heard an exclamation behind me, and Burbury sang out:

"Here's a big enamelled saucepan, nearly new!" It was so, and then again, "And here's another. What luck!"

Of course, if those saucepans had not been shut up in cases, they might have been considered treasure-trove. As it was, one did not need the deductive powers of a Sherlock Holmes to conclude that the travellers who had hidden these pots away so carefully meant to return, find, and once again use them. They belonged, as I knew, to Mr. Waag's Commission of Limits, as they call the Boundary Commission out there. When I met that gentleman in Buenos Aires I never dreamt that I should yet be reduced to stealing his cooking utensils. But we did not "steal" them, we only "availed" ourselves of them. I hope my readers see the difference as plainly as we saw it. And what do you think our companions said when they heard the story? Did they urge us to make restitution? What they said referred to the finding of some empty bottles among the rubbish, "A pity there was no whisky in them!" If there had been, of course we should not ... well, who knows?

FOOTNOTE:
[18] Pampa travel is like cricket in that it defies forecast. Sometimes everything falls in right, at other times nothing comes opportunely to hand.

CHAPTER IX

ROUND AND ABOUT LAKE BUENOS AIRES

Chain of lakes—Size of lake—Sterility and fertility—Trips to Cordillera—Bones of dead game—Shores of lake—Western shore—Tracks in marshes—Northern shore—Rosy camp by Fenix—Guanaco hunt— Horses stray—Cordillera wolf—Vain search for huemul—Return to Horsham Camp—Trip to River Deseado—Paradise of wildfowl—Shooting ostriches—Long-necked game of Patagonia—No ruins or vestiges of older civilisation in Patagonia—Hunting mornings—Wounded guanaco—Indian trail—Trip to River de los Antiguos—Meet ostrich-hunter—Wandering Gauchos—Wanton burning of grass— Second visit to Rosy Camp—Flamingoes—Danger-signals—Scrivenor returns to Horsham Camp—River de los Antiguos.

At last we had arrived at Lake Buenos Aires, a time long looked forward to. The pampas were crossed and left behind, and the lower line of the Andes was reached, the foothills of the great range whose upper summits we had watched for weeks lying high on the sky-line, blue and white and cold, sending the message of a great wind from them to us. We were now upon the shores of the largest of the wonderful network of lakes and lagoons which stretches parallel with the Cordillera hundreds of miles to the southward, ending not far from the Straits of Magellan.

There was to me something infinitely romantic about Lake Buenos Aires. Its aspect was ever changing, and so often you came on a scene supremely beautiful. The wild light of sunset upon the snow-peaks, the grey turbulent water of the lake, and the bull-like wind charging down at us day after day—all these things gave the place an individuality of its own.

The lake is of considerable extent, measuring seventy-five miles in length from S.S.W. to N.N.E., and its waters wage a continual war upon the thorns and scrub growing upon the margin. Vast masses of milk-white timber, blanched by the influences of sun and water and eloquent of the mountain-land of forest whence they have been washed down, lie at the lip of the flood level. When I was there in the dry season the upper rim of timber was about 200 yards distant from the edge of the water.

INLET OF LAKE BUENOS AIRES

The sharp contrast of fertility and sterility that one meets with in Patagonia is remarkable, the more so as they often lie in close proximity the one to the other. I have mentioned an arid spread of yellow mud and stones cut up by deep gorges which we crossed before reaching the lake. I do not think that any painter desiring to picture desolation could do better than descend the central gorge and there paint its gaunt and rugged outlines, tumbled together in a horror of barrenness that the eyes ached to look upon. Yet close to this place, within ten yards of it, a neck of land displayed green scrub, ay, and flowers—beautiful purple sweet-pea-like flowers in profusion! And on the farther side was a green gully with two blue peaty waterholes.

Near by, as I have said, we established a base camp, from which we made four expeditions towards the Cordillera, which lie on the westward of the lake, while, singularly enough, the continental divide appears to be to the eastward of it. On our trips we took with us merely a horse apiece, and carried provisions on our saddles. Meantime the remainder of the troop, which had suffered somewhat on our journey from Bahia Camerones, were turned out to rest and luxuriate upon the marsh grass, that extended in a broad strip for a couple of miles under the ridge, while downhill from the camp towards the south this rich pantano spread still farther.

Around the lake lay piled the skulls and bones of dead game, guanaco and a few huemules. These animals come down to live on the lower ground and near unfrozen water during the cold season, and there, when the weather is particularly severe, they die in crowds. We saw their skeletons, in one or two places literally heaped one upon the other.

During our stay in this neighbourhood I took the opportunity of examining most thoroughly the shores of the lake. The ground which descended to them was cut and intersected by pantanos of wet or drying mud and sand. Upon the eastern shore rose dunes, covered with dense low strips of scrub. In the pantanos the tracks made in the end of the winter, when the snow has melted and the ground is soft, remain visible for five or six months. And thus these hardened marshes offer a study of considerable interest.

Although the Indians declared that guanaco rarely visited the lake, this proved to be incorrect. In the winter a considerable number must live upon and about the shores, for their unmistakable tracks were always to be found. Towards Mount Pyramide on the western side, the number of these tracks was distinctly less—rheas, pumas, the animal known locally as the red fox or Cordillera wolf (Canis magellanicus).

A few huemules (Xenelaphus bisulcus) exist upon the northern shore. In the winter upland geese seem also to favour this spot in large numbers. So strongly does the mud retain the impression of tracks that I was able to follow the trail of a horse, which must have been ridden by one of Mr. Waag's party six months before, for a distance of a couple of miles.

In summer the north shore of Lake Buenos Aires is one of the poorest game centres in Patagonia. During the first fortnight of our stay there we shot but two guanacos. Sometimes for a week one would see nothing save an old ostrich, which was often observed at the far end of the marsh where the horses fed, but he was a wary bird with an experience of human methods, and he would never allow us to approach within shot.

It seemed probable, from the evidence of the tracks, that at the beginning of the hard weather the guanaco trekked down to the level of the lake. For one track made in November there were twenty made in July. The foregoing remarks only refer to the northern shore of the lake; on the eastern and southern sides things were very different, and about them we enjoyed good sport.

On November 21, Scrivenor, Jones and I made a little expedition to the River Fenix where it enters the lake, and there we came upon the most favourable camping-ground we had yet seen in the whole country. We pitched our camp—afterwards called Rosy Camp—in the midst of high yellow grass beside the narrow river that wound between banks, on which green low scrub ran riot, and enormous califate-bushes made impenetrable patches of thicket. Jones and I, on our arrival, went to examine the mouth of the river. Our camp was quite drowsy with the humming of insects, for, sheltered as it was from the wind by trees and by the cliffs of a lonely hummock, it gave us a delightful feeling of comfort and well-being after our many very different experiences of camps among the high dunes and rocks over which the wind whistled.

On the way Jones shot a Chiloe widgeon and I an upland goose. We found many tracks of puma and some of guanaco and huemul. As we walked towards the lake, I saw upon the outermost promontory of land a guanaco outlined against the evening sky. Hurrying on as fast as we could, which was not very fast, as I had poisoned my knee and was lame, we found the herd on a neck of land, to escape from which they would be obliged to pass within a hundred yards of us provided they did not take to the water. So we decided not to stalk them, but simply showed ourselves; as we expected, they broke landwards, passing within about seventy yards with their ears laid back, swaying their long necks and leaping and jinking among the stones. I pulled one over as she ranged up the side of the cliff. She turned out to be heavy with young, and the buck with her stopped at the top of the hill, but when I went towards him he fled. We were delighted at thus getting meat, especially as this guanaco was the fattest we had yet shot. Her flesh was, however, very strong.

When we were returning Jones, who was in front, suddenly said, "There go the horses!" It was so. They had stampeded, leaving us to get home as best we could. We threw off our coats, laid down our rifles carefully, and ran. Jones' horse was in hobbles, but being used to them kept up with his companions; we were, however, lucky enough to catch them after a couple of miles, and making bridles out of our waist-scarves rode them into camp. Scrivenor said the horses had suddenly started madly, broken their cabrestos, dashed together and then made off. We thought at the time they must have winded a puma, but this proved to be a mistake, for in the night two of them again escaped, and Jones retrieved them when the first streaks of dawn were etching the landscape in black and white. He woke me and we discovered that a wolf must have come into camp and stolen our duck and goose. This wolf had also eaten both my rifle-slings within three yards of where we were sleeping. While we were discussing our ill luck and lamenting the fact that we had carefully plucked the duck and goose upon the preceding evening, I observed the author of our misfortunes calmly watching us from under a bush. Revenge was, of course, uppermost in my thoughts. I killed her with a Mauser. She proved to be an old female 3 ft. 8 in. from the top of her teeth to the end of her tail.

It was beautifully warm all day in Rosy Camp, as we had named it, and we lay on the ground after making much-needed toilettes in the river.

The next night we had a visit from the mate of the wolf we had killed. It is a singular fact that the horses were at the least as much afraid of these wolves as they were of the pumas. While I was writing my diary and nursing my knee, which had swollen to a great size, the wolf crept within ten yards and had a look at me. I got up and limped across for my gun, but my movements did not in the least seem to discompose his serenity. He even advanced nearer, and showed not the smallest fear of me. This quality of fearlessness is very marked in the Cordillera wolves, which possess it in a greater degree than the pampa foxes. On one occasion when a wolf thus came to investigate our camp, my large deerhound, Tom, ran at him, and was met with a devastating bite. Indeed, I had to go to Tom's help. In the present instance I took up the shot-gun and gave the brute a charge of No. 4. He leaped straight upwards into the air, howling and snarling, and sank down quite dead.

These wolves kill young guanaco, and I have observed them pursuing a huemul. They kill sheep when a flock is brought into the neighbourhood of the Cordillera, generally remaining by their quarry after daylight. I have never observed them farther from the Cordillera than the northern shores of Lake Buenos Aires.

On November 24, Scrivenor went back to the base camp, as he had toothache. Jones and I rode south across the Fenix. Although we saw the track of a huemul in the sand we failed to catch any glimpse of the animals themselves on that day, but shot four bandurias, locally called by the Welshmen "land-ducks." This is the black-faced ibis (Theristicus caudatus). I was very eager to secure a specimen of the huemul in his summer coat, and to observe as much as possible of this beautiful deer, but no luck attended us then in that particular. Finally, we went back to Horsham Camp still unsuccessful. During our absence Burbury had killed a large Cordillera wolf near Horsham Camp.

THE HORSES RETRIEVED

On November 28, Barckhausen and I camped in the cañadon or valley of River Deseado, a swampy, reedy spot, tenanted by great numbers of upland geese, flocks of Chiloe widgeon (Mareca sibilatrix) and brown pintails. I also observed here the rosy-billed duck (Metopiana peposaca), the blue-winged teal (Querquedula cyanoptera), and what I took to be the red shoveller (Spatula platalea). But this last-named bird I did not shoot, and so I cannot speak with absolute certainty upon the point. Besides these, I saw flamingoes (Phœnicopterus ignipalliatus) and the black-necked swan (Cygnis nigricollis). A flock of parrots were flying about the heights, but of these I was unable to procure a specimen. The reedy pools and backwaters in this cañadon were, without exception, the most glorious paradise of wildfowl that I have ever seen.

On our way back from the River Deseado I secured the first Rhea darwini shot during the expedition. With the exception of wild cattle, the ostrich is the most difficult to procure of Patagonian game. These birds are always on the alert, and generally make off when you are still a mile away. They never pause save upon commanding ground. The most usual method of obtaining them is to run them down with dogs or to bolas them after the manner of the Indians and Gauchos on horseback. They are indeed a quarry well worthy of the attention of the still-hunter. The male is sometimes killed with a rifle when attending to the chickens, towards whom—with the exception of laying the eggs—he stands in place of a mother. At such times he will, when approached, pretend to be wounded and limp away with wings outspread to attract the hunters after him. An ostrich when shot through the body will always run from thirty to forty yards before dropping. This first ostrich, which I shot, was about four hundred yards away, and I should not have secured him had he not allowed me to get my range with a couple of preliminary shots. Down he went at last, and, immediately afterwards, as I was congratulating myself, appeared an ostrich running low through the grass. I thought it was the one I had shot and struck back for my horse. While I was galloping after the fast-disappearing bird, I rode right on to the first bird, which had been shot through the lungs. On measurement I found him to be five feet in height and three feet high at the shoulder.

The greatest number of adult ostriches I ever saw together was seven. This in a cañadon off the River Deseado. At a later date I saw forty-two together, but this included many small and immature birds.

The long-necked game of Patagonia is difficult to stalk owing to their having such a field of vision. The ruse of tying up one's horse in full view gained me many a guanaco, but was quite a useless trick in the case of ostriches. The Cruzado was by this time an A1 shooting-horse. He would stand anywhere and wait my return, he would also allow me to fire quite close to him, but he would never allow any white object to be put upon his back. If this was done, he would at once rear and throw himself back.

There is one thing which strikes me forcibly with regard to Patagonia. Here is small vestige of the elder peoples, and little of any older civilisations.[19] Even in the hearts of deserts in the old world are to be found traces of ancient cities, where men lived long ages ago. But nothing that bears farthest resemblance to a ruin, to the "one stone laid upon another" that tells of man's settled home, exists in Patagonia. Yet though the ruined cities of other countries are old, Patagonia is older yet. The nomad tribes have roamed here through the centuries, leaving the grass to grow over their old camp-fires, but never altering or marking with any permanent mark the face of this old land. No, though Patagonia is in a sense the oldest of all, for here we come face to face with prehistoric times—the skeletons of the greater beasts, the flint weapons of primitive man with practically nothing save the years to intervene. A lean humanity, untouched by aught save nature, has run out its appointed course until very recent years; and there is little to testify to its wanderings but the brown trail of generations of footsteps, which ten years of disuse would blot out for ever. You cannot there gaze over the ruins of a once populous city and say, "Here lived a dead people." No, you can but think by lonely river or lagoon, "The bygone Indians may here have had their camp, or the greater beasts their lair." The netted lakes, the gaunt Cordillera, the limitless pampa and the unceasing wind—that is all. Cañadon follows cañadon, pampa succeeds pampa, you have the Atlantic to the east of you and the Andes to the west of you, and between, in all the vast country, beside the Indian trail, the only paths are game-tracks!

On December 2 we were again short of meat, therefore Jones and I went hunting. These early mornings upon the high ground above the lake will never, I think, be forgotten by any of us who shared them. It was a vivid and pulsating life, and the hunting was carried on under conditions unique to Patagonia.

In the slight depression through which the River Fenix winds, herds of guanaco were to be found, each point containing any number between half a dozen to forty head. On the morning I write of we were not long in finding our game. A large herd, including several guanaco chicos, were to be seen from the heights dotted about upon the faded greenish grass of the valley beneath us. The sun, newly risen, had just begun to suck up the balls of white mist that rolled up and down the cuplike hollows, and as the light strengthened it brought out the gold and white colouring of the guanacos feeding in the valley. The horse I was riding had done no work for three weeks, and was fit to gallop for his life.

STERILE GROUND TO NORTH OF LAKE BUENOS AIRES

The herds were in a place quite inaccessible to stalking, but it was certain that they would break for the hills to the south. Immediately they saw us they took to flight in the direction we expected, and we dashed away to cut them off. The Patagonian horse soon begins to take an interest of his own in galloping game. We arrived within two hundred yards of where the herds had begun to straggle in a long line up the bare side of a range of round bald-headed hummocks, but we were not in time to get a shot before they disappeared over the sky-line. When we reached the top of the hills the guanacos were, of course, nowhere to be seen, but after an hour's tracking we again located them among the hummocks in a depression filled with dry thorn. This time we separated and Jones showed himself at the far end of the gorge, while I made a circuit and lay down upon the top of a hill towards which I thought they were likely to break. This they did the instant they saw Jones, who got a shot, breaking the leg of one. I killed another as they passed. We jumped upon our horses to overtake Jones' wounded guanaco, that was keeping up with the herd.

My horse, the Alazan, had recently received some jumping lessons, and being an animal with no sense of proportion, had been seized with a mania for jumping everything. Jones nearly fell off his horse with laughing when the Alazan valiantly charged a califate-bush, eight feet high and full of thorns, through which he dashed in one jump and two supplementary bucks. Emerging upon the other side we set off after our guanaco and enjoyed one of the most glorious gallops that ever fell to the lot of man. I could not help admiring the way in which Jones, who was a born rider, and, like most Gauchos, had lived all his life on the outside of a horse, picked his way among the great fragments of rock that filled the hollows. The Alazan jumped them, and proceeded upon his appointed path to his own evident satisfaction, the infinite amusement of Jones, and the terror of myself. However, though one might take exception to his methods, the Alazan had a turn for speed and bore my fourteen stone nobly to the front.

Presently the guanaco we were pursuing dashed across a shallow lagoon and fell upon the farther side of it. As we dismounted we observed fresh tracks of a wild bull, which was heading north-west towards the Cordillera. Although we followed these tracks for twenty miles and came upon ample evidence of their being quite recently made, evening fell upon us and we were obliged to turn campwards.

On our arrival we had a look at the horses and sat up late expecting the return of Barckhausen and Burbury, who had gone to look for the Indian trail, which the Indians told us led under the foothills of the Cordillera to the end of the continent. I have given a description of the trail in another place. It is in its way as remarkable a highroad as the Grand Trunk Road in India. Were it not for the tracks of horses, and the occasional dead camp-fire to which it leads you, it would be impossible to distinguish it from a series of guanaco-tracks running parallel. Nevertheless, many an ostrich-hunter has by its aid found his way into the settlements, when without it he would have wandered far and wide upon the pampas.

It was not before the next day, however, that Burbury and Barckhausen returned with the news that they had found the trail some twenty leagues away near the cañadon of the River Deseado.

I have mentioned my great desire to shoot a huemul (Xenelaphus bisulcus), and, as we had been disappointed in this respect in our former expeditions, I decided to penetrate into the gorge of the River de los Antiguos. We made arrangements for an absence of some duration from the base camp, leaving Jones and Burbury in charge.

On the 5th we started, and, while riding to Rosy Camp, saw columns of smoke arising from amongst the hills on the other side of the Fenix. We thought they were signals of Indians and answered them. By here and there burning a bush we signalled to the unknown, and in this way drew together. It was upon the yellow shores of a dry lagoon that we met with the first white man we had seen since leaving Colohuapi. This man and his errand were so typical of the country and its methods of life that I do not apologise for sketching his portrait at full length.

As he came riding towards us we perceived that he was seated upon a saddle of sheepskins, and rode a yellow horse, whose condition told its own story. In Patagonia one gets into the habit of noticing the horse before the rider. The practised eye can learn from its appearance and condition the answers to at least three questions. The rider was a very small Argentine, and he had, he informed us, come up from

San Julian. You who do not know Patagonia may think it strange that one should meet with one's fellow creatures miles from anywhere, but the Patagonian Gaucho is in his way unique. He is as much a pioneer of civilisation as were the fur-clad hunters of the Bad Lands of North America. By habit and by choice the Gaucho is a nomad. It is not too much to say that, grumbler as he is when upon the pampas, there is a deep-seated instinct in his heart ever leading him back to that peculiar mode of life which has become second nature to him. There is an idea in England that Patagonia is as untrodden as the Polar regions. But this is a fallacy. The tides of civilisation are moving slowly westwards, and will so continue to move until they are thrown back by the great natural barrier of the Andes. But as the tide will often fling a little wreath of foam far ahead of its advance—a wreath that disappears for the moment perhaps, but yet its fall has marked a spot that in course of time will be swept over by the rising water; so in Patagonia these few wanderers break away from the settlements upon the coast, and set out with their little store of flour, fariña, and maté, their troop of horses, and their half-dozen hounds. They say that they are looking for good ground or, as they call it, good camp to settle upon, but few of them actually carry out this final intention. It is the free life that they love, the wild gallops after the ostriches and the guanacos, the sound slumbers under the stars, and the absence of all control.

Such a wanderer was our small friend. He had, he said, two companions, whom he had lost when running ostriches. As we sat there upon our horses and looked from the man to the great clouds of smoke which were arising from the direction of the Fenix, of which he was the miserable author, one felt inclined to throw him in his own fire. For whereas, whenever I or my men lit a smoke, we were careful that it should burn but one bush, and not spread to scar and disfigure the face of the country, this irresponsible little being, who had, as it were, ridden to meet us out of the nowhere, persistently lit his reckless fires among the best grass, so that they burnt huge areas. It was a remarkable, and in its way a painful, reflection that this puny bit of humanity with his box of cheap matches could do more harm in half an hour than he would be likely to be able to repair during a lifetime. The fact is, a fire will burn a very small area upon the pampas near the coast, where there is little for the flames to take hold upon, while here in the high grass, near the Cordillera, it may rage for two or three days, devastating and blackening the landscape.

Rather annoyed with the small man, I directed Barckhausen to ask him why he had lighted so many smokes. He replied that he had done so in order to recall his companions. As the man was, after the fashion of the pampa, our guest, there was nothing more to be said on the matter, but had I foreseen how much trouble his mania for raising smokes was yet to cause us, I should probably have remonstrated with him.

That evening, as we rode into Rosy Camp, we saw a number of flamingos upon the lagoon, and shot an upland goose. The following morning I woke up in the grey of the dawn to see a Cordillera wolf nosing among the ashes of our camp-fire. I shot it, to the great delight of the small man, from whom after breakfast we parted. We had not advanced a mile before the little demon was again sending up a smoke to heaven. Burbury, who met him afterwards, said he believed that he carried a cargo of nothing but matches in order to be able to indulge to the utmost his passion for destroying the country through which he happened to be passing.

On December 7 we arrived above the River de los Antiguos, and, as we were about to descend the barranca, saw two columns of smoke rising some two miles off. Two columns of smoke close together were our danger-signal, and meant "Something very wrong, come at once." I was morally certain that they were the work of the small man, whom we had nicknamed "the Snipe," especially as the smokes were lit at a distance from the position of Horsham Camp, and if anything serious had happened, it seemed most probable that the two men left in charge there would have lit their signal-fires on the hill close behind the camp, instead of riding to some distance for that purpose. However, there was nothing for it but to send Scrivenor back, with instructions to show a smoke upon the shore of the lake behind an island in our view if my presence were really required.

While he returned to Horsham Camp, Barckhausen and I rode on towards the cañadon of the River de los Antiguos.

FOOTNOTE:
[19] I believe, as does Dr. Moreno, that a race of Indians, now extinct, once dwelled among the foothills of the Cordillera.

CHAPTER X

THE GORGE OF THE RIVER DE LOS ANTIGUOS

Descent into Gorge of the River de los Antiguos—Rest-and-be-Thankful Camp—First huemul—Greed of condors—Aspect of Gorge—Tameness of guanaco—Join Van Plaaten's route—Stinging flies—Signal-smokes—De los Antiguos in flood—Difficulty of crossing—Attempt to swim over—Washed away—Loss of rifle and gun—Return to western bank—Cold night—Start next morning—Upper ford impassable—Scanty diet—Fording torrent—Long ride to Horsham Camp—Fire-blackened landscape—News of red puma.

Barckhausen and I continued along the south shore of the lake until we struck the River de los Antiguos, a small but rapid torrent flowing through a huge frowning gorge, between very steep barrancas. Farther to the west a second river, the River Jeinemeni, runs for some distance almost parallel with it and discharges itself into the lake some little distance beyond the mouth of the Antiguos. Between these two rivers lies a tableland, which I was anxious to visit. We, therefore, looked for a favourable place to descend into the valley of the River de los Antiguos, and presently discovered a spot where the cliffs were rather less perpendicular. The barranca, which was about one hundred and fifty feet in height, being composed of sliding sand and stones, covered with a high growth of bushes, presented a troublesome route for the horses. They had been tied together by their headstalls, the only way in which it was possible to drive them. It was now necessary to dismount and take them down singly. Two of them, Mula and Luna, refused to face the slope, and had to be urged on by persuasions from behind. When Mula at last consented to begin the descent, he lost his head and slid down the barranca, almost carrying Barckhausen, who was pulling at his cabresto from below, with him.

When we all arrived safely at the bottom, we found the bed of the river was formed of large boulders, and progress was consequently very slow. After a time we forded across, the water barely reaching to the horses' knees, but flowing so rapidly as to bring down good-sized tree-trunks with it. We made a camp in a bare place backed by a deep green forest. After our meal, which consisted of half an emergency ration each, a couple of two-ounce dumplings and some tea, we climbed the western barranca, and discovered an open space in the forest, where the grass rose to our middles, and we were greeted by the wet smell of earth, to which we had long been strangers on the dry stretches of the pampas. We called the spot Rest-and-be-thankful Camp, and at once moved the horses up to it, and on the way Fritz, who happened to be in an obstinate mood, lay down among the stones. Little did we think at the time how often we were destined to climb up and down that weary barranca.

LAKE BUENOS AIRES FROM THE CAÑADON OF THE RIVER DE LOS ANTIGUOS

A number of animals live in the Gorge of the River de los Antiguos. Quite close to the camp I found tracks of wolves, guanaco, huemul, a wild cat, and the smaller rodents. There was a little story to be read on the wet sand. A huemul had come down to drink the preceding evening, and had been stalked by a puma and her cub. The puma must have been giving her offspring a lesson in killing. You could see that the puma had leaped upon the huemul from a neighbouring thicket, and there had been a struggle. The huemul, however, managed to dash back into the trees and finally made his escape upon the other side of the patch of forest.

After resting the night we rode up the Gorge, where we saw some guanaco and found an ostrich egg. We left the three extra horses tethered in the camp, and rode along the heights above the river. The going was bad all the time. Stones, cliffs and rifts hindered our advance, but presently we began to leave the bush behind and entered into a bare tract of iron-grey hillsides and black boulders. Here we stopped for a meal, for which we made an omelette of the ostrich egg, and ate it powdered with chocolate. We cooked it in a tin plate with a little mutton-fat, and uncommonly good we found it.

About two leagues farther on I shot a guanaco, but my desire was to see a huemul. Every new variety of game was of interest to us, not only from the zoological point of view, but also from that of the hungry man, for we had had a very long spell of guanaco meat. We spent the night in a spot where the horses fed on some fair grass.

We climbed the highest eminence at dawn and looked out for a smoke behind the island, but seeing none we pushed on. I was riding far ahead along the tableland above the river valley when I saw a huemul. It sprang out from some rocks ahead of me. It was a young buck, and when he caught sight of me he stood at gaze. The huemul is one of the most beautiful deer in the world, although he only carries small spiked horns of no great size. His summer coat is of a rich reddish-brown, which, when examined closely, is found to be thickly mingled with white hairs. In shape huemules are rather strongly built, being about the size of fallow-deer. I have given a detailed account of the habits of the huemul, of which no other record exists, in a later chapter, so will say no more upon that subject here. I was most unwillingly obliged to shoot the buck, for we were in need of food. Leaving the meat, after tying a handkerchief above it to scare away the condors, we hastened back to fetch the extra horses. We had

had scanty diet for some days, and the thought of a full meal put strength into us. We were not long in bringing up the remainder of our troop, but when returning we saw three condors drop suspiciously near the dead huemul. By the time we arrived there was hardly an ounce of meat left on the bones, and only the quarter, which we had hidden in the bushes, remained, even that being a good deal torn and mangled.

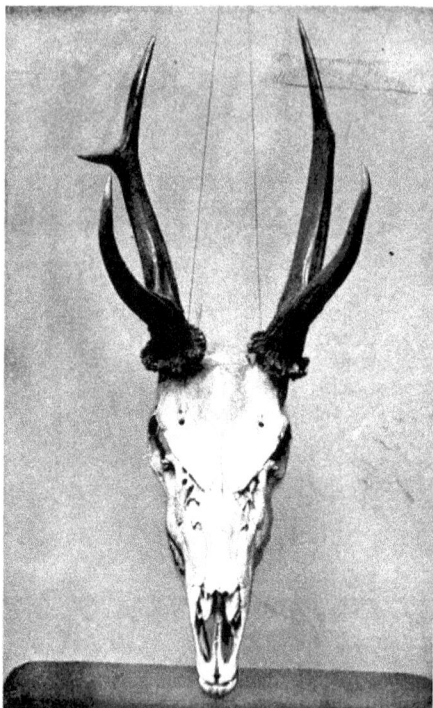

BEST HEAD OF HUEMUL (XENELAPHUS BISULCUS)

Such as it was, however, we made the best of it, and after cutting away the damaged parts, found enough for a meal. It turned out to be the driest, stringiest, worst meat I have ever for my sins been forced to eat.[20]

As night fell, the Gorge—it became the Gorge to us—assumed a more and more sinister aspect. Of all the scenes I had up to that time beheld in Patagonia, this was the most repellent and inhospitable. The little torrent (which was destined to play us such a trick), the high iron-grey bluffs and escarpments, the soaring condors, the scavenger caranchos, and the black shadows of the Cordillera, made up a picture that was both grand and menacing.

Next day I shot a guanaco. Very much easier work than it had been on the pampas. A guanaco would remain lying down until you were within a long shot, and one actually watched us and neighed while we discussed our porridge. Man had never, I fancy, molested them before.

We advanced for a good distance up the river over terribly bad ground, all boulders and steep cliffs, and then we attempted to ford to the other side. The two black horses, however, seemed to have conceived a horror of the river and could not be induced to cross. They simply made us very wet, and we had to go forward on foot. We were now within easy distance of the end of the Gorge, and had joined the route of Von Plaaten[21] from the south.

On December 10 I went out in the evening to shoot something for the pot. On the first ridge I came to I stalked and killed a big guanaco buck, putting a bullet into his lungs. Then I signalled to Barckhausen to come and help to cut him up. As I waited there in the fading light, wondering at the desolation of the place, a little huemul buck came bounding along and "paid the penalty," as the cricket reporters say. I had some trouble to keep off the condors while I went to some distance to call Barckhausen.

Altogether the Gorge was not an inviting spot with its hot marshy valleys and fat stinging flies. After sweating among the boulders in the lower ground, if we climbed the barranca, the chill wind from the Cordillera nipped our very bones.

As I sat writing my diary during those days, diabolical-looking insects with upturned tails used to crawl across the page.

My desire to penetrate farther at that time seemed likely to be fulfilled, as so far we had seen no warning smoke from the lake direction. The chief difficulties hindering our advance were the treacherous footing on the barrancas, which we were obliged to scale very frequently, and the trouble with the horses both on them and at the fords.

Finally I decided to leave Barckhausen with the horses and to walk on as long as food held out, for the boulders made riding impossible. But next morning, just as I had fixed up my kit preparatory to starting, a column of smoke began to arise somewhere in the direction of the lake. We fancied at first it was Scrivenor, who had come back to rejoin us, and we hastened up the cliff. But in that clear air distances are very deceptive, and the smoke, which from the depth of the Gorge had looked so near, turned out to be on the farther shore of Lake Buenos Aires. Then we perceived there were two fires throwing up their smoke in the morning sun—the "Come-at-once" signal.

We did not loiter, but in a quarter of an hour were climbing the barranca from our camp. The old game with the horses had to be gone through again. We made our way straight down the strip of tableland towards the lake, along the high sliding cliffs of the river's cañadon. It was a long ride, and as we went along the fact became obvious that the river had risen during the night and was still rising. The waters had grown earth-coloured and large trees were being hurtled down-stream.

The warm weather which we had been experiencing must have melted the snows which feed the torrents of the Cordillera. Rivers inside and in the neighbourhood of the Cordillera vary during the spring very much in volume, changing in a single day or night from a mere trickle of water to a torrent 100 yards in width. In the present instance the River de los Antiguos had begun to rise in the day while we were hunting. At length we saw a place where a big shelf of stone and shingle rising in the middle of the river divided it into two streams. To reach the bank nearest to this island of shingle it was necessary to climb down some two hundred feet of an uncommonly nasty slope. On the way the horses struck a bed of rolling stones and arrived very suddenly. The gut of the Gorge was choked with green forest and decaying vegetation; large dead trees, mostly trunks of antarctic beech, were jammed together, intersected by a dozen miniature torrents all sluicing down full of water since the melting of the snows.

Arrived at the river, my horse took the ford at once and went in straightly to his shoulders. The current was running like a mill-race—overstrong for us, but fortunately we had not plunged in too deeply, and so got back to the shore.

Had it not been for the two smokes, which we had arranged were not to be used save in the greatest extremity, I should have made a camp and waited to see if the river would fall. As things were, it seemed absolutely necessary to cross at once.

We now went a little up-stream, and I stripped off some of my clothes and waded down into the river. It was so cold that it took away all feeling from my feet. I had my precious rifle with me as well as a dear old shot-gun. The strip of water I was about to cross was quite narrow. I thought of leaving the guns behind me, but that would have meant another crossing of the river, which was so cold that it seemed to burn like fire.

I had not reached the middle when my left foot went into a hole, the current caught me, and the banks began to run backwards. As long as the water was deep I stuck to the two guns, but a little down-stream the river ran through boulders just awash, and among these I got rather knocked about. I dropped the shot-gun and clung to the Mauser, which was to us the more valuable of the two. Lower down the river was a shallow waterfall, studded with rocks and boulders. My knee caught between two rocks, and as I was afraid of having my leg broken, and had sustained rather a bad knock on the back of the head, I let the rifle go, and, with the help of my hands, got clear. I was washed down the fall into deeper water, where swimming was possible. The current carried me a yard down-stream for every inch I made across it, but in time I reached the end of the bank of shingle before mentioned.

After all, disappointment awaited me, for I found the second branch of the river, beyond the shingle bank, was running so furiously that, unless I had the help of a rope, crossing it would be too dangerous. Barckhausen could not follow me in any case, as he was unable to swim, so that eventually I was obliged to cross back again and rejoin him. On regaining the shore my plight was sufficiently miserable. I had kept on my shirt and jersey to save me from the stones, but of course they were soaking. It was six o'clock in the evening, the sun had lost its power, a cold wind was blowing, and I had nothing to pass the night in save some oilskins and my wet clothes; besides, I was rather badly cut about the head and knees.

I must explain that during my swim Barckhausen had succeeded in driving the horses into the river, and they were come to anchor on the shingle island in mid-stream. Our bedding was upon the back of one of them, and the river was still rising rapidly. We therefore decided to return to the camp, as being more sheltered. Barckhausen kindly lent me his shirt, as he had his vest, coat and great-coat, which were dry. We started once more to climb that weary two hundred feet of barranca, and were much beset by rolling stones and sliding sand. Scarcely had we reached the top when the horses, after standing for an hour and a half on their mid-stream island, took it into their heads to turn about and swim back, so we scrambled down our cliff-side again and made a camp amongst the sand and bushes. Here I saw a wild cat with young, the only one I met with in Patagonia.

REST-AND-BE-THANKFUL CAMP

We now reviewed our sleeping accommodation. The blankets were too wet to be of any service. Barckhausen luckily was in the habit of carrying a portion of his bedding upon his saddle, and this had escaped the water and was dry. I had a horse-rug and a small blanket. It came on a bone-wet night, the most miserable we had either of us spent.

Besides, I was very anxious about the possible condition of things at Horsham Camp, for the two smokes must have meant something serious, and yet we were unable to go to the help of our comrades. We made some thin porridge for supper and turned in. All night long the river continued to rise, we could hear it gulping and swallowing at the sand and shingle of the bank. I determined to try the higher ford, by which we had originally crossed, in the morning.

I find the following in my diary, written while the porridge was cooking:

"December 12.—Only a sportsman can realise my feelings. At one fell swoop both my guns, my old friends, gone! The more serious loss of the two is the Mauser. It has accompanied me upon my travels 10,000 miles, and was always to be relied on. And now to fancy it probably glimmering up through the deep waters of Buenos Aires Lake! Is there any use in saying more? When we get back to camp I shall have to fall back on the reserve Mauser, which has no back-sight, or I should say has a back-sight fastened on with a strip of raw hide. You arrange it before the shot, and when you have it balanced you loose off, and if the gun does not misfire you may hit something. How different to the rifle that is gone! And the shot-gun, which has also departed with the Mauser, was a gun with a history. Given to my uncle for gallant services in another part of the world—a Purdey double-hammerless 12-bore, I regarded it as an heirloom. Why did I ever bring it to Patagonia? Many a time have I, out of the shooting season, cuddled the stock and shot imaginary birds, and dreamed of the phalanx of geese bearing down on me in Scotland in the coming October! It is all over. His glittering locks "clutch the sand," or in fragments he shifts with the waters of the inhospitable torrent. Oh, my guns! my guns! Well, it was a congenial death to you, and I am glad to think the Mauser had killed a couple of Patagonian huemules before he came to his end. But, sentiment apart—and there is a great deal of it in this affair—the loss is very serious. True I have still at Horsham Camp four rifles and a shot-gun (two Colts, a Paradox, a 12-bore and the sick Mauser), but none of them are in the same class with the lost ones."

Before leaving the camp I went down again to the river brink to seek for wreckage. Nothing was to be seen save rock and stone, overturned trees and boulders. My regrets for the losses which had befallen us were, however, moderated by the reflection that I might well be thankful I was not personally keeping the two guns cold company in the bottom of the lake.

We were astir at four o'clock by moonlight, and started three-quarters of an hour later. To us, knocked about and dog-tired as we were, the going was difficult. The barrancas seemed endless. The river was now a yellow flood, crashing and rushing down the cañadon, bearing trees, bushes, and logs with its whirl and flurry. When we arrived at the upper ford it was only to find six feet of water there and a fall formed beyond it—quite impassable in fact.

Our position, in the face of this difficulty, was rather a serious one. We had food for three days, that is, porridge, and though "parritch is gran' food," it is not, alone, good to work very hard on. The snows were still melting in the hills, and, given a protracted period of warm weather, it might be days before the river would allow of our passing through it. I lit a signal-fire on the hills in the hope that my party at Horsham Camp would reply.

HUEMUL (XENELAPHUS BISULCUS) IN SUMMER COAT

It was possible that our small Argentine friend had again been lost "running ostriches" and had again lit up half the countryside to call his companions' attention to that important fact. The only weapon left us was a broken Colt and the cartridges in it. But apart from our own position was the far more serious fact that our companions were signalling to us to "Come at once—something wrong."

All the day through we patrolled the river banks, riding up and down searching for a ford. About six in the evening we found a place where an island broke the force of the torrent, and we fancied the water was falling.

The river everywhere was shut in by high cliffs. At the foot of the cliff we descended the ground was so soft that the horses sank, and we had to haul them through. When we came down to the level of the river, it appeared very different, viewed close at hand, to the encouraging idea we had formed, even through the telescope, from the cliffs above. But the set of the current was for once towards the farther bank, where it culminated in rapids.

I decided to leave the three worst horses, and we found them a fine stretch of grass and water at Roblé Camp. There we left them. They fell to feeding very quietly, and we rode away to the barranca we had so often surmounted that at length we had formed a road through its bushes.

The river appeared to be still rising, and was at that spot sixty yards or so broad. Large trees went whirling by us as we waded down on our horses into the outer plash of the stream. The horses took it bravely and slowly, tired as they were. We now found there were two islands, a smaller and a larger one, on our line of crossing, upon which we rested, and soon nothing remained save a twenty-foot stream between us and the farther bank.

Once my horse fell but recovered himself. Small blame to him, brave beast, he had been carrying fourteen stone all day. At last, after a strenuous moment, the water grew shallower, and we came out on the farther side into a belt of green scrub.

Luck never comes alone. As we rode on three huemules dashed out of a glade and I broke the neck of an old buck with the damaged Colt. I had taken a careful sight for a shoulder-shot! We cut up the huemul, skinned the head and rode on, and soon were out of the cañadon of the de los Antiguos River and riding through the bushes towards our companions. The moon, on her rising, found us still going, and the camp we made was a dozen miles from the river.

GRASSY CAMP

That night we put the horses in splendid grass, and in the false dawn of the next morning were in the saddle again. We had about fifty miles to cover before reaching Horsham Camp, and never in my life have I so regretted my weight as on that day. About noon, as we were crossing a white dry lake-bed, a column of smoke went up on Fenix Ford; our comrades were then hurrying to us as we were to them. We answered at once, and a couple of hours later perceived two horsemen on a distant rise. Two! Nothing wrong in camp then! Hurrah! They turned out to be Scrivenor and Burbury.

At last the vega, two miles out of Horsham Camp, began. I had ridden so much off my horse that the cinch would not hold him. An awful wind arose and the country round—burned by those miserable Santa Cruz people—sent up dust in clouds and blinded us. At last the green tents came in sight, one of which held, I knew, a reindeer sleeping-bag, wherein was to be found warmth and sleep.

When we met my first question was, of course, to ask as to who might be the perpetrator of the two fires we had seen upon the previous day, and which were still burning.

"As to those," said Burbury, "they must have been lighted by the little man whom you entertained at the Fenix. He came into our camp after he left you, as also did his companions. We knew that you would wonder who had lit the smokes. When we saw yours, we at once came to meet you." As we rode along towards our base camp we passed through acres of fire-blackened land and cursed the small man (his name is still a mystery to us) by bell, book, and candle. I had carefully informed him that two fires was our "Come-at-once" signal, and can only suppose that the irresponsible little creature had forgotten. After all, our resentment against the author of our misfortunes was not uncalled for. He had given Scrivenor a fifty-mile ride, had been the direct cause of our losing two guns, had made us abandon three horses, and had given Barckhausen and myself eighty or ninety miles of extra marches, besides compelling us to cross the River de los Antiguos when in flood. We had also to thank him for our miserable night upon the shores of the river. Against all this he had left us a lame hound which we feared could travel no farther.

His companions had in my absence visited our camp and had conversed with Burbury. This conversation, however, left us a much more valuable legacy. One of these men, an Austrian, had informed Burbury that the Indians had told him of a puma which lived farther to the south among the foothills of the Cordillera, and which differed in some essential respects from the grey puma of the plains. He described it as being "of a reddish colour, more fierce than the silver puma, and much smaller!" This was the first time I heard of the animal now named Felis concolor pearsoni, of which I afterwards was fortunate enough to obtain a skin.

When we arrived in camp, which we did late upon that afternoon, we ourselves as well as our horses were pretty well tired out, but a couple of days in the tent, a tin of cocoa, and some ointment for the cuts received from the rocks in the river, soon reinvigorated us, and we were ready to start for the River de los Antiguos, the scene of our petty disasters, once more.

FOOTNOTES:
[20] This was a very lean buck; a fat doe is excellent.

[21] Louis von Plaaten Hallermund, of the Argentine Boundary Commission, almost reached Lake Buenos Aires from Lake Puerrydon about two years previously. Mr. Waag had completed the journey, but we did not know this.

YOUNG GUANACO

CHAPTER XI

SOME HUNTING CAMPS

Second trip to De los Antiguos River—Pass Rosy Camp—Fenix flood gone down—Wounded guanaco takes to water—Mauser and shot-gun retrieved—Losing and seeking in Patagonia—Recover horses at Rest-and-be-Thankful Camp—Visit to River Jeinemeni—Trained horse for hunting—Shooting guanaco—Condors—Cañadon of Jeinemeni—Huemul hunting—Ostriches and their habits—Return to Horsham Camp—Night in camp.

On December 16, the interval having been taken out by me in sleeping off my chill and fatigue, Scrivenor, Jones and I made a start to retrieve the horses abandoned in the Los Antiguos cañadon by Barckhausen and myself. We each took a horse and a spare animal which carried the tent, for the weather was breaking to the westward. It was our intention to ride the fifty miles back on the horses which we had left behind in the Gorge.

On arriving at the Fenix we were delighted to find that its waters had fallen considerably, and that the pebbly bank in mid-stream, at the ford by Rosy Camp, was once more visible. Almost upon our old camping-ground we found, as we rode over the sand-hills by the lake, a pair of guanaco feeding. Jones dismounted and had a couple of shots, neither of which took effect. The animals had, however, not perceived Scrivenor and myself, and came past us upon the shores of the lake, and here Jones and I ran down and met the female, killing her after a long chase, which ended by her trying to swim out into the lake.

Upon the evening of the second day we saw again the ill-fated River de los Antiguos, and striking south we made a camp, as nearly as I could judge, opposite to where I had spent the night shivering in oilskins. Of course, at starting, the question had been mooted: Might we not, provided the river had fallen sufficiently, find the lost guns, and at any rate that treasure, the Mauser?

The probabilities were, of course, very much against such good fortune, and it was almost certain, that even did we find either of them, it would be useless after being knocked about by the violent handling of the river.

Immediately we arrived at the Gorge of the de los Antiguos, Jones and I rode down to the water's edge. I had small hope of success as regarded retrieving the guns, but the water had fallen as quickly as it had risen. We soon came upon my tracks going down to the stream, made during my last visit. We then rode along the bank. Trees, sand and débris filled the river-bed, and I had reached a spot some hundred yards below the place where I had been beached on the shingle island, and Jones was still engaged in searching another channel, when I saw something brown upon a sandbank.

There, half in and half out of the water, lay the Mauser, caked with rust, choked with sand and pebbles, but whole, unbent, though the stock was pitted with the battering of many stones. I picked it up, and there seemed but little hope of its ever becoming serviceable again. However, the sights, by a miracle, were intact, save the half of the bead of the foresight. After this we resumed our search, hoping with luck to come upon the shot-gun, and presently we discovered that also, lying half-buried among the wreckage at the lip of the flood. Being in a case, it was practically undamaged. We carried the two in triumph to the camp. Upon examination the Mauser bolt was found to be fixed and immovable, and we feared it would never fire again. For tools we had only an axe and a weak pocket-knife, but with the help of these two we took the Mauser to pieces, cleaned it, and fixed it together again, to find, however, that it would not stay on cock. As soon as we shut the bolt, the rifle went off. We examined it, but could discover nothing broken or bent, and, night falling, we went to bed.

I was awakened by Jones with the welcome news that breakfast was ready, and that he had got up early and been at work upon the Mauser, which he said had haunted his dreams. It was, he declared, as good as ever, and this proved to be the case. The trigger had been slightly bent, and a small stone lodged in the mechanism had been overlooked in the bad light of the previous evening. Altogether the affair stands out as one gigantic piece of luck.

It was not now at all a presentable weapon. It was, indeed, an object any gunmaker would have shied at, but it started business again by taking a particular stone out of the neighbouring cliff with all its old accuracy. To celebrate the event we made a plum duff of flour, which we ate with a tin of Swiss milk. Afterwards we made quite a bag of pigeons (Columba maculosa), which frequented the scrub of the river in great numbers.

Patagonia is a land so far from shops that one must not lose anything, and if you do lose anything, it is strange how persistent one becomes in looking for it. Scrivenor once rode twenty-five miles for a pipe; I have spent half a weary day following my old tracks for a similar purpose. I think the only article lost upon the expedition, and left lost, was Barker's large knife, and we had ridden fifty miles the day he dropped it. Jones lost a pair of pipes one day galloping, and after four days searching—at odd times— found them both again! Burbury lost a knife at the Fenix River—but I might go on multiplying instances for ever.

Well, now that we had found the guns, remained the horses, and after these we started next morning, moving our small camp up to where they had been abandoned.

I remember that day, for I was riding the roughest horse in all our troop, a stout little Zaino, which shook and vibrated like a miniature torpedo-boat. At length we came to the high barranca above the river, down which Mula had fallen and nearly immolated poor Barckhausen. We human beings tobogganed down—the measured angle being 38°—and the horses slid down upon their haunches. Part of the cliff accompanied us in our descent. Then followed that nasty boulder-strewn piece of journeying I have before described, until at length we crossed the river and rode in among the trees towards Rest-and-be-thankful Camp.

DESCENDING THE BARRANCA

That was one of the most picturesque camps which fell to our lot in Patagonia. The grass there, though coarse, was very good; deep green scrub and incensio bushes bounded it on three sides, the barranca leading up to the tableland being on the fourth. As we were riding through the trees we discovered the three horses, led by Fritz the Zaino, descending the barrancas to water. Truly our snakes were standing upright, as the Zulus say. Of course, immediately the horses under General Fritz perceived us, they stood still. Before that they were coming down the steep side of the cliff with the grace and swing of wild things, now they at once pretended that it was a very difficult business. We caught them, and found them to be in excellent condition, glossy, bright-eyed and fat. We at once put them upon sogas, lest their love of liberty might have been increased by the week-end they had spent alone. They were evidently in the habit of drinking each evening and feeding in the rich grass of the Gorge, and in the morning ascending to the tableland and enjoying themselves there.

After settling the camp, Jones and I saddled up Luna and General Fritz and went up to look for a guanaco. We found that the fire lit by Barckhausen and myself had burned over a largish area and driven the game backwards into the higher basaltic hills. Among these, and upon the western river, the

Jeinemeni, we had a most lovely evening. Fresh horses, keen air, a soft wind out of the west, and the most glorious of views—the lake, placid for once, in its gigantic setting of peaked and pinnacled Cordillera, the tint of yellow marshes in the lowland, and the whole background of the picture painted with mist and distance in a dozen shades of dusky and far-off blue.

In the course of that day's wanderings we first reached the Jeinemeni, the more westerly river, which shut in the farther side of the tableland. The ravine through which it flowed down to the lake was magnificent, a wonderful vista of broken white cliffs. The conformation of its cañadon was very different to that of the de los Antiguos. Seen from a distance the valley appeared almost treeless, and upon its west bank rose the lower hills of the Cordillera into needles and peaks of red rock and virgin snow. The plateau between the rivers we found to be an excellent game country. Upon a fast horse the ground was good enough, though rather too broken to admit of "running" young guanaco, one of the finest and most exhilarating pastimes that I have ever enjoyed.

There is an element in Patagonian hunting quite unique: so much depends upon your horse. There were but two in all our forty-seven which could be trusted to stand and not gallop off when we fired. These two I trained myself on the way up from Trelew to Colohuapi, and they were a great ease and comfort to me. But to go shooting on a wild horse, then probably to find your game in a bushless country, where you are quite unable to shoot because you cannot tie up your mount, is a most disappointing affair. Also you have on many occasions to gallop down your game—if you hit it a little too far back, for instance. Wearier work than chasing a wounded guanaco afoot over the bald and endless ridges of the pampas, or up and down the steep unstable slides of a barranca, I do not know.

GUANACOS DESCENDING A HILLSIDE

With my trained horse the Cruzado, and the Little Zaino, all that was necessary was just to drop to the ground—you could rein up in the middle of a fast canter and slip off—the horse would stand where you left him until you came for him again. There were others, of course, who, if you loosed the cabresto, were off to camp at a gallop, and where quickness is so important, they made sport a little of a penance.

But to return to our first visit to the Jeinemeni. In the cañadon we came upon a guanaco, and I stalked him. The bullet took effect, and the poor beast plunged into the abyss below. We followed him down a few hundred feet, but finding the way beset with loose stones, and, consequently, on the raw bare cliff, rather dangerous, we returned with much toil to our horses. It had taken us one and three-quarter hours to climb five hundred feet.

"Any horse, even that old Fritz, is better than a man's own legs," said Jones feelingly. Arrived in time—the fulness of time—at the top of the cliff, we sat down and rested. As we were doing so Jones perceived a cloud of dust uprising in the valley and drew my attention to it. It was coming towards us, but we were quite unable at that distance to make out the cause of it. We marked the place and I took a couple of bearings, and in the early dark we rode back into camp.

The next morning we sogaed up the horses and set out.

We wanted some meat, having only a little left of the last guanaco. We saw a number of guanacos on the hills and one half-grown one, which we attempted to gallop, but had to desist, as the ground was too false for the horses, and the basalt rocks and hills told in the guanaco's favour. At length, quite near the spot where I had shot one on the previous evening, we found a big old buck standing alone, and we speedily made a plan of campaign. I rode round and hid in the rocks far above him. Scrivenor tried stalking him and Jones headed him off from the north.

He went towards Jones, who sent a bullet through his heart at good range.

Immediately on our killing, the condors, caranchos, and chimangos began to gather and almost to drop upon the meat in our presence. I have before remarked on the number of these uncanny birds which haunted the Gorge. They were huge, black, ragged, bald, wrinkled, and offensive in odour, incarnations of lust and evil. The horrible flesh-colour of the bare skin on head and neck was glassy and livid. And how wonderful was their instinct! You shot your game, and within a few minutes a condor appeared far away in the heavens; then another and another! Perhaps they had some signal bidding to the feast.

Having cut up the guanaco, we descended into the cañadon of the Jeinemeni, where we had on the previous evening seen the rising dust—which meant the movement of living things. At first it was one of the nastiest of horseback climbs, all loose stones, and sand and sandstone chippings. The gorge below us was a chessboard of small-looking round folds set in the bases of the higher hills and hummocks. Among these were many boulders, with two or three deep black waterholes, eye-shaped; and, of course, there were condors. We arrived at the place where we had perceived the cloud of dust. A large herd of guanaco had passed at the gallop, as was evident from the tracks.

We rode on to the gorge of the Jeinemeni and made our camp by a little pool. Here we had a maté by the fire and gave our horses grass. Then came our climb up the ragged cliffs by which we had descended. They were very high, rising fold on fold, set as always with loose stones and shifting sand, a needle or two of black rock sticking out gauntly from their steep faces.

FIRST HUEMUL CAMP

The next day Jones and I went hunting. We desired to secure a few heads and skins of the huemul and we determined to devote a day to that purpose. I will describe that excursion at full length, as it was one typical of Patagonian sport.

Of course we rode. You ride everywhere in Patagonia. I rode Luna, and Jones one of the Zainos—Fritz the younger, a very rough horse.

When we started a light rain was falling and the summits of the Cordillera were purple with threatening cloud. The rain gave the mountain wind the softness which the pampero lacks. We quickly crossed the lower hills and saw some guanacos in the valleys. We did not shoot any but rode on upwards until we came to the high ground, where bushes of maté negra and black fragments of basalt made a desolate picture with the low clouds rolling over the wet hills. Presently a cloud enveloped us and we took shelter beneath a rock. It looked as if we were in for a wet day, but to our delight, after an hour of waiting the wind blew away the clouds and showed the pale blue sky beyond, the weather turned colder and set in fine. We jumped on our horses and jogged on until the high ground was reached. Here we dismounted and spied the country with the telescope. We had come to the conclusion that nothing was in sight when, moving a little higher, I saw an ostrich in a marsh not more than two hundred yards away. The bird had not perceived us, and fortunately the ground was favourable for stalking. Under cover of a hummock, we advanced to within about seventy yards, when I shot the bird. As always happens, on receiving the shot it ran thirty yards forward and fell.

During the whole of our travels we observed but one kind of rhea (Rhea darwini). The remarks that Darwin makes concerning the habits of this bird have little to be added to them. The male bird, which hatches out the young, will, when approached, feign to be wounded in order to draw off the intruder from the nest of the chicks. I have never seen more than nineteen chicks with a single ostrich at any period within a month or two of the hatching, but I was informed by the Gauchos that this number is not an outside limit. When started, Rhea darwini does not usually open his wings, as does the Rhea americana. This fact has been noticed by Darwin. On one occasion, shortly after leaving Trelew, we chased an ostrich, which, having run a couple of hundred yards, opened its wings. We did not, however, secure the bird.

Only when with young will the ostrich, on starting, expand the wings, but, as I have said, this is a ruse; yet I have seen them proceed for a short distance with wings full open at times when hard pressed. In the present instance we cut up our ostrich, taking the stomach, which, cooked as an asado, or roast, is esteemed a luxury by the Gauchos. The stomach was full of the grass of the marsh. Up to the end of December we found eggs. When fresh they were of a transparent and pale green, which after some days merged into a pallid white.

While we were yet engaged in cutting up the bird, the neck-skin of which came in very usefully as a tobacco-pouch, we paused in the work and took a look round with the telescope. On the heights above us, two brown objects were to be descried, which on examination proved to be huemules. They had evidently seen us, and their curiosity had been excited by our movements. Hesitatingly they began to descend the hillside towards us. We cut some antics and so decoyed the unlucky animals within range. After killing them, we took the skins of both, as there is no example of this deer in summer coat in any of our British collections. They were still shedding their winter coat.

After riding on, our next spy showed us a young huemul buck beneath us, but as I had already secured a specimen I was only too glad to let him go in peace.

I am sorry that I cannot give my readers any interesting story of huemul-shooting; that will be reserved for the pen of some future traveller, who will find the animal wild, because used to man and his ways. As for our experience of them, the interest turns rather on their confidingness and their behaviour towards man as an unknown entity.

We were riding home, my desire to shoot huemul completely evaporated, when we perceived among the basalt fragments above us the black face of a really magnificent buck. In approaching him I purposely gave him the wind. He had not seen us, but immediately on getting our wind dashed away to a short distance. On my showing myself, he stood quite still, snorted twice or thrice, and was just bounding off when the crack of the Mauser cut short his career.

There were by this time thirty or forty condors already gathered upon the carcases of the two we had previously slain. Indeed in no part of Patagonia did we see such numbers of Sarcorhamphus gryphus as among these hills. I understand that there is in Paris a considerable demand for the feathers of the condor. Here is the place to find them. On our homeward way we saw two huemul does and a pricket. They stayed and stared at us as we rode down the lower levels. When nearing camp a couple of guanacos started over a cliff within ten yards of us, and descended the sheer hillside, giving me an excellent opportunity of observing their extraordinary movements. All the huemules we had shot were so lean as to be practically useless for the pot, so when later on we came in sight of a herd of guanaco, and Jones asked me if he might have a shot, I said yes. He picked out one and bowled it over at three hundred paces with my Mauser. He was very delighted with his success, and said that the Mauser was better than any of the guns in Chubut.

On the day after, the river, upon which we had been keeping a very careful watch, again began to rise. So we packed up and camped that night in the end of the cañadon near the spot where I had shot my first huemul. Although we hunted during the afternoon we saw nothing, but on the following day, when starting for our ride, we sighted three huemules, two does and a young buck, in the scrub of a stream which enters the lake some miles to the east of the River de los Antiguos. In the evening of that day, after fording the River Fenix, and about eight miles out of Horsham Camp, a huemul buck dashed across about a couple of hundred yards ahead of us, and I, taking a very hasty aim, was fortunate enough to bring him to the ground. We had difficulty for a few moments in finding him, as he had gone head over heels into some scrub in a fissure of the hillside.

THE OFF-SADDLE

During this hunting trip, which I have described, we neither desired nor endeavoured to make a large bag; in fact, I think that one could very easily over that ground shoot ten huemules and an indefinite number of guanaco in one day, but such a proceeding would be little short of a crime. Very different indeed were my experiences after wild cattle, which I followed steadily at a later date of the expedition, for eleven days before I had any chance of a shot.

Another good hour of the day during our expedition was that when, pretty tired, one rode into camp, and saw the little green tent pitched among the tussocks, the horses scattered round, the big black pot upon the fire. You drank your maté, smoked a pipe while the black pot boiled, and you talked over the day's doings. And so on until dark began to fall, and in the night you could hear the sounds of the open, the rush of some river, the moaning of wind across the plain or through the forests—when near the Cordillera—perhaps the cries of wildfowl, or the whistle of the Chiloe widgeon as the shadows closed down. Then came preparations for the morrow—the beans were cut, the meat put on, the fire raked up about to-morrow's breakfast; and presently you turned in, the shadows waxed and waned, and when you woke the stars were paling in the western sky.

JONES SMOKES THE PIPE OF VICTORY

CHAPTER XII

BACK TO CIVILISATION

Christmas Day at Horsham Camp—Horse races—Menu of dinner—Leave Horsham Camp—Basalt plateaus—Large herds of guanacos—Sterile region—Birth of filly—Father of guanacos—Search for Indian trail—Pebble hills—Finding of trail—Filly's first march—Hunting—Mirages—Rain—Tent pleasures—River Olin—Meeting Mr. Waag's party—News from outer world—River Chico—Sierra Ventana—Indian toldo—Shepherd's hut—Houses, sheep and cattle—Night in huts—Antennæ of civilisation—La Gaviota—Santa Cruz.

"HORSHAM CAMP, Christmas Day, 1900.—Here the weather is warm; large, soft and poisonous flies haunt the marsh in the camp. The horses neigh. An ostrich, the greatest delicacy of wild game in Patagonia, hangs with three legs of guanaco on the meat gallows." So runs my diary.

We spent a very humble Christmas up there at Little Horsham Camp, and made what mild cheer we might. In the morning of Christmas Day we had horse races, a mile and a half-mile. We rode the best horses in our respective troops. Barckhausen, however, rode the Azulejo, which he decorated with a towel and a red handkerchief, to our great amusement. We were almost ready for the second race when he came in from the first, having had a difference of opinion on the way with his steed, which thought it would be much nicer to rejoin his friends and companions feeding on the green marsh than to run races.

The surprise of the day was the winning of the races by the Little Zaino, as we christened him. He was very timid and wild to saddle and mount, but once up he proved himself a treasure. In appearance he was a comely enough little horse, plump and well picked up, and had been used occasionally to carry a cargo on the way to the lake.

The day before Christmas I wanted to go for a bathe, so I caught our little friend, and, liking his pace, let him stretch himself a little on the way back over the edge of the marsh. He stretched himself to such good purpose that he was ridden in the next day's races and won the three events, although he was carrying a stone and a half more than the others! Our course lay through a belt of thick bushes, but, barring these, was good enough. At any rate, it turned out excellent fun, and we all enjoyed our races.

The only one of us who did not get a prize was riding a horse which came to us with rather a bad name, and which, immediately the others started, dashed back to the troop.

During the afternoon we made up our cargoes ready for the morrow's start, after our Christmas dinner, of which I print the menu:

LAGO BUENOS AIRES, 1900. CHRISTMAS DAY.

At 5 o'clock P.M.

NOTICE.—Come early to get a good helping.

MENU.

Common or Garden Duff à la Azulejo. Condiment au lait Suisse.

GRAND DUFF à la H. Jones avec muscatelles.

Bœuf.

Ostrich à la Patagonie. (If you want it.)

Gigot de Guanaco. (Order beforehand.)

Cocao au lait} Suisse.
Thé au lait }

Vieux Cognac avec vulcanite.

Plug Tobacco.

GOD SAVE THE QUEEN.

In the evening after dinner we indulged in some shooting matches—with the damaged Colt—which Barckhausen won.

A PATAGONIAN LAGOON

On December 26 we bade good-bye to Horsham Camp. After a long interval the cargueros were once more loaded up, and the whole troop tailed away to the eastward. Is any sight sadder than a deserted camp? The dead or dying camp-fire, the broken remains of food surprised by the sun, the litter, the bare rubbed grass, and the occasional fox. We left some tins of corned beef behind us, as I hoped to travel very fast to Santa Cruz. That day we made anything from eight to ten leagues, and camped in Seven Ostriches cañadon, the spot that Barckhausen and I had previously visited and named after the birds we saw there.

The following day (27th) we made a good march and encamped by a lagoon, upon which I shot two yellow-billed teal, and Jones and Burbury four ducks, which were plucked before we came into camp. On the morning after a very difficult part of our journey commenced. All day we travelled over a pampa covered with basaltic fragments and thorny bushes; some of these bushes bore a red tulip-like flower.

Enormous numbers of guanaco haunt these grim plateaus. Jones and I galloped a half-grown one, and killed it with the help of a dog. The going was extremely bad, our path lying through gorges and up steep-sided ridges, rough with basaltic fragments and powdered with sharp clinkers of lava. It is not easy to describe the changing fortunes of such a day. For instance, we were turned again and again by gullies and rifts in the hollows of the hills, and, what with shifting cargoes on these cruel and almost perpendicular slopes, the difficulty of keeping the troop of horses straight and of taking care of one's own limbs, was extreme. Literally thousands of guanaco appeared on the summits of the surrounding barren ridges, and fled galloping down the rock-faces with jerking necks and flying hoofs. Sometimes the old bucks would come and look at us, running towards us and neighing and laughing, and then ducking their long necks and cantering off. What they lived on in so sterile a region still remains a mystery to me.

I saw one condor poised high.

Our Indian baqueano, Como No, had told us that we must strike "between two hills." Barckhausen asserted that he had indicated to him a couple of round peaks on the summit or rather forming the culminating-points of this high basalt range. We made our way up these monstrous steps, as it were, of rock, steering by the compass, and after some twenty miles of travelling found ourselves upon a bare black highland over which the wind was tearing in heavy gusts. No wood, no water, no grass. I was afraid we should have to remain there for the night, and also afraid that Mrs. Trelew, the madrina of the Trelew troop, whose udder was big, might drop her foal in that sterile spot. Another danger which menaced us, was that the horses would certainly become lame if they had to travel far over these broken rocks. We therefore rode on perhaps another fourteen miles, and the dark was falling when we found a camp in a cañadon—a bad approach strewn with basalt fragments, but a fair camp at the end with a little stream and good grass.

On December 29 the Trelew mare dropped her foal, a little disproportionately-boned, huge-jointed alazan filly. During the day Scrivenor and I explored the cañadon and I shot a guanaco and an ostrich. The guanaco was a very father of guanacos, old, scarred, black-faced and war-worn. His meat was worse than that of a he-goat.

To all sides of us stretched the limitless expanses of basalt, and our outlook was not a cheerful one. An examination of the horses' hoofs convinced us that another day's marching such as the last would work great havoc amongst them. I did not know how far this wilderness of basalt might extend, so on December 30 set out with Burbury to attempt to find its boundary.

Our intention had been to strike the Indian trail under the Cordillera and follow it until we reached the neighbourhood of the River Belgrano, when we would keep the course of that river to its junction with the River Chico, which in its turn would lead us down to the settlement of Santa Cruz, our destination. When I left the Cordillera I had made up my mind to return to them farther south at the Lake Argentino near lat. 50°. To cover a large area of country, and at the same time to collect specimens, is a physical impossibility. I had therefore decided to leave Scrivenor at Santa Cruz to collect fossils in that vicinity, while I myself again crossed the continent to the Andes, some part of which I hoped to explore, and my dreams were not uninfluenced by the stories of the red puma, of the existence of which, however, Scrivenor was very dubious.

THE INDIAN TRAIL

Such, then, were the reasons that were taking us to the eastern coast, and my desire was to arrive there as soon as possible in order to have plenty of time to carry out my projects before winter made travelling of any kind impossible. Once we reached the River Belgrano our difficulties would be over, that we knew; but in order to attain this end we had to pass through a region somewhat waterless and stony lying on the verge of the basalt wilderness, into which we had strayed.

To get away from this basalt region was, of course, our first desire. Could we but find the Indian trail, which we were sure must be at no great distance, and which stretches, leading one from camp to camp, all the way from Lake Buenos Aires to Punta Arenas, with a branch in the direction of Santa Cruz, our troubles would be at an end. Owing, however, to the lessening number of Indians, the track is now only clearly visible for half a mile at a time in the neighbourhood of fords and other difficult places.

To return to our search. Burbury and I had started early. The going at first was over basalt clinker, fearful for the horses' feet, but presently we came to a low round hillock of pebble—a hopeful sight, for I had been half afraid we might be deep in the basalt wilderness. Following on we discovered other pebbly hillocks, on one of which I found a single horse-track, stamped when the ground was soft some time previously. After a while, as we rounded a slope, we saw a bit of green camp. We were bearing a little west of south, and there we struck the full Indian trail—that wonderful trail, which runs league after league, worn by the footsteps of generations upon generations of Indians as they migrated up and down the length of the country with their women and children, their guanaco-skin tents and their few possessions.

The trail is much like a guanaco-track, or rather like several running side by side. So the Tehuelches leave their footmarks, which resemble those of the game they live by, and they leave little else to show to those who come after, that here hundreds of men have existed through the centuries, knowing such joys and sufferings as lie between birth and death, only a trodden line across the waste and a few burnt bushes by the wayside.

RIVER OLIN

We rode back to the camp, and decided to try the little filly with a short march, as much delay was out of the question. The horses all appeared to be interested in the arrangement, and refused to be driven unless the filly led. This she did, making her first journey trotting beside her mother. We had to cross a ford, and Barckhausen brought the filly over gently by the ear, Mrs. Trelew objecting extremely to such treatment of her offspring. We are all very careful and tender over our loose-limbed baby. During the short march we saw many guanacos.

The duration of the expedition might be divided into periods: first, the biscuit period, when every one toasted biscuits, hard camp biscuits, shiny and of a great size; followed by the dumpling period. Now it was the damper period, which was the most appetising of them all.

THE EASTERN PORTION OF LAKE BUENOS AIRES

On the last day of the year we managed seven leagues, and camped in a bare cañadon. New Year's Day we covered eight leagues of bare and arid steppes of pampa. At this time we had a great deal of hunting. A lame dog, left behind by our Argentine ostrich-hunter, turned out to be excellent for sport. We named him Chichi. We camped by a lagoon of muddy water with a thin strip of feed half encircling it, but the grass was rich with seed. Mirages haunted our marches through this desolate region. This chapter might be called "Through the Land of Distant Hills." There was a savage loneliness between those wide horizons that thrust itself upon you. One felt a mere atom, and the thought of finding oneself condemned to live there alone seemed too awful to face. The bare, round-headed hills looked old and bald, eternal winds (though not so strong as nearer to the lake) whistled sadly as before, and on all sides pampa pebbly and grassless, ridge on ridge, horizon on horizon, mirage on mirage.

Suddenly, during that night, the sky became black over the distant Cordillera and the rain began. Immediately we slung up the tents. Oh, those tents, what a comfort they were at the end of a weary march! We had no adequate poles and no bushes or pegs to hang them upon, but we got them up somehow and put the cargo round them. Then we crept inside and listened to the rain. The warm beds, the rugs, the candle and tobacco and books. It was homelike. And the dry shirt one could put on within that shelter, with the rain, rain outside! When you have slept out in all weathers you begin to understand the full luxury of a tent like ours, with its furs and warmth and a decent pipe out of the wind. It is a moving home. To be free of the weather, to let it rain if it wants to, to lie and listen to it, these are all thrilling pleasures, pleasures because of the contrast to the wet open camp where, in spite of the covered and sweating head and body, the pitiless rain trickles in pools into your bed. And the spell of reading at night inside the tent, the company of thoughts new and old of wise men, these are pleasures of which only the wanderer knows the true sweetness.

During the next day or two we continued to travel over the same waterless stony pampa; there were pigmy hillocks, many guanaco and a lagoon of wonderful shades of blue, also the wind ahead, and dust blowing back into our eyes. We crossed the River Olin and pushed on for the River Chico. One cold night as we sat round the fire some one suggested we should have an exhibition of our effects when we reached Santa Cruz. Beyond a broken cup or two, a bombilla, and a shattered kettle, we could produce little else. It was hinted that Barckhausen's trousers might figure in it, and I offered to contribute my old coat.

Before reaching the River Belgrano we came in sight of a troop of horses being driven across the pampa by a couple of Gauchos. At first sight we thought them a mirage. On inquiry I was told that my friend Señor Waag was in command, news at which I was naturally delighted. I had made Mr. Waag's acquaintance in Buenos Aires, and we had arranged to meet in Patagonia if possible. Mr. Waag was on the Argentine Boundary Commission, and has done more valuable geographical work in the Cordillera than any other man. Being told that he was only a couple of hours behind the troop, I galloped on to meet him, for I heard that his waggon had broken down, and so made sure of coming upon him. After a few hours going, I arrived at the camp of his assistants, where were two Italian engineers, and also some piratical-looking peones in red caps making bread in an oven dug into the ground. But Mr. Waag himself was not there, having gone off the track to camp in a cañadon. I was greatly disappointed, for I had looked forward to this meeting.

RIVER BELGRANO

However, we were greedy to hear news of the outer world, from which we had been cut off for four months. We were far behind the times. I think our first question was about the war and Kruger. We learned that he was in Europe and that guerilla warfare was still going on. The Italians' news only carried up to November.

THE ITALIAN ENGINEERS' WAGGON

We made our camp a little way from theirs, and our hounds strayed over to them and stayed with their waggons, deserting us altogether. As for ourselves, we were most kindly entertained by the Italian engineers, and enjoyed the luxuries of a tin of butter, biscuit, bread, tea, milk, sugar and some cognac. Flies abounded and bothered us as we ate our meal on a packing-case, an ostentatious comfort which made us feel very civilised.

We were now in the valley of the Chico, which is a large stream with a swift current, its cañadon bordered with bare ridges. It felt like old times to be in a river valley once more, reminding us of those we had passed through on our way to Lake Buenos Aires. We saw geese again, of which I shot two, and also a pigeon. The valley here was very rich with red seed-bearing grass, and beyond, nearer to the water, a glorious green pantano, dotted with deep clear pools.

Before parting with the Italians they presented us with some sugar and I gave them some tea and tobacco. The valley through which we marched continued to be very fertile. The grass was like that of an English meadow with sweet far-off scents, but lacking the dewiness of our English scents of wood and wold.

On January 7 we travelled eleven leagues, taking a short cut through a bare cañadon of dry mud-hills. Leaving this behind us we again came in sight of the River Chico and crossed a high pampa of yellow tussocks and gravel. The morning dawned hot with the usual accompaniment of mosquitoes and sand-flies. As we sighted the river this heat gave place to a fresh rain-smelling wind, inexpressibly grateful.

In the afternoon, as we rode along, there appeared against the sky a keen peak of rock—Sierra Ventana. We had long been looking forward to our first glimpse of it, knowing it would be a sign that we were nearing civilisation. Blue, distant, perhaps thirty miles away, behind the basalt hills, it raised its strange castle-like head, only the castle is of nature's building, not man's. I think we all welcomed this token of the old kindly inhabited world again, after our months spent on houseless plains and inhospitable mountains.

A herd of guanaco some twenty strong showed at almost the same moment. I galloped forward, feeling glad that our dinner no longer depended on my shot. I was a mere sportsman once more. The doe I shot had fat on her, the first we had seen during our wanderings, "just as we've got the chance of fat mutton, too," as someone remarked. Rain fell at night, and the wind blew, but with the razor-edge of cold off. We camped in some flowering grasses with the bare steppes of the pampa on one side and the dark hills on the other; behind these, among some bright streaks in the stormy billowy sky, the Sierra Ventana thrust up its crest.

THE HOME OF THE INDIAN WHO GAVE US MUTTON

Next day we came upon a hut of Indians, who gave me some mutton, for which they would accept no payment. Perhaps they did not like to take money from a man in so old a coat! I, however, gave them some tobacco.

Later we came upon a bush-shelter of some tender of sheep and cattle. It was a forlorn little place—just a hut of poles and bushes and skins by the river bank. It was doorless, and the dweller must have been a very small man, judging by his bed, which was a hole in the earth, pillowed with a broken wooden cargo-saddle. On one of the props was fastened a card with the word "Salido" (Gone out). A bag of canvas, old and stained, was tied up to the roof, a cracked tiny mirror hung from the central pole. He seemed to have no provisions, only a bag of yerba. He had recently killed a lion, for we found its skull. We saw some half-wild cattle near by. It was a grey evening, and, as always when out of the river valleys, the scene around was colourless basaltic desolation.

SIERRA VENTANA

LA GAVIOTA

On the 9th we struck three habitations. Strong squalls with gusts of rain accompanied us on our way. Sheep and cattle could be seen in the valley below, and at last we stopped at an estancia, where we bought fariña, flour, biscuit, sugar, and mutton—luxuries to which we had for some time been strangers.

The owner allowed us to sleep in some mud-houses by the river, and we enjoyed the shelter, partial as it was.

Our next day's march took us across four fords, and by evening we reached an estancia, where I was kindly received and given afternoon tea. Estancia is a word with a fine sound. It may, however, mean anything from a real house, full of comfort, to a mud hut. This estancia was a delightful change to us; we could sit on chairs and saw prints on the wall and a sideboard once more. The night fell very cold, with an empty heaven overhead, but its lower arcs set with slate-blue cloud.

On the 11th we hit civilisation after a march of over forty miles, the last part of which lay across a travesia. Civilisation took the form of an undersized drinking-shop perched on the rim of the bare pampa. How we had longed for civilisation—and now we had found it! I sat writing in a room with pink fly-blown walls and green fittings of the grimiest. Four Gauchos of the lower sort were playing cards for beans and shrieking over their game. The little innkeeper, a small, dark, aquiline, black-bearded Argentine, in a dirty white vest and a black neck-rag, held rule inside. Any camp is better than these antennæ of civilisation, that seem to have touched and always to bear onwards with them things unclean and repulsive. Jones' homely face was good to see, when he came in and said, "I should like to be away from here."

SANTA CRUZ

I realised suddenly how I loved the camp and the cold clean hills, when I heard the raucous music of that unlovely place. It was scarcely a pleasure to see cognac advertisements again, and to smell the dregs of yesterday yet awash on the greasy grey metal counter! A concertina was playing the old aching tunes that always seem to carry with them tags of vice and crime.

RESIDENTS OF SANTA CRUZ

We pushed on for Santa Cruz, and on the way passed the house of another trader, who also sold liquor. It squatted beside the river, which here flowed blue and estuary-like between white-faced cliffs backed by bald hills. A board over the door of the shop bore the legend "La Gaviota," or Seagull. It was evidently part of the wreckage of some boat washed up on these beaches.

Santa Cruz town is situated on the banks of a large estuary formed by the junction of the rivers Santa Cruz and the Southern Chico before they fall into the Atlantic. It is a straggling place, a collection of wooden houses with roofs of corrugated iron. The chief export is wool, which in the season lies in long rows of bales upon the shore ready to be embarked. The town lies beyond sandhills, which separate it from the sea. Concertinas and jack-boots ring in its galvanised-iron huts; mules, horses, dogs, and cattle house in its formless plazas. It is a place which you hate and like at one and the same time. You long to get away from it while you are there, yet find yourself looking back sometimes and wishing to see again its vague streets and its drag-net agglomeration of humanity.

CHAPTER XIII

JOURNEY TO LAKE ARGENTINO

Dividing expedition—Darwin's trip up the Santa Cruz—Provisions—Shoeing horses—Pampa grass and marsh grass—Start for Lake Argentino—Burbury and Bernardo—Visit various estancias—Negro—Suspicious wayfarers—Hospitality—Cañadon of the Santa Cruz—Dry pampa—Sunsets—Game and wildfowl—Flamingos—Sandflies—Mystery Plain—Lake Argentino—River del Bote—Mount Viscachas —Lonely lagoon—Death-place of guanaco—Neigh of guanaco—Large herds—Thorny grass— Description of Lake Argentino—A tragedy of wild life—Condors—Numerous birds and beasts of prey—

Severities of winters—Snowfall—Burmeister Peninsula—Lake Rica or South Fjord—Bad weather—The Wild Man of Santa Cruz.

I spent a few days in Santa Cruz making arrangements to divide my expedition into two parts, leaving Scrivenor with the peones to collect fossils and specimens in the neighbourhood of the River Santa Cruz, where most interesting deposits exist, while I with Burbury and a peon, whom I picked up at Santa Cruz, recrossed the continent to the lake-region.

In a huge country like Patagonia, to explore and to collect at the same time is practically out of the question, but by dividing our forces I hoped to achieve both ends more satisfactorily.

The lake which I now wished to visit is the last very large piece of water in the long chain of Andean lakes and lagoons. It is a little to the south of 50° S. lat. From this lake, Lake Argentino, the River Santa Cruz flows eastwards and empties itself into the Atlantic, the settlement of Santa Cruz being situated at the mouth of the river. It was by following the course of this river upwards for some 140 miles that Darwin made his only serious expedition into the interior of Patagonia. His party found the passage of the river both dangerous and laborious, and Captain FitzRoy decided to return to Santa Cruz on the fifth day, after they sighted the snowy summits of the Cordillera. Thus they never reached Lake Argentino.

We also followed the course of the river, but on horseback instead of by boat, and thus for the early part of our journey we passed through the identical country traversed by Darwin.

THE MAIN STREET, SANTA CRUZ

I desired above all things to be able to move rapidly, and accordingly cut down the amount and weight of our baggage as far as prudence permitted. I append a list of the provisions, which I intended—with the help of guanaco meat—to last us for the four months which remained before we must return to the coast if we wished to escape the severities of the Andean winter:

35 kilos fariña.
25 kilos oatmeal.
15 kilos sugar.
6 lb. tea.
12 tins cocoa.

Besides these we took a spare change of underclothing, one of the tents, fifty rounds of 12-bore ball and the same quantity of shot cartridges and 150 for the Mauser rifle.

We were able to put everything on two cargueros, and even then they were not very heavily loaded. I took two madrinas, the Zaino mare and Mrs. Trelew, with their respective troops, the horses numbering in all twenty-one. During their rest in Santa Cruz they had attained to quite fair condition, and were in consequence ready for the road. It was necessary to shoe such as would permit the operation, as their hoofs had been worn down by the basalt fragments which had strewed our path from the north. The operation, by the way, was one which we had to perform ourselves, as the blacksmith at Santa Cruz, on being asked to do it, said he preferred the trade of building wooden houses, but consented to lend us his forge and tools for three dollars a day. We had some difficulty in finding shoes to fit, and I warn any future traveller against the nails which they keep for shoeing purposes in the settlement.

The short harsh grass usually to be had on the pampa is certainly a very much better food for horses destined to travel long and hard journeys than the beautiful meadowy vegas of the Cordillera, which look so inviting. The richer grass of the latter naturally fattens them in a wonderfully short space of time, but the first hard day's march cuts up their condition like so much butter.

We left Santa Cruz on January 22. I was accompanied by Burbury and a Swede, Bernardo Hähansen, who proved in the event to be a useful and courageous fellow. Our first march took us to Mr. Campbell's estancia. We saw a good number of guanaco and some ostriches on the way, which at first lay across the open pampa, afterwards diving into a deep cañadon some seven and a half leagues long. The little Blanco showed his appreciation of the excellent food he had been enjoying by behaving badly. On arrival we found Mr. Campbell was away from the farm repairing fences, so we were obliged to await his return. When he came, he took us up to the house, where we had some tea. We remained at the estancia for the night, and next day went on about three leagues over good pampa to Messrs. Cressard and Dobree's. The manager, Mr. John Noble, received us kindly. The cook at this farm, a former New Zealand hand, had come with us to Puerto Madryn in the Primero de Mayo, and said he would have applied to go with us had he known how to cargo horses. As he cooked very well I should have been glad to have received his application. On January 24 we reached Clementi's estancia. We were accompanied on the march by an old Irish sailor with a Hibernian cast of countenance. The señora asked us into the house and at once gave us hot milk and bread, which was very grateful after a long day in the saddle. The valley near by was full of sheep, and several healthy-looking children were playing about the buildings. Here also I saw the first and only negro I met with in Patagonia. The sight of his face gave me a sudden vivid recollection of Hayti. A long-bearded Argentine patriarch, whom I descried first in the half-lights of the kitchen during the evening, looked a very Abraham and most venerable, but daylight on the morrow robbed him of all romance.

On this day (the 25th) we pushed on to the Sub-prefecto's estancia. It consisted of the usual corrugated iron shanty and barn. We marched on the following morning and reached La Ultima Casa, where we were hospitably entertained by Mrs. Hardy. She was indeed very kind. Her husband had been an Englishman, but she herself was an Argentine. It is certainly a fact in Patagonia that the Argentines are far more ready to show hospitality than are our own countrymen. One hardly wonders, however, at people being a little cautious and suspicious, as the wayfarer is not always a wandering angel in Patagonia, or, for that matter, in any thinly populated country that is being newly opened up. Therefore we were the more grateful to our hostess of La Ultima Casa. At the shanty of another farmer, a

Scotchman, we had had the door bolted against us, and been told to await his home-coming if we wished to enter the house.

FORD ON THE RIVER SANTA CRUZ

We ate our meal at Mrs. Hardy's sitting on up-turned boxes, and she brought out some magazines for our reading. Hers was a strange existence, poor old lady! She appeared to be regarded or—it comes to the same thing—thought she was regarded a little in the light of an Ishmaelite by her neighbours, who were trying (she told me) to acquire her land. Her position did not seem to be prosperous. The casa had the usual corrugated roof, and her one window could boast no glass. From this main building a sort of barn jutted out to the left. Later on, I decided that this annex, which I at first took to be a barn, must be the old lady's private sanctum, for from it she produced five magazines, some lions' claws, a skunk-skin rug, some hen's eggs, and the hen herself. A regular widow's cruse of a place. The blackened roof of the kitchen was supported by four beams lengthways and four across, these last shiny as if tarred with the smoke of many winters. An old step-ladder in the corner answered the uses of a cupboard, cups and so forth being kept on a couple of wooden shelves, and lumps of sheep's fat decorated the room. We sat on the old wooden bedstead with its pile of sheepskins for bed-clothes and wrote our diary. Our hostess, who wore her hair in two plaits hanging down at each side of her face, sat on a case and talked while she drank the inevitable maté through a bombilla. She asked us to remain over a second day, which was most good of her, but we had to continue our journey.

We marched until about three o'clock, when, coming up to an empty shanty, we took shelter in it for a while, as it happened to be very hot. Later we started again, and made a long march across a pampa above the cañadon of the Santa Cruz, which is here two miles or more in breadth. Speaking of this cañadon, I cannot do better than give Darwin's words: "This valley varies from five to ten miles in breadth: it is bounded by step-formed terraces, which rise in most parts one above the other to the height of 500 feet, and have on the opposite sides a remarkable correspondence."

The river winds considerably as it flows through the cañadon, the sides of which are very bare and grassless, excepting where springs break through and flow down the cliff-side, their course being marked by a line of vivid green. The pampa above, along which we travelled, was made up of bare yellow levels, broken here and there by strips and patches of a very dark green bush, so dark as to seem almost black. We found a good deal of difficulty in getting to a camp with water, as the pampa was very dry, so we prolonged our march till 7.15 P.M., when we came upon a shallow and turbid stream running down in a southerly direction from the barranca. In the end we had to descend into the cañadon of the river. Not far from the spot which we chose for camping lay the bodies of some eighty guanaco with their skins on, which had died during the previous winter.

The landscape immediately on the banks of the Santa Cruz is arid and hopeless in the extreme, but one can never forget the glory of Patagonia, its wonderful sunsets, which gleam out over the dull-hued empty wastes in a splendour of colour. So on that night as I stood in the shadow that steeped all my side of the river, the other bank was lit up with a translucent glow of sunset as delicately yellow as if it shone through the petals of a buttercup.

On January 27 we started along the cañadon, which continued to be desolate and rather stony. We saw many guanaco, living and dead. After a time we made for the pampa above, from where we looked once again upon the Cordillera, gleaming very dim and faint on the horizon. Finding a lagoon with some grass about it, we off-saddled for an hour. Later we marched on rather more slowly than usual, and camped in such a place as a wildfowler might see in dreams of the night. A lagoon of sword-blue water, but in shape like an arrowhead, rimmed in with low green rushes, above these yellow tussocks of coarse grass bending in the wind, behind all a bare promontory arched over by a sad evening sky. On the breeze came the "Honk, honk" of geese mixed with the thinner notes of snipe. Ducks, too, were there, and the snipe in wisps of thirty. Presently, as I sat writing, a guanaco came in sight, and later a flock of cayenne lapwings (Vanellus cayennensis). I might have been, as far as the aspect of things was concerned (save for the guanaco) in Uist and going home to a warm fireside, instead of journeying on and on for many days and weeks to come over the endless pampa and into the distant Cordillera.

THE DRINKING-PLACE

At this lagoon also I saw a condor (Sarcorhampus gryphus), and before this had seen a couple when at Mrs. Hardy's. It must have been near this spot that Darwin shot his condor, which he speaks of as measuring eight and a half feet from wing-tip to wing-tip, and four feet from head to tail.

By the middle of the next day (January 28) we reached a lagoon with a threshold of green meadowy marsh, a relief after a long pull over a waterless and bare stretch of country, and there took a needed half-hour of rest. On our second starting we managed to wander into a desert of basalt or lava, and could only advance very slowly and with difficulty.[22] Nor could we find water for a long time; at length we came in sight of a big pool lying ruffled in the saffron lights of the sunset. Upon its margin or in the water were flamingos (Phoenicopterus ignipalliatus), upland geese (Chloephaga magellanica), thirty-four bandurias (Theristicus caudatus). There were also guanaco within sight. Here we camped, and found yet another deep and rocky lagoon, on which were many divers which I could not identify. A heavy wind was blowing, which died down at night and gave occasion for hundreds of sandflies to rise and worry us. Each day, as we marched on, the Cordillera seemed to be advancing, as it were, towards us.

We woke to find the next day pale with thin sunlight glinting across the prospect of basalt, low bushes and far horizons. We were now well beyond Mystery Plain, which formed the limit of Darwin's expeditions up the river, and which he named with a strong desire to push on and find out what lay on its farther side.

On the 29th we made a long march. After some couple of hours' going we saw ahead of us clear pampa instead of the rocky stone-strewn surface of the region we had been passing through of late. Over this pampa, though it was tussocky and uneven, we were able to advance at a good rate towards a line of hills that rose in the west. As we approached we saw that they stood up ridge behind ridge, and over these we rode, passing many good camping-grounds and seeing herds of guanaco, but no wood or bush for fire. At last we got to the top of the last ridge of all, and there, standing in the teeth of a strong wind, we looked down upon Lake Argentino lying below us, and backed by the peaks and snow summits of the Cordillera.

Although there were many cañadones and grass of the richest, we could find no water, and so went on and on.

Presently, as we were descending towards the lake, we reached a lagoon, but found no feed there for the horses, so we were forced to leave it behind, although the troop was tired and we had been for several hours in the saddle. I perceived traces of horses at some distance, and we therefore left the bank of the lagoon and cut across the pampa heading for them. We wandered on through bare hills, which fell in perplexing folds, curve within curve, and at last we reached the River del Bote, which has but one ford by which we could cross. This we found, worked the troop over, and then encamped.

Day by day we had been leaving behind us the seemingly limitless pampas and were now drawing close to the full blue range of minaret-shaped mountains. Each march was adding to their height and making clearer the details hidden in the hedge-sparrow-egg hue of their distances. First we came in sight of Mount Viscachas one morning when, bearing a little too far out upon the pampa, we struck a tract of very bad going. The ground was covered with thorny bushes and basalt fragments, and here and there harsh tussocks of grass sprouted from the blackened wilderness of stones. The night we passed beside the lagoon on the high pampa left an impression on my mind as one of the most desolate and forbidding of camps. Flocks of flamingos were standing in the upland pool, and round about upon the little promontories that thrust out into the wind-whipped water bandurias were huddled in close order, while as the evening began to fall a wisp of snipe flew over, wailing most mournfully. Few things, indeed, seem to me to bring out into keener prominence the loneliness of a place than the cry of snipe heard in the windy gloaming. There is some suggestion of human sorrow in the sound.

MAP OF LAKE ARGENTINO AND DISTRICT. SHOWING ROUTES

So we had journeyed westward, having always upon the south the yellow pampa, and beside us on the north the river running through its deep cañadon, while every dawn the vast phalanx of the Andean peaks seemed to have moved nearer, as though the great mass of mountain was marching slowly and surely towards us like the battle-front of some destroying army.

Again we came upon a second death-place of guanaco, which made a scene strange and striking enough. There cannot have been less than five hundred lying there in positions as forced and ungainly as the most ill-taken snapshot photograph could produce. Their long necks were outstretched, the rime of weather upon their decaying hides, and their bone-joints glistening through the wounds made by the beaks of carrion-birds. They had died during the severities of the previous winter, and lay literally piled one upon another. A brown, almost chocolate-coloured, lagoon washed close to the front rank of the dead, and those in the rearmost line had evidently lain down to die while in the very act of descending the tall barranca for water. The mortality among guanaco in a really hard winter is tremendous. They die in batches, absolutely in hundreds. At that season they come down to the lower grounds for warmth and water, but desert them in the summer and take to the high pampa, where, as I have described in another place, the Indians hunt and slay them in great numbers for their pelts. The cry of the guanaco is a noise unique. It is something between a bleat, a laugh, and a neigh. Often the old macho of a herd would come to the high ground nearest to our camp, and from it neigh defiance at us, while the rest of the point would satisfy their curiosity by staring from a safer distance.

Upon the high pampa, across which, bearing north-west, we passed, we found guanaco to be extraordinarily plentiful, and fatter than any we had hitherto met with in our wanderings through the country. Upon this pampa was no firewood at all, nothing save rolling grass which pricked you with minute thorns, so that a walk through it left your putties spined like a porcupine. To stalk in this grass, where the guanacos were unusually wild, and long periods of crawling were necessary to attain success, one had to carry a piece of guanaco-skin in the left hand, which took up the grass spines that must otherwise have entered the palm of the hunter.

Our first glimpse of Lake Argentino was a strongly-marked and vivid picture as seen from the rim of the high pampa when we surmounted it. A great eye of blue water—for the sun was bright—set beneath white pent-house brows of the mountain range. A tremendous wind was blowing out of the north-west, and we could see the great southern lake was in a turmoil of short and angry seas. Deep channels cut away into the depths of the Cordillera at the western end, and at the eastern side the waters flowed out into the swift current of the River Santa Cruz. Farther along the northern shore the cañadon of the River Leona was also visible. We could not then guess how glad we should one day be to reach the haven of that river mouth. Beyond the lake, and partly surrounding it, the Cordillera raised their jagged line of peaks against the sky. From the bases upwards towards the higher altitudes the mountains were black with forests. Three large icebergs floated on the water at the farther side, one of which had drifted into shallows near the shore. No sign of life was to be observed anywhere in the great hollow stretching beneath us.

To my mind Argentino is a far more beautiful lake than Buenos Aires. After a long look we began to descend into the lower land by a sharp cleft that led down into a deep cañadon. It was, owing to a recent landslip, a nasty piece of travelling, and the horses, disliking it, broke back more than once, the Zaino overo taking the lead as usual.

FIORD OF LAKE ARGENTINO, SHOWING FOREST ON MOUNT AVELLANEDA

Emerging from this cleft we came on one of Nature's tragedies. Upon the side of the slope was a guanaco, fallen (when I first caught sight of it) upon its knees, and making frantic efforts to rise. Three huge condors were poised a few feet above the head of the unfortunate animal. I galloped towards them, and as I came near the guanaco fell over upon its side, still moving convulsively. At once one of the condors lit on the ground beside it. I cannot have been more than a minute approaching, and as I came close the condor rose into the air to some distance. A thin stream of blood was trickling down the surface of the rock upon which the guanaco lay, and the poor creature was jerking its legs and body. During the moment which I had taken to ride up the condor had torn out its eyes! The guanaco was evidently dying of scab, and had thinned down into a mere skeleton.

I own to a horror and a loathing of the condor. Seen against the pale hue of the sky, its stately flight and grand spread of motionless wing made it seem a noble bird, but near by it shared the repulsive appearance of other carrion-eaters. In size it is enormous. I shot one off Hellgate measuring nine feet three inches across the outstretched pinions. It rivals the vulture in its ability to quickly discover and arrive upon the scene of a feast, and is in the habit of gorging itself until it becomes practically powerless, and it is possible to slay it afoot with a stick. It is one thing to be well mounted on a good horse and to watch, as you ride along, the far specks in the intense blue, or to admire them wheeling in wide graceful circles with quiescent wings, but quite another aspect of them would be borne in upon you if your horse chanced to stumble, and left you, say, with a broken leg upon the empty pampa; long before help might come, or, indeed, if you were alone, would be at all likely to come, you would make a terribly close acquaintance with the methods a condor adopts when meat—be it dead or wounded—falls under his power of beak and claw.

Patagonia is certainly a wonderful country for birds and beasts of prey. You may travel leagues upon leagues and see no sign of life save chimangos (Milvago chimango), caranchos (Polyborus thaurus), and condors (Sarcorhampus gryphus) in the air and upon the bushes, and at your feet the tracks of lion and of fox and of skunk. Sometimes this fact strikes you with peculiar force. The landscape made up of thorny bushes and spike grass jagged rocks, and white and grey slime, in which live the puma, the wild-cat, and the fox; the air inhabited by birds of prey. What do they live upon, these creatures, there are so many of them? How do they eke out existence? Sparse herds of guanaco (I am now alluding to the sterile portions of the country, such as lie about the north shore of Lake Buenos Aires and also part of the north shore of Lake Argentino), a few small birds, and abundant rodent life of the smaller species—that is all. Curiously enough, in the richer lands of Patagonia, it seemed to me that, though there was more game, there were fewer birds and beasts of prey.

In the winter and in the spring the country, as far as wild life is concerned, is but a thin and gaunt place. Nothing that wanders carries any fat, for the food has been reduced to a minimum. It is on this sterile battlefield of nature that living creatures enter into a death-grapple with the conditions of life, and swing to and fro in a contest whose outcome is only decided when the dark days of storm are over; for at this season the richer lands are often under snow, and it is about the bare margins of lakes and lagoons that the game gathers and remains.

All the way up the River Santa Cruz we were able to recognise the points marked and named by Darwin, until finally his party was forced through lack of provisions to turn back just when he had arrived within reasonable distance of the great lake. He named this last prospect he looked out over in Patagonia,

"Mystery Plain." Now it no longer is mysterious, but Darwin's map remains to this day the best chart made of the river.

His description and his opinion of the country are sufficiently dismal, but he passed through a waste and empty land, before colonising on the coasts had reached its present state, or much of the country within reach of the sea had been partitioned, as it now is, into sheep farms. And it must be admitted that the neighbourhood of the Santa Cruz is somewhat sterile, and would be likely to give a false idea of Patagonia as a forbidding land to a stranger who knew no more of the country than the coast and this boulder and sand-strewn river valley. This cañadon is, in fact, covered with glacial detritus.

END OF SOUTHERN FIORD OF LAKE ARGENTINO

Leaving the shore of the lake well to our right we rode parallel with it for some miles, crossed the Rivers Calafate and de los Perros, and finally arrived upon a peninsula which culminates in Mount Buenos Aires. This peninsula is called the Burmeister Peninsula. Here, many days' ride into the interior, and under the very shadow of the Andes, lives an English pioneer, Mr. Cattle, whom we visited, and who was kind enough to help me in every way and to give us hospitality.

During the first night we spent upon the shores of Lake Argentino there was a heavy snowfall on the tops of the nearer mountains.

ESTANCIA OF MR. E. CATTLE

Our first move was in the direction of Lake Rica—so-called locally. Upon the maps we had with us it was marked as a separate lake connected by a river with Lake Argentino. We soon proved this to be a mistake, the so-called Lake Rica being an arm of the large lake, connected with the parent volume of water by a channel of considerable width, which is occasionally blocked, or nearly so, by icebergs. I should mention that we had left England before the publication of Dr. Moreno's excellent map, in which this and many other errors had already been set right.

Taking our horses, we made our way to the south-west along the shores of Lake Rica. We were forced to make détours, as the steep banks were cut up by innumerable rifts, at the bottom of nearly every one of which streams of varying size emptied themselves into the fjord. Heavy forests clothed the slopes of the hills almost to the margin of the water. Very little animal life was to be observed. I picked up a number of iron-ore stalactites on the shores and also from the mud of the shallow water near them. When approaching the end of this South Fjord—as Lake Rica should properly be called—of Lake Argentino we crossed a river or rather, I should say, a torrent, that after a riotous course between very steep cliffs flowed over a rocky bed into the South Fjord. This river would have been, I should say, impassable at an earlier date in the season.

Our advance was finally stopped by cliffs which descended clear to the water's edge. We camped on the shingle at the foot of the cliffs just short of the spot where their bases plunged under the level of the water, and all night long we could hear the rushing thunder of masses of ice breaking from the parent glaciers and crashing down into the fjord.

The weather now completely broke up. Rain fell in, close steady lines all across our outlook over the western fjord, and the drenched forests behind us tossed and creaked in the wind. Nothing more dismal and depressing can be imagined than this forest-land dim with lowering skies and a downpour of rain. For four days the heavy rain, sometimes mixed with sleet, continued to fall, and through it we rode back to the Burmeister Peninsula.

It was upon the shores of Lake Argentino that a great Gaucho, perhaps I should say the greatest of all Gauchos, one Ascensio Brunel, at one time found a hiding-place. We visited the spot later on, but here I may as well tell some part of the story of his life. He was very generally known for many years as the "Wild Man of Santa Cruz," and his history was an extraordinary one—one of those smears of high and vivid colour which circumstance occasionally paints in upon the dull humdrum picture of the daily life of a district.

Let us set out his antecedents.

He and his brother were Gauchos. They lived in camp, and were partners in a small business. Cattle, sheep, and horses formed their stock.

Once they went together on a long journey, and became acquainted with a lady, whom we will call Bathsheba. They both loved her; yet she was another's.

THE WILD MAN

The two brothers descended upon that other and slew him. Then they made off with the lady to the wilder districts. There they quarrelled about her. Ascensio waited until his brother happened to be away tracking horses in a particularly wild part, and then he rounded up the remainder of the stock, and he and the lady fled yet deeper into the interior. For a space they covered their tracks and escaped the brother.

In the course of time the lady left her lover, as ladies will, and he, his brain turned by some strange passion, went mad.

When we strike his trail again he was known as the "Wild Man of Santa Cruz."

He began to steal horses, found the sport to his liking, and stole more. Unable to use or keep them, he merely drove them to some sleepy hollow, where he killed them in hundreds. (We once counted eighty-three of these skeletons in one place.) He dressed in the skins of pumas from head to foot. His saddle was of puma-skin, and armed only with boleadores he ranged the land stealing. His career was a long one, and he became such a Gaucho as has never been known. To-day he might be heard of as lifting a dozen horses on the Santa Cruz River; a week later he was spiriting away tropillas in Chubut.

He had the run of 300,000 square miles, the whole of Patagonia was his farm, his stock what he could steal.

You may remember that I described a meeting with Indians, a tribe who lived in tents of guanaco-skins on the River Mayo. The Wild Man paid them a visit, and stole a hundred mares; and they, discovering it, rode down his trail and caught him. They took him alive and haled him as a prisoner to the nearest settlement, where he was put in gaol.

He escaped, made straight back, and lifted another big batch of the Mayo Indians' horses.

Again they pursued him, but he was fain to escape, being mounted on a very good horse. At last, only one Indian continued to hold on his trail, and he, when he neared the wild figure clad in puma-skins, grew afraid and turned back.

The Wild Man rode on, and also out of our story and all human ken. That was four years ago. He has not been heard of since. But I daresay that the Mayo Indians could finish off the story with a different ending.

FOOTNOTE:
[22] *A guide who applied to me at Santa Cruz warned me that, if we went without him, we would have great difficulty at this point. He asked ten dollars a day for his services, which I, however, declined.*

CHAPTER XIV

THE DOWN-STREAM NAVIGATION OF THE RIVER LEONA

Boat necessary for farther exploration—Steam-launch on shores of Lake Viedma our only hope—Start to find her—Difficulty of crossing Santa Cruz River—River Leona—Old camp—Hills and guanaco-tracks—Lake Viedma—Finding launch—Damaged by wanderers—Down-stream trip discussed—Repairing launch—Our one chance of penetrating Cordillera—Risks of down-stream passage—Gathering firewood—Cold work—Launch of Ariel—Aspect of Leona River—Good intentions—Califate fuel—Desolate evening—Getting up stream—Start in bad weather—Obliged to put back—Second start—Sucked into current of Leona—Bernardo puts on steam—Rain—Stop for the night—Dangers of Leona channel—Second day's trip—Launch turns in squall—Rushing downstream—Racing ahead of the current—Awaiting the finish—Reach after reach—Rounding a cliff—Choice of many channels—Narrow passage—Safe—Sup off armadillo—"If."

As it was impossible to make any further exploration without a craft of some sort, I began to cast about for materials for boat-building or, rather, for boat-repairing. There were a couple of canvas boats on the spot, left on the shore by a Commission some three years previously, with which I thought perhaps something might be done. But these, on examination, proved to be so worn with the stress of weather, and when launched shipped so much water, that it seemed hardly practicable to use them for our purpose, the more especially as their holding capacity made it impossible to take more than a small quantity of provisions.

I next heard of a boat on the River Santa Cruz, but that was also in very evil plight, added to which the odds were against our being able to get her up to Lake Argentino, owing to the fact that the River Santa Cruz was in flood and the current more than usually fierce.

Note.—The author regrets the comparative absence of illustration to this chapter. The launch shipped so much water through her broken plate and in other ways that the photographs taken were destroyed.

I have mentioned in an earlier chapter the boat which Dr. Moreno had during his last expedition in the year 1897 brought, at much cost and labour, to Lake Viedma. There lay our hope. It was a steam-launch, and the Argentine Commission had packed her up carefully and snugly on the shore; but, although we knew nothing of her present condition, we were aware that the chances against her remaining undisturbed for that period of time were small, as Lake Viedma is not difficult of access, and in all probability wandering bands of Indians or Gauchos had got at the boat, stripped off her covering of canvas, and looted such of her contents as seemed to possess any value in their eyes.

THE LAUNCH WITH MR. CATTLE AND BERNARDO ON BOARD

However that might be, this launch appeared to be our only resource, and I was lucky indeed to have been given leave to use her if necessary. On my speaking to Cattle on the matter, he was kind enough to offer to accompany me. Burbury possessed a good knowledge of engineering, which would be of invaluable service to us, and, as it happened, Bernardo, in the course of his adventurous career, had had some experience in the engine-room of a Brazilian steamer.

So on February 15 we set out for Lake Viedma, with the idea of bringing the launch, if possible, down the River Leona, which is the connecting waterway between the Lakes Viedma and Argentino.

To travel from our starting point at the foot of Mount Buenos Aires to Lake Viedma it was necessary to skirt Lake Argentino until the southern outlet of the Leona was reached, and then to follow that river to its source in Lake Viedma. The distance was about eighty miles more or less, and included the fording of the River Santa Cruz.

Our party was made up of four men and twenty-one horses, and upon one of the packs we took a light canvas collapsible boat and a pair of oars with which to negotiate the Santa Cruz.

On the following evening we arrived on its southern bank. There we found an old Commission boat that was used as a ferry, but it was beached, with the usual contrariety of things, on the wrong side of the stream, which is from one hundred and fifty to two hundred yards wide at this spot and runs with a swift current. Many a Gaucho has lost his life in attempting to cross lower down.

Next morning it was still dark when the plume of smoke rose from our camp-fire of califate-wood, and as we sat round it waiting for the asado to cook, we smoked (a bad habit when indulged in before breakfast, against which one would warn everybody else) and drank maté. It was a cool dawn I remember that developed later into a hot day. We put the collapsible boat together, and Cattle, after a mishap with a rowlock, brought the old and leaky ford-boat across, as we needed her to transport our baggage. We piled the cargo into her, and such weak places as we could deal with we strengthened.

The theory was to take the filly through the river behind the boat, trusting that the old black bell-mare would follow her offspring, and the troop in its turn follow the mare, as had occurred on the occasion of our former crossing of the river near the settlement of Santa Cruz.

So we dragged the reluctant and much-protesting filly down to the riverside, conveyed the boat a few hundred yards up-stream, and then Bernardo and I got aboard and shoved off. I had put a collar round the filly's neck, and by this supported her in the wake of the boat. All would have gone well had not one of the rowlocks, worn by weather and worm-eaten, struck work and smashed. Left with but one oar the current took charge of us. Soon the unfortunate filly began to turn over in the water like a catherine-wheel, and I was unable to help her much, as I was holding a rowlock in place with one hand and supporting the filly with the other. Eventually we were obliged to put back, and were lucky enough to make the south bank just in time, for at that part of the shore there is but a small stretch upon which it is possible to land; immediately below high cliffs descend sheer to the water.

After this we resolved to drive the troop over before us, but although they had had a long-journey experience of river-crossing they did not care to face the Santa Cruz. In spite of our efforts they broke back five or six times. Once we nearly had them in the water, when the little Zaino got away and galloped up the bank. At last, however, by dint of bellowing and brandishing oars or anything that came handy, we succeeded in convincing them that the south shore of the Santa Cruz had become unhealthy to remain upon, and so they swam over. We started at once with a boatful of gear, and landed barely in time to defeat the ambitious intentions of the leading spirits of the troop, who on getting out of the water decided to make off and regain a life of freedom.

As soon as we got the baggage over we saddled-up and rode through a very sandy tract of land, and by evening made our camp under a bare hillside by the River Leona.

I believe that a German expedition had once encamped there. Both wheat and beans were growing near the long-deserted camp-fire. No doubt the seed had fallen from some of the provision-bags of the Germans. There was also a miniature corral formed of bushes.

On the next day we made a very long and tiresome march, which led us into more than one difficult place. We rode on league after league over the worst sort of ground, including the descent of two or three really bad barrancas. Bernardo, who acted as guide, became shy after awhile of telling us that Lake Viedma lay only two leagues ahead. As the day wore on we rather pressed the question, and he grew correspondingly coy in his replies.

One of the barrancas led us into a sort of maze of conical mud hills, confusedly huddled together. Through them lay a tangle of guanaco-tracks, which mostly ended on the tops of the hills. The troop followed these tracks in various directions, and you were surprised at all points by the startled faces of the horses glaring down at you over unexpected bluffs. The going was very heavy, and deep holes betrayed the horses' feet. Altogether it was some time before the troop was put through.

Late in the evening we reached the shores of Lake Viedma, and found the launch. She was lying behind a bare and very low promontory. The Commission which had used her three years previously had packed her up with care in canvas and raised her on rollers. But I was sorry to find that needless and wanton damage had been inflicted upon her by some roving passers-by. They had torn off the canvas covering and appropriated many important tools, including quite a number that could have been of no possible use to any save a party meaning to use the launch herself. A few of these missing details we picked up in the adjacent bushes, where the irresponsible unknowns had thrown them.

As to the condition of the boat, her three-years sojourn on an isolated beach had not improved it. Her boiler was in rather a bad state with rust, and one of her plates was cracked. Originally built for a pleasure-launch, the Argentine Commission had raised her gunwales and decked her in; without these alterations she could not have lived in the rough waters of the lakes of Patagonia.

The evening and the surrounding scenery were equally grey and depressing, but with an ostrich, and a guanaco I had shot in the morning, we made ourselves very comfortable round the fire, while we talked over our contemplated voyage down the Leona. Cattle, whose knowledge of the subject under consideration was of immense help, agreed with me in thinking the thing could be done.

Next day Burbury, who was, as I have said, a very fair engineer, set to work with Bernardo's help to get the launch into working order, while the rest of us went to cut and gather fuel.

The two canvas boats which belonged to the launch were later found a couple of leagues down the shore, but a bit of wind began to blow, so it was impossible to bring them up, and in the event they had to be left where they were.

In making ready the launch Burbury was much hampered by having only a small supply of screws to draw upon. Time and exposure had dealt hardly with her, her pump was strained as well as being imperfect, some portion of it having been taken away. The craft was about thirty-five feet long with a displacement of about three parts of a ton. She was by no means an ideal boat for the kind of navigation that lay before us, for which a good wooden craft would have been much more safe and handy. Had her length been less it would have been another advantage, as the seas upon the lakes are very short. Weather-worn as she was, however, she represented our sole chance of getting really deep into the unpenetrated Cordillera. It was a case of take it or leave it, and which of the two it was to be gave me some thought that night.

I could not conceal from myself that it was a peculiarly risky affair taking her down the River Leona. The up-stream navigation of the river had been made by the launch when the Commission brought her up-stream, towing her through the difficult places from the bank. But that, of course, was a very different matter.

The Leona is a comparatively large river, very cold, and running, when in flood, from five to eight knots an hour, with, in places, a very strong rip. There are a good many rocks and shoals, but at the time I write of the water was high, snow-fed by the warmth of the preceding months, and therefore with luck we might hope to slip over most of the reefs in safety. This was fortunate, as what with the cold, the eddies and the cross-currents the chance of a swimmer reaching the bank was not great.

Should the current, however, get the launch broadside on, we would have to give her full steam ahead, and charge down the unknown and rock-set river. Besides, the channel was, we knew, very hard to follow, for among the islands the stream divided into four or five arms, and we had no guide to help us to choose the main channel.

The risks were very real and looked large enough in my eyes that night, but in case I should be charged with foolhardiness in deciding to carry out our design, I think I may say that the average man would have decided as we did. Few, after so many weary miles and months, coming at last to such a crucial moment, would very closely consider the risks, since outside of running them the single course open was to turn back defeated, leaving one of the most interesting unexplored portions of the Cordillera unvisited and untrodden.

In the course of the next day or two we worked hard at the launch and in gathering firewood. On the 18th we got the boat afloat after eight hours of hard labour, for during her three years rest she had sunk deep into the shingle and sand. It was quite impossible to use the horses, as they would not pull forward into the lake, and thus into the water, so we got at the work ourselves. About mid-day a wind sprang up, and the water, fed by the melting snows, was perishingly cold. It seemed for a time as if we should never succeed in getting her afloat, and as we had not been able to bring up either of the canvas boats, wading was very much the order of the day, and after every few stretches of work we were uncommonly glad to take spells in the sleeping-bags to warm our half-frozen limbs. Hot cocoa, also, was kept going from time to time.

THE WORLD OF ICE

At length we got her off into the little shallow bay, where the waves were breaking, for a wind was rising out of the north-west.

During the day Cattle and I went down and viewed the Leona. We fixed upon a little backwater some distance down stream, where wood was abundant, as the goal of our first venture. The river had swollen and was rising, and the current looked menacing, but we thought that with great care and slow movement we might bring the launch through all right. Care and slow movement! We did not foresee to what an extent the elements were destined to take charge of our affairs.

Our plan was to descend the river stern-first with only enough steam to enable the boat to answer her tiller; for fuel we had no choice but to burn wood, and although califate made no bad firing, still the results to be expected were not by any means the same as if we had been able to put coal into the furnace.

In the evening the horses strayed, and I went to bring them in. The landscape on this side of Viedma is the most desolate imaginable, being made up chiefly of sand, sparse yellow grass, low thorn-bushes, and the skeletons of dead game. It is a place only fit to die in, a fact the guanacos seem to have grasped, for their bones lay all over the ground in far greater profusion even than upon the shores of Lake Buenos Aires. The mountains about Viedma differ in outline from most of the other ranges in Patagonia. The peaks are more pointed and rise against the cold sky in a line of pinnacles and minarets.

My way led me along the banks of the Leona. It was a grey and miserable afternoon verging towards evening, and the strong wind was sending a large volume of water racing and moaning between the bare and treeless banks of the river. I remember thinking with great longing of warm and comfortable England, of good friends and true, of home, and of all the many small things which make life worth having. I suppose every one is attacked with this kind of feeling sometimes. Not very often, luckily, nor when the sun is shining, but on these miserable, grey, whimpering evenings everything takes on a sombre shade.

I found the horses collected in a rincon, beneath the shelter of a few thorn-bushes; they were looking very forlorn, especially the Alazan, who was etched out darkly against the bleak sky. They seemed a bit tucked up too after the tiring marches of the previous days.

We hoped to start in the launch on the following morning. When we woke it was still blowing half a gale. I, however, told Bernardo to get up steam, and we put the baggage aboard, and as the boat had no name we christened her the Ariel. She was given other names before we were done with her!

Burbury was to take the horses by the banks of the river, while we steamed down the channel. It was blowing pretty strong when all was ready, and Bernardo, to inaugurate the start, raised a feeble whistle, thereby seriously diminishing the amount of steam in the boiler. The Ariel got under way with some wheezing and groaning, and soon we were heaving up and down, head to swell. The waves were all breaking, and the seas short, with the consequence that we had several duckings. Presently, however, the wind lulled and I thought all was about to go well with us.

But soon I noticed that the figure of Burbury, standing upon the shore, remained ominously stationary. The wind was rising again, two or three heavy seas broke over us, and the launch would not answer her tiller. Bernardo shouted that the boiler was leaking, and it looked as if we should soon be in trouble.

Ultimately we were obliged to put back into the bay, which we managed with difficulty, and there anchored.

We determined to try again to-morrow, and then got up the tent and turned in.

On the morrow the wind had dropped somewhat, though the lake was still white with breakers. We had a maté by the fire on the promontory and prepared to start again. It was 9.30 when all was ready, and by that time the Cordillera was shut out by a big purple rain-cloud. As the rain began to fall we took our places and heaved in the anchor.

We started at one knot full steam ahead, and the Ariel creaked as she crept out into the lake. The rain and mist from the direction of the Cordillera had blotted out all sight of them, and were beating down on us steadily. The rain, however, was in reality favourable to our attempt, as it served to smooth the water. The short waves leaped up under every puff of wind, but the launch ran along past the mouth of the river, attaining to a quite respectable speed as she proceeded.

A nasty little squall struck us for a moment as we were broadside on, but it passed, and then, with her nose pointed toward the Cordillera, the launch described a large circle, and we allowed her to be slowly sucked stern first into the power of the fierce current of the Leona. At length it got hold of her, and, adopting a cautious policy, we gave her full speed ahead against the current, which had the effect of letting us drop down stream at about two knots an hour.

Just before we entered the rip of the current I saw a rock a couple of feet off on the starboard side; it was only a few inches under the surface, but luckily we slipped by without harm. We got on pretty well in this fashion through the whole afternoon; it was raining pitilessly all the time. Bernardo, who was acting as engineer, at one period ran the engine at a pressure of 30 lb. above safety, until it was explained to him that, if he continued doing so, it was probable he would see Sweden no more.

Towards evening the weather cleared into the most lovely blue afternoon, and we camped for the night at the spot we had before chosen, having some fifteen miles of our voyage behind us. We pitched the tent and I crawled into it and lit a pipe with a vivid question in my mind as to when I should do so again. You could hear the river growling and gulping at its banks. I felt I had never before realised how warm and comfortable that little tent was. The next day would decide the success of our expedition or otherwise, and all the worst of the river lay before us. I cannot deny that I disliked the thought of the morrow. Familiarity with the River Leona is not apt to breed contempt. Its channel was made up of sharp bends and curves, and if the launch by any untoward accident were to swing round, we should be forced to steam faster than the current, and at that speed she would certainly split herself from stem to stern if she touched. Besides, she answered her helm badly, and the river in places was very narrow.

But, for all this, our success so far had had its effect, and we resumed our voyage next morning in high spirits. We began by negotiating a nasty passage among the rocks with neatness. The river then became very erratic and winding in its course, and almost at once the current caught us, and it seemed as it some gigantic hand were pushing the panting launch slowly round. Steering was no easy matter, she was canted badly, and we discarded some of our heavy clothes, raw as the air was, preferring the cold to the chance of sinking should anything happen.

In places the rip was very strong and the curving pearl-grey water gave but a poor opportunity of observing any rocks that might lie in our course. We were by this time able to manage the launch better and were beginning to understand more or less her special peculiarities.

Then the dreaded event came to pass. We were sagging down with about 70 lb. of steam in the boiler, when a heavy squall, which had long been brooding darkly over the Cordillera, rushed suddenly upon us. The launch, under the fury of the wind, turned almost broadside on to the current, and it became necessary to give her her head.

Bernardo, who had had his orders as to what to do in case such an eventuality occurred, flung open the furnace-door and piled on wood to get a heavy head of steam on. The Ariel's powers had much improved with use, and she was able to race along ahead of the current, a fact which gave her steerage-way.

"She's steering a bit better," shouted Cattle; "if Bernardo can keep up the pressure it may be all right." Bernardo, evidently feeling that the moment needed commemoration, blew the whistle and grinned.

Now that she was turned prow-first, any attempt to get the boat back to her old position would have been more risky than to go forward, for the river at this part was much narrower and the current proportionately more rapid. Bernardo poked his head up from the engine-hatch and laughed, "She go fine this way," he remarked. At the moment a rock glimmered up close to the bows, but we slipped over it with a few inches to spare.

BERNARDO HÄHANSEN

There was now no straining and grunting from the engines as there had been while we were battling against the current. You barely felt the throb and vibration, and it was only when you looked at the banks that you realised how swiftly the boat was rushing onwards. Perhaps we achieved seventeen knots. The shores slid by.

We were now shut in in a world of our own, whose boundaries were the curving banks and the reaches of the river as they opened out in front of us. One's senses were too much occupied, one's nerves too much on the stretch to be aware of anything beyond. We, the launch and the river were playing a gigantic gamble, in which the stakes on our part were perilously heavy. This continued to be for five minutes one's most prominent idea. It was very exciting, for we had nothing to do but await developments.

Very soon, however, this feeling wore off. It seems that a very strong emotion cannot in the nature of things last long. Undoubtedly c'est le premier pas qui coûte. I looked round and saw the other two grinning.

At the pace we were then going our voyage was not likely to last more than four hours. This was a rough calculation allowing for the windings of the river that lay between us and Lake Argentino. We afterwards found that we ran the distance in three and a half hours, but they passed like a quarter of an hour. I do not suppose that any suicide club has ever invented a more acute form of excitement.

We rarely saw half a mile in front of us. At first the banks were low and the coarse grass upon them blew and shook against the pale blue of the sky-rim, but soon they began to give place to high and rocky slopes. Now and then one caught the glitter of a submerged rock. The wind and the current made the main channel difficult to follow with the eye, and round several corners we were positively feeling for it.

In places it seemed as if the launch were running into an impasse, and at such times it was necessary to send her along at her highest pressure in order to have the more command of the tiller. We would rush down upon such a place, and not until we were within forty yards would the river open out grey and shining, the helm be put over, and we find ourselves flying down another reach. We always kept to the rip, and by so doing attempted to follow the main channel.

About midway down the river came some more difficult places where the cliffs narrowed. One of these gave us a curious experience for the water seemed to absolutely go downhill, so steep was the angle of incline. Before reaching this spot we had come in sight of the top of the cliff that overhung it, and whose base, we could judge by the line of the channel, must be washed by the water. On turning a corner we came within full view of the place, and a strange view it was. The river appeared to race downhill and to end in a froth of yeasty foam at the foot of the towering black bluff. Look as we might, we could not see any way out of that tumbled smother of water; we knew there must be one, of course, but the question was in which direction did it lie. There was nothing for it but to pile on fuel to make the boat answer handily.

The sun striking obliquely on the river dazzled our eyes and turned all our forward course into a golden splendour. We knew that somewhere lower down the river there was a bad place where its bed was thick-set with rocks, but we had no idea how soon we might come upon the spot. Presently, as we drew rapidly nearer and nearer to the cliff face, it became evident that the channel bent very sharply to starboard, and that we should have uncommonly little room to turn in. We were now running in shadow, the high banks having blotted out the sun. We rushed on towards the cliff, and almost at the last moment saw that the channel bent away to the right; Cattle put the helm hard over, and our craft whirled round the point with small space to spare, and we found ourselves snaking through the eddies of another reach.

We shouted to each other that the worst of it lay behind us, and such for a time seemed to be the case, the river widening out to about eighty yards across. Here the main channel was clearly marked. It might be supposed that we should have taken this opportunity to turn the launch into her original position, but we had twice during the morning been in difficulties with the pump, which, as the injector would not work, was our sole means of filling the boiler. I was afraid that the strain of steaming against the current might prove too much for the launch. The decision to go on without turning her was, I think, under the circumstances, the right one, the more so as directly after the descent of the river the pump became further strained, with the result that it was impossible to refill the boiler save by hand.

Presently the hilly shores once more gave place to low banks, and islands began to appear in the stream. The lower river has many of these groups of flat islands covered with stones and coarse grass. When we got in among them the river broke up into a dozen channels which all looked alike. We, of course, chose the largest. Again it branched. Again we chose the largest, and again.

At length the channel we were following, instead of opening off into the main river, subdivided into a couple of very small streams. The current was as strong as ever, and the depth of water appeared to be about three feet. A small crested grebe was uttering its peculiar, melancholy cry. Ahead the banks seemed to draw together to a jutting corner, beyond which we could not see. Cattle was at the helm, I was standing up on the fore-hatch trying to catch sight of what we were coming to.

All this time we could not slacken speed, for the current tore along and we outdid the current. The water had the same strange appearance of running downhill; it seemed to drop away from us at an extraordinary angle. The force of the current forced us to keep steam up to a high degree of pressure, up to 45 lb., which was 15 lb. beyond safety.

At this point the stream was not above eighteen feet wide, and we could almost touch the banks on either side. We were now about half-way downhill, so to speak. The rush of the water, the zipp of the wind as it swept past our ears mingled with the cry of the astonished waterfowl. Nearer and nearer, clear water showed under the left bank, and in a moment more we had swept round the corner of rock and out into the main channel of the river once more. We flew along in the strong rip, the launch shook and quivered, and we discovered with joy that we had gained the wide lower reaches.

Our troubles were at an end for the day. A dozen miles still lay before us, but in fair and open water. In due time we recognised a big stone which marked the site of our old camp where we had rested on the way up. We secured the launch a little way below it, where the Leona enters Lake Argentino.

After landing we pitched the tent and sat down to talk it all over. In the meantime we cooked and ate an armadillo, which Burbury had caught on the previous day. It tasted very like sucking-pig.

Then a curious thing happened. The launch, which was bumping slightly at her anchorage, had to be moved, and going on board we found that the pump had again struck work, as it did on many subsequent occasions. One could not help thinking what the result might have been if it had broken down a little earlier in the day. What a wonderful word that little "if" is! Two letters long, but it may mark the distance from pole to pole, the difference between life and death.

That night a series of heavy squalls blew out of the west. We lay in the tent and listened to the wind with the luxurious feeling that comes of good shelter.

CHAPTER XV

A HARD STRUGGLE

Running an ostrich with dogs—Crossing Santa Cruz River—Horses troublesome—Lose my way— Launch refitted—Diary of rough days—Crossing the bar—Nasty predicament—Wreck imminent— Storm—Ascensio's Bay—Changeable weather—Dangerous lakes—Squalls rushing down from gorges of the Cordillera—Icebergs—Ashore for fuel—Squall comes on—Cut off from launch—Miserable night—Wind lulls—Aboard again—Crossing Hell-gate—Cow Monte harbour—Bernardo's fire— Fighting the fire—News of the world—Rumours of war—Death of the Queen.

Late in the evening of the same day Burbury arrived with the horses, and upon the following morning I rode on with him to pass the troop over the Santa Cruz River. We took with us one of Cattle's hounds, and sighting some ostriches on the way we gave chase. The dog had a rope affixed to his collar, by which Burbury had been leading him, and I had no time to take it off before letting him go. In spite of this disability, with the rope trailing behind him, the big black hound pulled down one of the birds. I did not then know how valuable that ostrich was to be to us.

We reached the Santa Cruz about 7 A.M., and, after a considerable amount of persuasion, we managed to induce the horses to enter the water.

One of the great dangers of driving a tropilla into a river is the chance that, when they do take to the water, your own mount is very likely to rush in after them, and, before you can free yourself, he will have carried you into the pull of the current, and, of course, beyond your depth. Therefore it is always well to do this kind of work bare-back, with only a bridle in your horse's mouth, so that you can fling yourself off at any moment. It is also well to unbuckle the loop of the rein; the omission of the latter precaution has resulted in the drowning of horses on many occasions.

After seeing Burbury safely across, I started on my tramp back to the camp at the mouth of the Leona. Fortunately, I carried the whole ostrich with me, as I thought it was quite possible we might be held back by bad weather in our voyage up the lake.

Cattle and Bernardo had stayed with the launch to prepare her for probable rough handling by the waters of Lake Argentino, and it was lucky they did so, as events proved. Cattle lighted a smoke to give me my direction, and I was tempted to try a short cut, which led me across an interminable series of sandhills mottled with the tracks of foxes and lions (pumas).

When I got into camp we held a small festival in honour of the launch's good behaviour, and drank to her health and good luck in a cup of tea sweetened with the last of our sugar. But it never does to rejoice prematurely, and our way along the north shore of the lake turned out to be a battle with adverse winds, rain, and vindictive bad weather.

The launch presented quite a different appearance by the time I returned. The engine-room hatch had been covered by a canvas hood, and bulwarks formed by lashing oars to strengthen the wire railing which ran round the deck. The wheel had been rigged up forward and protected by a weather-dodger. The cargo had been carefully stowed, and, in fact, every precaution taken to ensure the safety of the boat and to make her seaworthy.

The following is taken from my diary, which carries us from hour to hour of the next few troubled days:

"February 21.—It blew pretty hard all through the morning, and the bar of the Leona was quite impassable; but towards evening the wind dropped slightly, so we got up steam and started. We ran out over the bar, fighting our way by inches through the heavy surf, but just beyond it the engine broke down, and we were at the mercy of the wind and waves. It looked as if we were being driven back to certain shipwreck, for the launch could not live in the seas that were breaking on the bar. I cut loose one of the oars which formed our bulwark, and both Cattle and I did what we could to prevent her turning broadside on.

"I was engaged in this work at the stern when I heard Bernardo shout, 'Mr. Preechard! Mr. Preechard!'

"I lay my full length along the deck and looked down at Bernardo in the engine-room. He was holding on to the pump, which was spouting steam and water. There was no room for two people in the engine-room, nor in that angry sea was there much possibility of my getting down there. So I lay along the port decking, and slipped my feet under the after-hatch, thanking Providence for my length, and so managed to hold the pump down while Bernardo tried to repair the damage.

"Every now and then the seas caught us almost broadside on and broke heavily, nearly sweeping me over with them. My head being outside, I could see Cattle clinging on like a cat, and doing all that man could do to keep us from swinging round. We were on the bar, and scarcely twenty yards outside the fiercest of the breakers. As it was, big seas kept sweeping over the launch and crashing on her plates, making her roll appallingly.

"Between us and the shore was from one hundred to one hundred and fifty yards of yeasty surge, dominated by a heavy current setting south. The anchor continued to drag, and we hung on while Bernardo fought with screws and nuts for our lives. While we drifted back over the bar, nearly capsizing as we did so, it became obvious that our only course lay in first getting in the anchor and then putting it out again with a good length of chain. In spite of the almost inconceivable rolling of our craft, Cattle was successful in his attempt to do this, and the launch came prow on to the breakers, which were losing something of their fury as they crashed across the bar, twenty yards in front of us.

"Meantime, Bernardo did not relax his efforts to get the engines working once more. We were, as I have explained, a couple of hundred yards from the shore, towards which the full force of the wind, aided by the current I have mentioned as setting south towards the mouth of the Santa Cruz, was drifting us.

"The anchor dragged again, and we had to undertake the difficult business of getting it in, and taking a second chance of dropping it on better holding ground.

"We were tossing upon the bar for an hour and twenty minutes, during which time poor Bernardo was violently seasick. It made us laugh to hear him apostrophising the launch in the words, 'Be—she make me—' I will not conclude his sentence.

"At length, however, the Swede coaxed the engines into once more performing their appointed duties, and as putting back would have been a more difficult business than going forward, we began to forge slowly ahead. It was now between five and six o'clock, and there was a freezing south-west wind booming out of the Cordillera, but when darkness fell this lulled for a short time and we made the most of our chances to push forward. But, later, it came on to blow heavily, the seas rose high and short, and in the night-sky overhead only a few stars were visible through the racing clouds. The wind veered to the south-west, and we were off a lee shore set with rocks and icebergs, and there was no anchorage for another twelve miles at least.

"The wind again veered a point to the southward after a time, and it soon became evident that the launch, quivering and swept continually by the waves, was making but little headway, while our stock of fuel was growing low, and would not last us for the run to the anchorage.

"I shouted the facts to Cattle, who was steering at the time, and he suggested that we should try to make Ascensio's Bay—the place where the famous horse-stealer and Gaucho, Brunel, used to hide and slay the tropillas he robbed from the Indians. As Cattle and I were discussing the question in shouts, a big sea swamped us, almost carrying Cattle overboard with it and billowing along the deck and nearly drowning out the engine-room.

"Cattle had made some trips about Lake Argentino in a canvas boat, but had never been in Ascensio's Bay. But, as the night was growing darker and the gale rising, we resolved to make for it. At last, through the noise and battering of the grey-black water, we reached the shelter of the promontory by the bay and succeeded in feeling our way in. There we dropped anchors from both bow and stern, drew off some water from the boiler to make a maté which we drank, and afterwards lying down in the after-hatch instantly fell asleep. Bernardo occupied the fore-hatch. We were too tired to dream of eating anything, and, in spite of our close quarters and the cold, we did not wake till morning.

WHERE THE SQUALLS CAME FROM

"The 23rd dawned calm and fine, and the first view of the spot in which we were anchored made me think that something more than mere luck had been with us during our entry upon the previous night. The mouth of the bay was dotted with an outcrop of toothlike rocks.

"The dawn developed into a morning with strong sun, and we were off early. For two hours all went well. Then came a shiver creeping across the glassy surface of the lake, after that a swell, and in a matter of twenty minutes the quiet lake had become as nasty and as angry a piece of water as can be imagined. This change is eminently typical of the temper of the Andean lakes; they cannot be depended upon from hour to hour. In the present instance at 7.45 A.M. we were steaming, as I have said, through calm water, yet at 8.15 one sea of every four was dashing in a cloud of spray over the boat. The reason of these sudden changes is not far to seek.[23]

"Here, encircled by snow-capped mountains and bounded by high cliffs, the waters of Argentino are often struck by swift squalls descending from the gorges. The voyager may be, as we were, many miles distant from the actual spot where the storm first strikes, but the squall rushes down the funnel-like openings, bringing a heavy sea with it. The seas are also very short, which more than doubles the difficulty of navigation.

"On this occasion the sun was obscured and the outlook to the westward became more and more menacing. The launch began to creak and groan as usual, and to make but slight headway. Far away glimmered an iceberg, which lay at the entrance of the bay that marked our next harbourage. Soon it became clear that we should never be able to reach its friendly shelter without gathering a fresh supply of fuel. There was only one alternative left to us, and that was to put in close to the shore, and either wade or swim off to get more.

"The squall had now more or less spent itself, so we ran in close, gaining some small shelter from a promontory which ended in a big boulder.

"To attain such shelter as the promontory offered it was necessary to make our way through a group of rocks. This we did, and the wind sinking, Cattle and I scrambled ashore with the axes and fell to work while Bernardo remained on board.

"Before, however, we had gathered half the required quantity of wood a second squall, more heavy than the first, came screaming across the lake, tearing the launch from her anchorage and almost driving her upon the beach. We stripped off some of our clothes and waded down into the water, and after a ten-minutes hard struggle we succeeded in getting her back into deep water, where she again dropped anchor.

"We returned to our work ashore, and cut and piled a good store of fuel, almost as much as we needed, on the shingle ready to carry aboard, but the violence of the waves put all hope of embarkation out of the question for the time. This was about 10 A.M., and all day the wind increased in violence. A stately procession of icebergs began to float down from the northerly arms of the lake and squall succeeded squall. Soon it became evident that the launch was drifting again, and I shouted to Bernardo, who was now within hearing distance of the shore, to break up an oar and use it for fuel. Luckily he had kept up fire in the furnace and steam in the boiler, and as the weather was growing rapidly worse, I ordered him to steam up over the anchor, and afterwards to take the boat a quarter of a mile out and there drop anchor with all the length of chain out that we possessed.

"What followed gave to us, I think, perhaps the most heartbreaking moments we experienced throughout the whole trip. While Bernardo was getting up enough steam to carry out orders, the launch, still drifting, swooped nearer and nearer a reef of submerged rocks. As she was in deep water, Cattle and I could do nothing to help; we were compelled to watch helplessly from the shore and rage at our own impotence. We called to Bernardo to keep her off with an oar, and while he was unlashing one the stern of the launch and, more than all, her precious propeller barely escaped being smashed to pieces as she rose and fell on the rollers. To us, looking from the shore, it seemed as if her last hour was come, and it appeared hard indeed that she should have run safely through so many perils only to end her existence in the lake before we had had time to carry out any part of the exploration on which we had set our hearts.

"At the crucial moment, however, Bernardo managed to pole her clear and give her steam. She moved slowly out and anchored far off shore.

"Evening drew on, but the wind showed no signs of dropping, as it usually did at the rising or setting of the sun. There was nothing for it but to make up our minds to a night ashore. We found ourselves in a dilemma, for we had our whole supply of food on shore, while, with the exception of my poncho, which I brought with me to dry, Bernardo had all the rugs and blankets in the launch. However, we made the best of it by building up a big shelter of drift-wood and bushes. Then we lit a huge fire, for our clothes were soaking, and essayed to dry them.

"Meantime the launch was riding out the storm as well as could be expected, but taking a good deal of water aboard all the same. It grew dark and the last we saw of her that night, her anchor was holding and a big sea was racing aft. Bernardo had got on the hatches and gone to bed, we supposed, for we did not see him the whole time save once, and then he was bailing furiously."

The sky was black with the promise of rain, so we heaped up the big fire, filled the cooking-pots with water, and spreading the poncho on the ground took our places upon it. It was not such a very bad night after all. Things rarely fulfil their promise of disagreeableness—things of this kind anyway. We passed the night somehow with the help of our pipes and an occasional brew of sugarless tea. I never desired sugar so much as then. Sugarless tea is far less warming than sugared. Sleep was well-nigh impossible. It was too cold for that, and, besides, one or other of us was always up and trying to pick out the launch from the surrounding mass of spindrift and tumbling black and grey waters.

In those latitudes the wind generally rises or falls, as the case may be, with the setting or rising of the sun, and eagerly we waited to see if the dawn would bring any change in our uncomfortable position. But at dawn it was blowing, if anything, harder than ever. The launch, however, was all right, although there was no sign of Bernardo. We were driven to make a breakfast of berries from the califate-bushes, of which a few mean specimens grew sparsely on the hillside. It is a desolate place, that northern shore of Argentino.

When the sun came out we lay down and slept in its liquid rays. A little after midday we cooked some fariña with mutton fat and ate it. The gale was still tearing across the water, and we began to count over our resources. We still had the greater part of the ostrich which the hound Moses had killed on the way to the River Santa Cruz, but it was an immature bird, and would provide us with no more than three meagre meals. A couple of handfuls of fariña were yet in the bottom of the bag, we had a half-tin of tea and three-parts of a plug of tobacco.

As for Bernardo, he had now been nearly thirty hours without food; indeed, to be accurate, he had been fifty hours without food, thirty of them in the launch, for we had started work on a maté. If we could have made him hear, he might have attached a line to the life-buoy and floated her off, and we could have sent him back supplies.

We had made certain of another night of discomfort, so we gathered another big pile of firewood. Cattle's leg, that he had strained on the previous day, was giving him much pain. But when the sun was already dipping behind the summits of the Cordillera the storm began to lull. We had little hope that Bernardo could stand out much longer against starvation, so after half an hour, as the seas were going down, we thought it well to try and get off to the launch.

We went down to the beach, and, after much hailing, roused the Swede. By signs I told him to come in as close as he dared, which meant to within twenty or twenty-five yards of the shingle. This time he got her in a better position, and we stripped and waded in with the wood. It took us about forty journeys, and the water was abominably cold. I do not think two men ever worked much harder during the time we were at it, so before very long we were on board with everything.

Fearing to remain near the shore we got up steam, and with exceeding thankfulness bade good-bye to that inhospitable beach. I asked Bernardo how much longer he thought he could have held out. He said two days, and, in fact, appeared to think he had been better off with the blankets and his pipe and the warmth of the fore-hatch than we with food on shore. First and last he was a fine fellow, patient, quiet and hard-working. As to his being better off than Cattle and myself, that was a matter of individual taste, I suppose. As a rule, indeed, the average man will, as far as my experience goes, sacrifice his food to his bed nearly every time, especially when the wind is blowing out of the snows.

Evening soon settled down into night, and we ran on by starlight to our next anchorage, an almost land-locked bay, where we made merry on the remains of the ostrich. I also discovered some flour in the afterhold which had been overlooked, enough to make three small dampers. We were uncommonly glad to resume our rugs that night.

On the 24th we gathered more wood and put to sea. We meant to reach the southern shore of the lake on the Burmeister Peninsula, and there put in to a good anchorage not far from Cattle's headquarters. But to do this it was necessary to pass across Hell-gate, the opening to the north arm or North Fjord of the lake, always a difficult stretch of water owing to the fact that squalls perpetually blew down upon it from the funnel formed by the winding gorges of the upper lake. We soon saw the two dark bluffs beyond which the water wound away behind the outlying buttresses of the mountains, whose snow-caps glimmered against the wintry sky. We did not escape scot-free, for a squall duly caught us, and the tossing sent everything in the launch adrift. We ran by five icebergs and once the pump refused to act, and things looked awkward, but in the end, to make a long story short, we steamed into our shelter, which we called Cow Monte Harbour, and tied up the launch with no small thankfulness, for she was leaking badly through the cracked plate I have before referred to.

As the grass was dry we could not, with safety, make a fire sufficiently large to signal Burbury to bring up the horses, as had been arranged, so we sent on Bernardo with a message. He started off in his big boots and we had no idea of the mischief he was to drop into before we saw him again. He was accustomed to the pampas round about the town of Santa Cruz, where you can light a fire with impunity, but amongst the high grass growing in the valleys of the foothills of the Cordillera a fire is certain to spread over an immense area. Finding the way long, perhaps, Bernardo sent up a brace of smokes as signals. We saw them, and knew at once what was likely to happen.

THE FIRE

When the horses arrived we bundled on to them and rode away to try and stop the conflagration. There were two fires raging, and our only chance lay in being able to arrest their spreading beyond the shores of a dry lagoon, which mercifully extended between them and the summer-dried, well-grassed marsh lying under Mount Buenos Aires and Mount Frias, where Cattle's pioneer-farm was situated. It would have been a distressing return for his co-operation and help had one of my men raised a fire to sweep over his land and destroy his whole stock of horses, sheep and cattle, a result that was for a time imminent.

We all provided ourselves with sheepskins and began our attempt to beat out the fire. It was raging in bone-dry grass and thorn and the flames leaped up and scorched our faces. Every blow with the sheepskin sent up a shower of sparks that got into one's eyes and ears, and it appeared as if we should never make headway against the blaze. We might clear ten feet for a moment, but as we turned away the flames would eat their way back and, rekindling, flare up in waving tongues and roar again. Of course we were to windward, on the lee side the smoke rolled away in a solid cloud. I do not know how long we worked on that upper ring of fire, but slowly we succeeded in beating it out by sheer weight and repetition of blows.

The wind had by this time dropped a little, and the course of the main blaze set downhill. At length we had beaten out a half-circle and came to the crux of the affair. If we could but blot out the fire to the south, where it was burning savagely among high bushes and dry thorn, it was probable the situation would be saved.

We took a short rest of four or five minutes and began again. The smoke was gathering and rolling in great gouts, and we could see nothing save the flames on the one side of us and the black blinding dust on the other. As for ourselves, we were as black and scorched as singed rats. We knew that the next ten minutes would decide the matter.

Beside the fire ran a meandering cow or game track, and it was at this line that we meant to try and cut off the flames, which were rapidly spreading and getting out of hand. One was conscious of nothing but the thud of the sheepskins and the figures of the workers leaping in and out of the smoke and flame. I have never witnessed a wilder scene. The men shouted as they worked. It was like a battle-picture seen in a dream. All along the cow-track, where the fire lipped it, the sheepskins rose and fell. A dense dun-coloured cloud rolled out and up, lit every moment by explosions of sparks.

Presently it became a race for a spot some 200 yards ahead, where a line of green damp grass might stop the fire and force it in another direction. To cut it off at this point would make the remainder of our task more easy. But just on the nearer side of the grass line a number of high bushes were growing, and their strong roots and lower branches gave the flames a definite hold. Now and again, too, one had to run back and stamp out some sudden recrudescence of the flame. There is no need to describe the last half-hour; only, when the yellow circle of fire had given place to a smouldering black ring, we were ready to lie down on our blackened sheepskins and feel neither glad nor sorry but only wearily tired.

To beat out a fire is about the hardest sort of effort a man can make, for no spell of rest can be obtained without losing the results of previous labour. Afterwards, when we made a round of the fires to make sure of safety, we found them sinking sullenly into black deadness.

We were especially lucky in the direction taken by the fire, as, had it burnt along any other line, it is almost certain that our camp and all that we possessed would have been destroyed. Such a disaster actually occurred to Cattle some years ago in the north of the country. He was then journeying with two companions, when a half-breed boy he had with him was foolish enough to allow a camp-fire to spread among the surrounding grass. The pioneers were able to save nothing but a pair of boleadores and a Winchester rifle with the seven cartridges that happened to be in it. The party fortunately possessed several hounds, by whose efforts the stock of meat was kept up, otherwise it is more than likely that their case would have been a serious one.

The interval between the time of our starting for Lake Viedma and our return was in all but eleven days. During those eleven days much happened that brought back most vividly to me old boyish dreams of travel and romance. I had realised some of them, but risk and adventure, which enchant us in the glamour of far-off contemplation, are apt on nearer view to lose in romance what they gain in reality.

On the same day of the fire, news, brought by some wandering Indian or Gaucho, reached us; rumours passing from mouth to mouth as they will in a wonderful manner over the most sparsely populated country. The first we heard was a report of war, a real war-scare, such as might have originated from the fertile imagination of a Haïtian journalist. The Russians were said to be marching upon India, and France had joined hands with them against England.

It was but the barest outline, yet it shook and excited us out there in the ends of the earth just as if we had formed items of a crowd in Fleet Street.

Following on this came that other heavy tidings indeed, the death of the Queen. We took off our hats, and at first nothing was said. The news struck each man of us. There was a sense of loss and of the blankness of a personal calamity, which expressed themselves at last in a few odd homely words.

There, 7000 miles away, the abstract idea of the nation became concrete. One had no picture in one's mind of England that did not bear in the foreground, filling the heart and eye, that gracious, royal, simple, noble figure, which for so long had drawn out towards itself the highest patriotism of the race. The tumult of a nation's mourning was taken up and echoed feebly here as in other remote corners of the earth. Thousands of pens have borne witness to the world-wide sorrow. No need to say more, but while I write the scene comes back, as some moments of one's life will and do come—the broad blue heavens, the wide lake, the wind, the smell of grass and califate-bushes, the grasping after shattered fancies, and the heavy acceptance of the hour assigned.

FOOTNOTE:
[23] This we came to understand very thoroughly at a later date, when we penetrated to the end of the long twisting arms of the lake.

CHAPTER XVI

WILD CATTLE

Denseness of forest—Wild cattle originally escaped from early settlers—Grown somewhat shaggy—Indians will not hunt them in forest—Patagonia not a big-game country—Hunting wild cattle—Disappointment—Hunters paradise—Twelve blank days—Sport on Punta Bandera—Big yellow bull—Losing the herd—Baffling ground—Charge of bull and cow—A shot at last—Hunting in forests on Mount Frias—String shoes—Winter hunting—Shoot bull—Shoot huemul five-pointer—Wild-cattle hunting first-class sport.

Very different to the easy sport afforded by the huemul was our experience of hunting wild cattle in the forests which clothe more or less densely the ravines and slopes of the lower Andes. These forests, which in some parts are absolutely impenetrable in the spring, because at that season the pantanos are saturated with the rains and melting snow, give shelter to many scattered herds of wild cattle.

FORESTS UNDER THE SNOWS WHERE WILD CATTLE BREED

Captain Musters, writing in 1871, speaks of hunting these animals under the Cordillera, but their existence in a wild state dates from a far earlier period—in fact, from the time of the first Spanish occupation, when cattle escaped from the Valdez Peninsula, and roaming over the pampas at length reached the high grass and sheltered places of the Cordillera. Finding these entirely to their liking, they have ever since lived and bred in that region; their numbers, no doubt, being from time to time increased by deserters from the unfenced farms on the east coast of Patagonia. It is a strange thing that cattle which escape almost invariably head north-west towards the Cordillera. This fact has been commented on to us by many different Gauchos and cattle-owners up and down the east coast.

The older herds have lost the smooth aspect of domesticated animals and thrown back to the shaggy front, longer horns and rough-haired hide characteristic of wild cattle. As to the special parts of Patagonia in which wild cattle are most plentiful, it would be of little use to give a list of them. Should a herd stray in the plains, the Indians will soon make them change their quarters and return to take refuge among the woods and ravines of the foothills. Inside this forest-land the Indians will never venture, and there the emancipated bull thoroughly enjoys himself. Even the beasts belonging to the farmers lead a wandering life, and at a short distance from the settlements are shy of the approach of man, and have to be rounded up by mounted Gauchos. Those of them that have been inside a corral and regained their liberty are every whit as wild as the wild cattle proper. Being caught with a lasso and branded is by no means an experience calculated to instil any deep confidence in mankind into the mind of a calf.

In the Cordillera the herds are extremely wideawake. When a point is disturbed, they always go higher up into the mountains, and almost invariably leave that particular neighbourhood under cover of the ensuing night. Their climbing powers are extraordinary. Wherever a guanaco can go, a wild bull can follow him. Their tracks are regularly and clearly marked, and they appear to move along precisely the same paths from feeding-place to feeding-place. The snows of winter force them to lower ground, but in my opinion the herds never penetrate very deep into the Cordillera. Precisely how far they go it would be hard to determine, but they seldom ascend to the higher levels, preferring to wander about the outer spurs of the lower hills. There is a spot on the south side of the Lake Rica where they appear to make their way farther into the recesses of the mountains than in any other district.

Patagonia, as the reader will by this time realise, cannot be called a big-game country in the sense of affording any variety of large animals for the benefit of the sportsman. But whoever goes into the Cordillera will find the wild bulls of their forests well worthy of his attention, for they give as excellent sport as any big game in the world. A point which must tell greatly in their favour in the eyes of some people is the fact that the pursuit of them is a pleasure by no means unattended by danger.

The first day on which I attempted to find wild cattle we sighted two herds, one about half way up the hillside and the other higher, almost upon the snow-line. We had gone out rather with the idea of prospecting, having but little hope of being so lucky as to get a shot. Mr. Cattle, Burbury, and myself made up the party, and while Cattle hid in the direction towards which the herd might be expected to break, Burbury and I undertook the stalk. We separated, and I finally got within two hundred yards of a dun-coloured bull; but his position was so bad that it seemed a pity to shoot. The herd ultimately moved into a strip of forest high on the shoulder of the mountain, and we failed to locate it again.

Upon this followed a period when the memory of the shot I might have taken rankled as a thorn in the flesh. The difficulty of finding a herd was very great. We went out several days in succession and failed to catch sight of a single horn. For twelve days we searched from dawn to dark and found nothing. Yet these days, which resulted in a total bag of two huemules, were infinitely more sporting than were those in the neighbourhood of the River de los Antiguos, where a large number of animals might have been secured. On four occasions fresh tracks were found, and in that keen invigorating air the hunting of such a quarry was a sport for the gods.

A GLADE IN THE LAKE RICA FOREST

There is a picturesque sentence in one of Mr. Kipling's writings, in which he speaks of a life "spent on blue water in the morning of the world." Each savage of us has, I suppose, some such ideal existence, and if that be so, mine would be passed in hunting some great horned quarry upon frozen hills in a land where no wind too strong should blow, and where the views of water and of peaks should be in all shades of separate and glorious blue. What a splendid place such a happy hunting-ground would be! Quite different to the happy hunting-grounds of the North American Indian, the Tehuelche or the Eskimo—the latter, by the way, looks forward to a paradise where he will lie for ever upon the sleeping-bench in the warmth and eat decomposed seals' heads! The nomad hunter races kill to eat in any manner or by any means, the romance of sport is in one sense lacking in them; but in my happy hunting-ground there will be Irish elk with mighty spreading horns upon those wondrous hills....

We have wandered far away from our subject. I think it may be said that during those twelve blank days every method of hunting wild cattle had a fair trial. Upon the northern slopes of Mount Buenos Aires (which, I must mention, is very far distant from Lake Buenos Aires, being, in fact, surrounded on three sides by the waters of Lake Argentino) there is comparatively little wood, although there is much thick high brush, so that—as in Sardinian moufflon-shooting—one may spy the ground two or three times in the day, and yet fail to discover a herd hidden in the brush or in one of the many water-worn ravines. Nevertheless, this place was the most open ground which we hunted, and was far superior to the Lake Rica side of the mountain, upon which cluster dense forests of antarctic beech, through which it is impossible to see more than twenty or thirty yards, and often not so far.

Once or twice I tried sitting up for bulls at their drinking-places, but never with any success. The fact is, that the forests they range through are so well watered with streams, pantanos and springs, that they have a score of drinking-places to choose from, therefore the chances are twenty to one against getting a shot. But in a district where water is scarce, it seems to me that this plan might meet with success. The best sport was undoubtedly that which we enjoyed towards Punta Bandera, a headland forming the north point of Mount Buenos Aires.

It was here, upon the thirteenth day of my hunting, about an hour and a half before dark, that I perceived a fine point of seventeen upon the hillside in front of me. They were, however, in a spot utterly impossible of approach, in the centre of a bald ridge upon the summit of which they were silhouetted against the black background of the mountain beyond them. Deep gullies cut up the intervening ground, and after advancing as near as might be, I lay down and possessed my soul in patience, waiting until the moment when the herd should choose to move. They had left me time enough and to spare for observing them through the glasses. Three black bulls, a yellow one and a red were the pick of the herd, there were some cows and well-grown calves also, and these last began to proceed very leisurely down a cow-track, which would ultimately lead them on to ground where they might be stalked. I had tied up my horse in a hollow among some bushes of Leña dura. It was a glorious evening and the shadows stood out very distinctly, so much so that from the slightly higher ground I could see with the telescope the movements of the shadows of the bulls. The bases of the mountain were steeped in clear still dusk, there was no wind, and the whole scene lived again fantastically in the smooth waters of the lake. When one is shooting, no matter how intent one may be upon the game, it is natural to observe these things and enjoy them, in a secondary sense possibly, but none the less keenly. Anyway, there was plenty of time to observe, for the herd took it easy, and now and then one of the big bulls would come to a standstill and stare about him. The yellow bull especially took my fancy, the spread of his horns must have been over four feet. At length, however, the last of the herd disappeared into a gully and I hastened forward. About a mile separated me from the point, and this I covered at good speed; the final bit necessitated a crawl, which ended on the edge of a low rocky plateau. Here I peered through some fuchsia-bushes. To my disgust the herd had quickened their pace, and were a little beyond range upon a space of level land beneath me; they lingered here for an uncommonly long time, giving me ample opportunity to study the surrounding cow-tracks and the grass-bare wallows. Meantime the precious light was fading, and the reflections of the snow-peaks were beginning to blur and darken in the mirror of the lake. Ahead of the herd were a number of tracks, which ran parallel with each other for a certain distance, but afterwards branched into different directions. I could see them dimly through the telescope. Should they happen to take the lowest of these, they would be delivered into my hands, for it led immediately under a cliff over which I could get within a few yards of them. This track finally emerged upon the shore of the lake. Under the leadership of a yellow cow, the whole point began presently to descend this very track. As soon as the last of them was out of sight, I rushed on to secure my shot. On the way I spied from behind a boulder on high ground the coveted old yellow bull knee-deep in the lake, drinking. Over the first part, which was high, I had to be very careful, but once this spot was passed, coming to the conclusion that as the light was fading so fast the race would probably be to the swift, I hurried. Alas! a deep gully again blocked my way, and it was necessary to make a détour of about half a mile through breast-high bushes. While passing amongst the brush much care had, of course, to be exercised to avoid the breaking of twigs or branches, as the herd was not far off. When at last I arrived at the cliff above the spot where the herd had disappeared, I could not see the sights of my rifle. I would have given much for two minutes of moonlight, for I could hear the noise of the bulls moving within twenty yards, and the smell of them was distinctly perceptible to my senses, sharpened by months of a natural life. The whole herd had packed pretty close together on the edge of the shingle, but it was already too dark for me to shoot, so I retired after a while, comforting myself with the prospect of following the herd in the morning.

Yet although I followed, I never found. The herd, as was to be read from the tracks, struck upwards after leaving the lake and entered a wide piece of forest, in which no day was ever long enough to find them. Several times after this we were on the tail of a herd, and again and again lost them in the dense forests. The ground over which one had to move was extremely baulking to success; it was covered with broken sticks, dead trees, and branches, dry, rotten, and ready to snap beneath the smallest pressure. Sometimes after a long stalk one found oneself in a patch of dry dead bushes, the breaking of any bough of which would certainly spoil all chance of success. Again, one could not see more than from twenty to fifty yards ahead, and in thick forests much less. A herd will stand quite still till within thirty yards if you have not perceived them, but the moment your eye catches one of theirs the animal makes off, taking his companions with him.

A bull, if you wound him and he charges, will charge but once, and if he misses you, will pass on. But a cow is quite another affair. She will return to the charge again and again, and will kneel down in order to horn her antagonist. She is at least twice as formidable an antagonist as a bull.

THE FATHER OF THE HERD

The next time I saw wild cattle was once again upon Punta Bandera, and upon this occasion I had my first shot. It was early in the morning when I made out the point with the glasses, feeding about half-way up a spur of the mountain-side. Determined this time not to be disappointed, a whole day was spent in a series of very careful manœuvres. All went well until I entered a patch of dry dead growth, so thick as to make it impossible to move without giving audible indication of one's presence. While lying among this stuff debating what course to pursue, to my delight a black and white bull, evidently the leader of the herd, rose, grunted once or twice, and, followed by the whole of his companions, began to come towards me. He got to within 150 yards, and there coming upon the edge of the dry stuff among which I lay hidden, turned tail and moved slowly in the opposite direction. To shoot through the undergrowth, which was about five feet high, was, of course, impossible. Yet there was no chance of the animals, while roving in search of pasture, reaching any better position with regard to me, while any movement on my part to approach them must have been through the dead bushes. There was nothing for it then but to stand up and take the chance of a shot. A twig snapped in my rising and the herd charged furiously away. A red bull, which had travelled higher than his fellows upon the slope of the mountain, gave very much the best chance as he raced along nearly broadside on.

He turned a complete somersault to the shot and lay so still that I thought I had killed him. As I went towards him, however, he scrambled to his feet and galloped after the retreating herd, and although upon their tracks for the greater part of the evening, at no point on the way, nor at the spot where he had fallen, did I find any traces of blood. I therefore concluded that he had put his foot in a hole, and that I had missed him clean. Since my return I have heard the end of the history. The red bull was found dead quite close to where I had shot him. He was, I understand, hit through the lungs.

After this shot on Punta Bandera, the herd left that locality, as they invariably do, and most of the remainder of our hunting took place upon the Lake Rica, or southern side, of the great mountain. One of the pleasantest days we enjoyed was upon Mount Frias where a large point of cattle had gone up beyond the snow-line. On that occasion, when above the snow-line, I saw a pampa-fox, some guanaco and a few ostriches. Quite a number of small birds that I was unable to identify, as I could not shoot them, were feeding upon a red berry which grows beneath the snow.

I think of earthly situations I would choose that for the location of my happy hunting-ground where life throbs and quickens in the keen air, and where, in the shelter of the black forest of antarctic beech-trees, one can hear the wind from the snows moaning and crying among the tree-tops, and dropping the leaves, painted with red and yellow, upon the soft mossy mid-forest carpet.

While on Mount Frias my attention was drawn away from the cattle by what I took to be an instance of albinism in the guanaco. There was an immense herd of five hundred or perhaps more in an open hollow, and among them I observed a very white specimen, but on looking at it through the glasses it proved to be piebald rather than truly white.

My next excursion was made on much lower ground in the direction of Lake Rica. We had observed some spots to which a herd returned night after night.[24] The success with which the herds can pick their way over bad ground such as this and through trees, and most of all across the giant trunks, decaying and rotten, many of which must have fallen years ago, is extraordinary. Had it not been for the openings broken by the passage of the cattle, we should have been unable to penetrate the denser parts of the woods without axes. In spite of his being such a heavy brute, a bull can always overtake a horse in these spongy swamps, or indeed in most cases over very bad ground.

In the winter, which was now only too quickly coming upon us, wild-cattle shooting becomes, as does the shooting of all game in Patagonia, much easier than it ever is during the rest of the year. The herds descend to the low ground, being driven downwards by degrees while the snows creep day by day lower on the mountain-sides. As they desert the heights the area in which one may expect to meet them naturally becomes smaller, and on the more level country they can be followed with less trouble. The hunting in this big forest was quite different to that on Punta Bandera, the sole method here being to find comparatively fresh tracks and follow them up, there being no possibility among that dense growth of spying animals from a distance.

One day I had entered an extremely wet and boggy strip of forest and came upon new tracks, which I followed in and out among the trees for some hours. At length they led me up another hill into another belt of forest. I remember that under the hill I took a "spell," and at that moment, although I could not see them, the cattle were within one hundred and fifty yards of me. Fortunately I was very quiet and did not light my pipe, but presently went on. Arrived at the top of the hill, I peered through the branches and saw a fine brindled bull just in the act of rising to his feet. One of the outlying cows had winded me and had given the alarm. My bull was off at a gallop, and there was nothing to do but to send the heavy Paradox bullet into the only part of him that was visible as he dashed away. The shot took effect, he staggered but the second barrel brought him down in good earnest. A third hit him in the centre of the forehead, which is a deadly shot indeed, but with a smallbore rifle one must be careful to place one's bullet clear of the shaggy curl. The first shot had, I discovered, gone forward and upward, touching the backbone; the second was a fair behind the shoulder shot. I write this to illustrate the amount of shooting that a wild bull will sometimes take.

AS IT WAS IN THE BEGINNING

There are few higher joys in a sportsman's life than the pipe which he smokes after a successful shot, but the skinning of the quarry that comes later is a very different matter. This is especially the case when the animal has dropped in such a spot that one cannot turn it over owing to its weight.

EDGE OF FOREST

For this forest shooting a 12-bore Paradox or jungle-gun is as good as any. I had one which was made for me by Jeffrey and Co., and with it one could make a very decent pattern at seventy yards. In open ground I generally used a Mauser, but this rifle was, of course, not heavy enough for forest shooting at a dangerous quarry, where most of the shots were within forty yards.

Once again on Punta Bandera I saw the big yellow bull. One day I watched the great herd of wild cattle straggling slowly down the opposite hillside, the cows with their calves trotting alongside them, and the magnificent yellow bull bringing up the rear in solitary state. They were in a hopelessly unget-at-able position, so that one could only watch them. The air was so clear that, with the telescope, it was possible to make out the tracks of each separate animal as the herd descended the incline.

While I was still engaged in watching the cattle, I saw something brown move on a knoll above me and about four hundred yards distant. A huemul doe had appeared upon it. She was not frightened, and was entirely unaware of my proximity. Soon she was joined by a buck, a four-pointer with nice clean horns. There were now two sporting interests in the landscape, the greater and the less. The cattle had turned and were moving relentlessly upwards over bare ground where a stalk was out of the question. I turned my attention therefore again upon the huemules, from whom I found myself separated by two deep gullies.

In an hour's time the cattle had diminished to mere specks upon the side of the mountain, and a strong wind having arisen, which blew from the huemules towards me, I thought I might safely try a shot at the buck. It knocked him clean head over heels. He proved to be in fine coat, and I at once set to work to skin him. By the time I had finished it had grown quite dark. As for the herd, they were too clever for me. I never sighted them again, but that big yellow bull I shall often see in dreams. Perhaps I may be permitted to meet with him when I attain to the happy hunting-ground of my desires.

Apart from the rifle, there are other ways of hunting wild cattle, but in the practice of these open ground is naturally a necessity. Boleadores will rarely stay on a bull, but the lasso is an efficient weapon, and on horseback a Mauser pistol will take a lot of beating. In the last instance the hunter gallops level with his quarry and trusts to his horse to carry him clear of danger in case of accident. As a rule, wild cattle avoid open ground, and if they chance to be away from the cover of the forest keep a sharp watch. Their hides are worth about £1 more or less when sold in the settlements, a value which is enough to turn every man's hand against them, were there any men in those districts whose hands might be so turned. But the wild cow will long continue to breed in her chosen solitudes, and indeed she is well able to take care of herself. From all I saw of wild cattle, they yield the palm as a sporting animal to few others in the world.

FOOTNOTE:
[24] To hunt this swampy ground in shooting-boots is an unnecessary handicap, for the footing is so soft that one sinks to the knee in the worst places. A pair of string-shoes called "alpargatas" are the most useful and suitable footgear for this work, and the gain of their lightness is an added advantage.

CHAPTER XVII

ON THE FIRST ATTITUDE OF WILD ANIMALS TOWARDS MAN

Opportunities for observation rare—Migration of guanaco limited—Guanaco and man—Upright and crawling attitudes—Will allow approach with horses—Tame near farms—Easily domesticated—Curious—Shyness of ostrich—Huemul curious and confiding—Instances—Easily rendered timid—Puma cowardly—Attacks upon man—Tame cubs—Cordillera wolf—Very fearless—Instances—Pampa-fox also fearless, but in less degree—Résumé of evidence.

It will be conceded that few subjects have more interest than the attitude assumed by wild animals towards man on first acquaintance with him. I think it may be claimed that we had exceptional opportunities for the study of this very important question. In most other districts into which white men have passed for the first time, they have usually been preceded by aborigines, who have made that declaration of war which must invariably be given forth between men and feræ naturæ. But in Patagonia, when the beat of the Tehuelches is left behind, there are many places to which one may penetrate where the animals have never before seen man. We here come to a question which is as old as the world—what were the original relations existing between man and beast? On man's side we know the position; on that of the wild animal we can rarely obtain evidence at first hand, especially in these latter days, when the earth is overrun and populated in almost every habitable region.

It will be seen from the description given of Patagonia that some of its remoter portions offer a unique field for observing the effect of man's appearance on the behaviour of animals that have had no previous knowledge of him. These places present some of the few localities left untouched by the presence of human beings. The value of any evidence still obtainable as to the bearing of wild creatures when brought into contact with human beings for the first time can therefore hardly be over-estimated. The chances of observing details of conduct and the spontaneous attitude of animals under these conditions have unfortunately become exceedingly rare and are daily growing rarer. Soon there will be no spot where such facts can be collected. Knowing this, I made every effort to gather all the data possible.

Large herds of guanaco patrol the country in all directions; how far they are local in their habits it is not easy to decide, but I was informed by several people that such and such a marked guanaco had been in such a district since such and such a winter, therefore I am led to conclude that the guanaco are more or less local in their movements. In the summer they are to be found on the high pampa, and in the winter the herds descend to the lower ground. But all the evidence that I could gather pointed to the fact that this periodic migration is limited in extent, and that certain herds belong, as it were, to certain districts and live and die within a comparatively small area.

During peculiarly hard winters, however, they will gather in very large herds and travel a good distance to the low grounds, where water and some pasture are still to be procured.

The guanacos that we met with on the basalt plateau to the south of Lake Buenos Aires probably visit the shores of the lake during the winter time. In the inverse order of things no travellers ever cross the basalt plateau in summer, nor do they visit the lake in winter; we may therefore conclude that the guanaco were in that region unacquainted with man. The following is taken from my diary while we were crossing the plateau:

GUANACOS ON SKY-LINE

"December 28.—To-day we saw great numbers of guanaco, many of which have in all probability never before beheld a human being. They were about as tame as English park deer, allowing us to approach on foot to within seventy or eighty yards, and, in the case of the old bucks, to within fifty yards. The females were, of course, much shyer. It was a beautiful sight to watch the great herd leaping up and down the hillside and dashing through the outcrop of black fragments of basalt. The bucks almost invariably kept between us and their females. On some occasions, when I came suddenly round a hill upon a herd, the old buck would gallop up between me and the herd and stalk along, uttering his peculiar neighing cry. There were numbers of young guanacos among these herds. These very quickly attain considerable speed, and at a fortnight old give the hounds some trouble to overtake them. Young guanacos, when cut off from the herd, can be approached by man. This morning I succeeded in galloping between one and the herd to which it belonged. He allowed me, on horseback, to come within six yards, but on a dog appearing in the distance he at once dashed away. Young guanacos, when separated from the herd, will follow a troop of horses, running fearlessly beside the riders."

In contrast to the above I give a record of another meeting with these animals at a later date. I find in my diary on May 13, 1901, written in the cañadon of the River Katarina at the upper end of the north-west arm of Lake Argentino, as follows:

"I saw two herds of guanacos, which were certainly unacquainted with man. They were extremely wild, not allowing me to approach within six hundred yards. I to-day hunted these guanacos with the idea of observing whether they would take to the water, or perhaps pass into the forest, which was plentiful in patches. They did neither, but kept to the bare cliffs on the edge of the peninsula, and when driven away from the cliffs at one end simply sought the shelter of the cliffs at the other."

Again, on the tableland between the River de los Antiguos and the River Jeinemeni the guanacos were extraordinarily tame. Only one traveller had been there before us (Mr. Waag). The guanacos permitted us to advance to within two hundred yards, and one, which was lying down, allowed me to come within sixty paces walking upright. At this distance I determined to see what effect the crawling attitude would produce, and for this purpose I retreated and again approached, this time on my hands and knees. I was still one hundred and fifty yards from the animal when he got up, and I had not proceeded many steps nearer before he bounded away. From this instance it may be deduced that while the herd evidently understood and feared the approach of predatory enemies in a crouching attitude, man upright in his natural position inspired relatively little fear but rather curiosity, for the guanaco remained lying down and staring at me as long as I appeared walking towards him.

On yet another occasion in the cañadon of the River Katarina, the first sight that a herd, seventeen strong, had of us, was when we were on board the launch. They raced up to the bank of the river and stared at us, only darting off ten or twelve paces when the irrepressible Bernardo saluted them with a whistle. Shortly afterwards we anchored and went ashore, but the guanacos would not allow us on foot to approach within half a mile, although when we were hidden they returned to the neighbourhood of the launch without fear. In the evening they retired far up the valley, where I again saw them upon the following day. They were very timid, and I could get no nearer to them than three hundred yards, although I made one or two attempts to do so.

There was one point which was distinctly noticeable, and which these observations bear out. Guanacos, unacquainted with man, will allow him to approach in the first instance much closer if he happens to be accompanied by a troop of horses, as was the case with us in our experience of the herds on the basalt plateau. In fact, guanacos will reconnoitre a troop of horses, even though there may be men among them, at a very much shorter distance than they will venture upon with regard to a camp or a group of men without horses.

Districts where the Indians hunt the guanaco may be passed over as having no bearing on the subject in hand. There the herds are, of course, extremely wild and hard of approach. But it is interesting to note that near the coast, where there are numbers of guanaco, they are comparatively tame. Shepherds on horseback from the farms pass and repass within sight of the herds, who grow accustomed to the experience and become easy of access to within one hundred yards.[25]

One day in the October of 1900, when at the farm of Mr. Greenshields at Bahia Camerones, I took a long ride through the cañadones where the shepherds were wont to pass. Again and again the guanaco herds allowed me to ride up close to them, and I invariably found that a single animal was shyer of approach than a herd.

Guanacos are very easily domesticated, and in time become obtrusively playful and affectionate. It is a favourite trick with them to come behind their human friends rearing and striking them in the back with their knees, which results in a more or less painful fall.

Curiosity is a largely developed mental characteristic in the feræ naturæ of Patagonia. The first and overwhelming impulse of nearly all the wild creatures (the ostrich, Rhea darwini, excepted) appeared to be to investigate the aspect and actions of man. Upon the coast-farms the guanaco, grown blasé by familiarity, will not take any interest in man's movements unless he indulges in some unusual and fantastic antics, such as lying on his back and kicking his legs in the air. Then an otherwise indifferent herd will gather and watch the proceedings with much attention.

As far as my experience goes, no wild creature, save the ostrich, on first beholding man, straightway travels out of sight. All the others, according to whether they naturally are shy or the reverse, retire to a more or less remote distance, and from there watch the doings of the intruder upon their solitudes.

Of Patagonian game the least hunted is the deer of the Andes (Xenelaphus bisulcus). We came in contact with these animals both near Lake Buenos Aires and Lake Argentino. At the former place, my friend, Mr. Waag, had marched through the Gorge of the River de los Antiguos, where most of my observations were made. As he was working very hard on his geographical surveys at the time, he did not shoot much, and I think it more than probable that man was an unknown factor of existence to the huemules of that region before we came upon the scene.

My observations of huemules consistently show that their first attitude towards man is one of curiosity and confidence. I instance some cases to bear out this assertion.

On December 9, 1900, I had just shot a guanaco upon the western shore of the River de los Antiguos, when a huemul buck about a year old, no doubt startled by the noise, dashed past me within twenty yards, and, catching sight of me, stopped quite still and fixed his eyes upon me. As I remained motionless, he advanced several paces and again halted, looking at me. I was sitting upon the body of the guanaco I had killed, the wind happening to be blowing from the deer towards me. We kept these respective positions for about five minutes. I then lit my pipe. At the scraping of the match he retreated a little, but gathering courage soon paused again. I rose slowly to my feet and advanced steadily towards him. He waited until I was quite close before he sprang away and disappeared from sight up the barranca.

Again in May 1901, being then in the cañadon of the River Katarina near Lake Argentino, I saw from the boat what I took to be the horns of a huemul against the background of the low forest. I landed and crossed the swamp in the direction of the thicket. Here, coming into an open space, I saw the buck to whom the horns belonged. Behind him the head and shoulders of a doe were visible projecting from a bush. I continued to walk on till I came within something like one hundred yards, when I sat down behind a fragment of rock and hid myself from their view. The sun was, I remember, but a hands-breadth above the Cordillera, and I made up my mind that I would not move until its lower rim had dipped beneath the snow-peaks. At the time I had set for myself I peered round the edge of the rock very carefully—as slowly as one peers when one is observing the movements of a gaggle of Scotch grey-lags. Imagine my surprise when there, not ten yards away, appeared the face of the doe, her gaze fixed upon mine! On seeing me thus suddenly she ran back to the shelter of the undergrowth from which she had originally emerged, and from which the buck during the interval had not stirred. The shades of evening were fast falling, and I was obliged to make an end of my watching for lack of light.

But undoubtedly the most remarkable example of the natural tameness of the huemul occurred on May 9. I was in the same cañadon, and on this occasion had the luck to secure a photograph of the doe as she went away. It was about noon that I, being on my way up the cañadon in a northerly direction, heard a stick break in a thicket near by, and a moment afterwards a huemul buck came into view. Fortunately I had not caught his eye, and he remained looking out from a patch of bushes, wondering, I suppose, what strange animal this could be that was coming towards him. Pretending that I had not observed him, I threw myself down among the high grass and waited for developments. The buck snorted twice or thrice and advanced to within thirty yards of where I lay. He stood upon the side of a hummock, flanked by his two hinds. They were shortly joined by a third, which came up out of the hollow behind them. I lay perfectly still. The buck halted, but the hinds came on till within a few feet of me. The buck now approached on the right; he was a four-pointer. The does had winded me. Two of them were mature, the third a half-grown hind. Before five minutes were over the hinds had come so near as to be almost touching me. Presently the half-grown hind sniffed my boot and started back, taking the other three with her. They drew nearer a second time, the buck coming within a yard of me, and dropping his horns as though to turn me over. I did not quite like the action, as it might have meant more than a mere push, and therefore raised myself gently to a sitting position. The deer retreated about thirty yards, and there stood, not taking their eyes from me for a considerable time. Seeing that no further approach of the deer was likely, I finally got up and went my way. The does followed me for fifty yards or so, the buck remaining stationary, and then all four bounded off into the woods whence they had come.

In spite of this original confidingness exhibited by the huemul to man when unknown, he appears to be readily rendered wild and timid. Burbury saw some of these animals near the Engineers' camp above Lake Buenos Aires. They had probably been hunted by Mr. Waag's party and were excessively wild, flying on the farthest glimpse of man. This observation was confirmed by Humphrey Jones, who told me that the huemules living in the woods near the Welsh colony of The 16th October are wilder than any other creature, and that to shoot one is a feather in the caps of the local hunters. I cannot say whether they are easily tamed when in captivity, for I came across no instance of a huemul kept by man.

So far, then, my observations on the huemul.

Concerning the puma, I have never heard of any man being attacked near the settlements by this animal, and, indeed, authentic instances of its acting as the assailant are very few and far between. All those of which I gathered reliable evidence occurred in remote places, distant from the beat of man. Mr. Waag told me of a puma which did not retreat from his party in the Cordillera, but gave manifest signs of anger and a readiness to attack. Another case is that of Dr. Francisco P. Moreno, who, upon the banks of the River Leona, a river which flows between Lake Argentino and Lake Viedma, and is seldom visited, was attacked by a puma. He was, he informs me, walking wrapped in the skin of a guanaco, and he fancies the animal may have mistaken him for a guanaco. It sprang upon his shoulders and tore him under the chin with its claws, but was luckily beaten off by his companion and killed. This puma was found to be in milk, a fact which, arguing the presence of her young near at hand, probably accounted for the unusual outbreak of fierceness. The young were searched for but not discovered.

A third instance is that of Mr. Arenberg, one of the Argentine Boundary Commissioners, who was mauled by a puma in the neighbourhood of Lake Buenos Aires, at a spot probably hitherto unvisited by man. He was seriously wounded in the face. As a rule, the puma is a cowardly animal, and is frequently killed by the Indians with a bolas.[26]

**THE HUEMUL DOE WHICH TOUCHED THE AUTHOR.
PHOTOGRAPHED WITH SMALL CAMERA AS SHE RETIRED**

Although, during the whole of our journey, we were constantly coming upon evidences of the presence of pumas round and about our camps, it was not until we had entered the Cordillera that they actually reconnoitred the camp. In a forest near Lake Argentino, one moonlight night, two pumas circled round our camp, and for upwards of half an hour kept uttering their peculiar cry. Pumas often stampeded our horses and left plain tracks near the camp, but in spite of this they killed no animal, not even a dog, belonging to us.

Puma cubs in captivity become very tame. One settler whom I met had two cubs about a year old. They were attached to their new home, and though they would follow a horse for two hundred yards or so, they invariably returned after a short distance to the shanty of their owner. Another puma cub had been kept by Mr. Cattle at Lake Argentino. This cub was wont to fight battles royal with the hounds, but in the cold of winter would lie among them for warmth. All these cubs were those of Felis concolor puma. So long as they were well fed they were docile, but when hungry their fierce nature reasserted itself. Mr.

Cattle had finally to shoot the cub that belonged to him. Mr. Waring, however, still had his at the time of my departure. I heard these two killed a colt in the month of May.

The study of the Cordillera wolf (Canis magellanicus) from the present point of view is exceptionally interesting. To this animal man is practically unknown, and it manifested the most utter fearlessness, when brought into contact with human beings, during our expedition. This wolf will advance within five or six yards of a man in open daylight; it will walk over him when asleep in camp. They haunted our camps about Lake Buenos Aires, lurking about all the night through and eating everything that came within their reach; then, instead of departing when daylight came, they usually remained crouching near by, and put in an appearance during breakfast-time with an absolute disregard or ignorance of probable danger from the neighbourhood of man.

On the River Fenix one of these wolves came into Rosy Camp during the night, stole a duck and a goose, and further gnawed my rifle-slings within a few feet of where I was sleeping. We only discovered our loss at dawn, and while we were still discussing it, I perceived the animal itself lying under a bush close at hand calmly watching us. Deprived of breakfast, I had no thought of mercy, and shot her with a Mauser. She was an old female. That night her mate paid us a visit, and frightened the horses, who seem to fear the large Cordillera wolf almost as much as the puma. I was rather crippled at the time with an injury to my knee, and was sitting by the fire. I happened to look up and caught sight of the wolf standing within a few yards of me. He quietly returned my look but made no movement to run away. In a moment or two I got up and limped across to fetch my gun, the wolf watching me with interest, but without the smallest sign of apprehension. As a matter of fact, he came a few steps nearer to me, still gazing at me fixedly. He also joined the majority in a very short space of time. We could not afford to have such desperate thieves about our camp. At another place in the same neighbourhood a wolf, coming in to investigate our camp, was attacked by my big deerhound Tom. The wolf made no attempt to escape but met his foe with a fearful bite, and in the end we had to go to Tom's assistance before the wolf could be killed.

CAMP THIEVES

From these instances it will be seen that the Cordillera wolf has absolutely no fear of man. The pampa fox shares this characteristic, but possesses it in a much less prominent degree. When I have been chasing one of these latter the animal has in more than one case stopped to regard me steadfastly, not with the timid curiosity of the huemul but with a fearless stare. Yet these foxes are hunted for their pelts. One evening I fired at a pampa fox and missed him. He retired at a slow lollop while I pursued him. When a couple of hundred yards had been covered, he halted, chose a bush, deliberately lay down and waited for me, his muzzle sunk upon his paws. I picked up a handful of gravel and tossed it at him. He rose, snarled, looked at me for a moment, and then walked slowly off.

The data given above suffice to show that different animals assume very various attitudes with regard to man on first introduction to knowledge of him. Not only this, but animals of the same species behave variously under these circumstances. My experience of Patagonian wild animals goes to prove that those to whom we were the first human visitors regarded us with extreme curiosity, and though in some cases there was a show of timidity, it was not to be confounded with any apprehension of violence at our hands.

To sum up the relative confidingness of the animals I met with, I propose to take the distance within which they will allow man to approach as a sort of scale:

Guanaco. The evidence is contradictory, but it may be taken that these animals will allow a man to proceed towards them to within eighty yards; at any rate, in most cases. But if a man remain stationary, they will be inclined to approach him a little nearer.

Huemules will allow man to approach within fifteen yards. If he remain perfectly still, they will go almost up to him.

Puma (Felis concolor puma). If unacquainted with man, will occasionally attack him.

Cordillera wolf. Utterly fearless of man. Will, if approached too closely, show signs of taking the offensive. Will stand over his kill until the human intruder is within a foot or so.

Pampa fox. Will allow approach to within twenty yards.

I have already described the attitude of all these animals towards man in the more settled districts, with the one exception of the Cordillera wolf. Concerning this animal no data, so far as I know, exists, as his range does not, in my experience—I am here open to correction—extend beyond the foothills of the Cordillera.

The whole of my personal knowledge as to the behaviour of animals toward man on first meeting with him leads me to believe that none but extremely broad rules can be laid down on the subject. It would be very difficult to prophesy the precise attitude likely to be adopted by any individual animal under this condition, for the evidence concerning animals of the same species varies so largely. I am, therefore, driven to believe that the conduct of any given animal depends on its own special turn of character; that it is, in fact, a matter of individual temperament. In the case of a group of animals, the note of the behaviour of the whole group would be given by either the leader of the herd, or would depend on the first instinctive action of that one of the group which was the first to perceive the strange object.

But, having stated the evidence which I gathered, it will be better to leave others to draw their own conclusions.

FOOTNOTES:

[25] Where there are sheep, and consequently mutton is procurable, the guanaco is rarely hunted.

[26] This method has been referred to in another chapter.

THE LARGER MAMMALS OF PATAGONIA

Little known of natural history of Patagonia—Distribution of principal mammals—Huemul—Range—Habits—Horns—Not timid in remote districts—Curiosity—Common puma—Immense numbers—Destructive habits—Method of attack—Silent—Expert in hiding lair—Pearson's puma—Points of difference—Characteristics—Guanaco—Wide range—Large herds—Quantities of bones at drinking-places—Hard winters—Habits—Lack of affection for young—Patagonian cavy—Arbitrary limit of range—Weight—Habits—Armadillo.

In commencing this chapter I may remark that, as far as English publications are concerned, I have found nothing bearing on the zoology of South-eastern Patagonia of later date than the book of Captain Musters, published in 1871, and no work whatever dealing with the mammals of the Cordillera.

Captain Musters traversed the country with a tribe of Tehuelche Indians, and only at one point touched the Cordillera. His book is essentially a book treating of these interesting Indians, and he does little more than refer now and then to the zoology of the land through which he passed.

Every one is, of course, familiar with the volumes to which the voyages of the Adventure and the Beagle gave rise, but it must be remembered that the most westerly point attained by the boat-party from the Beagle, which ascended the Santa Cruz River, was Mystery Plain. In no English work whatever has any mention been made of the huemul (Xenelaphus bisulcus), a deer peculiar to the Southern Cordillera, nor have we any account of the habits of the puma, or, I should rather say, the pumas of Patagonia. During the time we spent in Patagonia we covered a considerable portion of the country, and passed some five or six months within the Cordillera, or in their immediate neighbourhood, so that we had ample opportunity for making some interesting observations.

To begin with, I should like to say a few words concerning the distribution, broadly speaking, of the principal mammals of Patagonia.

Patagonia is divided practically into sections by its eastward-flowing rivers. To-day the jaguar (Felis onca) does not, I am informed, range south of the River Colorado, although specimens were killed in the vicinity of the River Negro fifteen years ago. The River Deseado forms the southern limit of the distribution of the Patagonian cavy (Dolichotis patagonica). The armadillo (Dasypus minutus) is never found south of the River Santa Cruz. During four months which I spent south of that river I did not see one, but when for three days we crossed to the north bank we met with four and killed one. Dasypus minutus is very common in the neighbourhood of Bahia Camerones. The range of the huemul

(Xenelaphus bisulcus) is confined to the Cordillera or their close proximity, according to my experience, while Felis concolor puma, and the guanaco may be said to cover the entire country as regards the plains, and I have seen the animals or their traces in various parts of the Cordillera.

So much for general distribution.

1. Huemul (Xenelaphus bisulcus).

(Huemul or Guemal of the Argentines and Chilians; Ciervo of the Gauchos of Southern Patagonia; Shóan of the Tehuelches.)

In the neighbourhood of Lake Buenos Aires this beautiful deer first came under my observation. On the south side of the River de los Antiguos I saw a buck (which I shot), two does and a pricket. I was told by my Gaucho, Humphrey Jones, that the huemul is found in the forests as far north as the Welsh colony of The 16th October, about lat. 43°; on the south its range extends to the Straits of Magellan. The easterly limit of their present habitat may be said to be the foothills of the Andes. Dr. F. P. Moreno, however, states that these animals have been seen in the hills in the vicinity of Port Desire, on the Atlantic Coast: I do not think that they are any longer to be found there. As far as my personal observations go, I never came across a specimen farther east than a couple of miles from the shore of Lake Buenos Aires upon its north-eastern side. The Indians said that these deer were at one time more numerous in that region.

BEST HEAD OF HUEMUL (XENELAPHUS BISULCUS) SHOT BY THE AUTHOR. SIDE VIEW

During the summer the huemules leave the lower grounds, where the mosquitoes trouble them, and travel up to the snow-line of the Cordillera and even beyond it. At this season I never saw a large herd, but in the winter Mr. Cattle, a pioneer living near Lake Argentino, informed me that he had seen a large herd of over a hundred strong that visited the lake. In the warmer weather I noticed them usually in small parties of two or three, seldom more.

These animals are in the habit of wandering outside the forests in the evening and forenoon, but in the afternoon they generally retire to their shelter, where they often lie down. I have found them inhabiting the margins of the dense forests upon the slopes of the Cordillera which border the lakes. They are excellent swimmers, and cross the broad arms of Lake Argentino without hesitation.

In December the huemules which I shot were shedding their winter coat, and I noticed the bucks were farther advanced in this matter than the does. There were a few scraps of velvet clinging to the horns of one of the bucks which I shot on December 9, 1901. It is curious to note that the Indians, on seeing my reindeer-skin sleeping-bag, triumphantly identified it as being made of the pelt of the huemul!

The best head that I secured carried five points. Mr. Von Plaaten Hallermund, of the Argentine Boundary Commission, told me he had seen a huemul's head carrying eight points in the neighbourhood of Lake San Martin. One of my peones, Bernardo Hähansen, who had penetrated into the same district, said he had also seen an eight-pointer. Mr. Cattle and his companions shot two bucks, both of which were four-pointers.

Save for the attacks of pumas, the huemul lives pretty well undisturbed in his fastnesses. The Indians do not hunt them, as in the forest-land horses and boleadores are comparatively useless. They do occasionally kill a few of these deer, however, which may have strayed to the foothills or to the shores of the lakes.

Huemules are, in general, very confiding, for their range is confined for the most part to districts where they have little chance of making acquaintance with the human race. But near the colony of The 16th October, Jones told me that they had become very wary and difficult of access, as was to be expected in a region where they are constantly hunted. In the more unpenetrated parts the buck is very courageous in the rutting season, and has been known to make some show of attacking man. On open ground, in my own experience, they manifested wonderfully little timidity, and would wait for the approach of man, but inside the forests they invariably dashed away on catching a glimpse of one of our party. If, however, you have a dog with you, they will in all cases take to flight.

In the preceding chapter I have given various illustrations of the natural tameness of the huemul.

When it has observed something unusual in its surroundings, this deer will remain watching, and without moving, for a great length of time. On one occasion I saw near Lake Argentino a buck and doe about a quarter of a mile away. I was lying under a bush watching some wild cattle, a herd of which were above me against the snow-line, and the huemules stood and watched me for nearly an hour. They were some ten yards from each other. Presently the cattle moved, and I followed them upwards. I returned unsuccessful in the evening to the spot, not having fired a shot, and found the two deer still watching my horse, which was tied up on the shore of the lake.

On one or two occasions when I have fired at a huemul the others of the herd have run towards the noise. Once this happened when I was in full sight of the animals.

Musters, in his travels through Patagonia, mentions a "red" deer. Of this I could find no trace, so that in all probability he alluded to the huemul under that name; the reddish tinge of the huemul's hair lends likelihood to this suggestion.

No. 2. Puma (Felis concolor puma).

(Leon of the Argentines; Gol of the Tehuelches.)

This is the silver-grey variety of puma most commonly met with in Patagonia. The distribution of this animal extends over the entire country. It is to be found in the Cordillera as on the pampas. I came upon tracks of this animal at the end of the north-west fjord of Lake Argentino about long. 73° 14′, and I also saw a puma at the south-western extremity of that lake.

Evidence of their existence accompanied the whole itinerary of the expedition throughout the entire route it covered. The number of pumas in Patagonia is very great, more so than any zoologist has yet given an idea of. During one winter two pioneers killed seventy-three near Lake Argentino. Near San Julian immense numbers are yearly destroyed, but lately, owing to the advent of settlers, they are becoming less numerous. At Bahia Camerones, on the farm of Mr. Greenshields, fourteen pumas were killed during the winter of 1900.

A female killed near Santa Cruz measured 6 ft. 10 in., and a male killed near Lake Argentino 8 ft. 1 in.

The puma can easily be galloped down, as it rarely runs more than 300 yards or a quarter of a mile when pursued on horseback. It invariably stands at bay with its back to a bush or a rock.

In strong contradistinction to the habit of the Felis onca (jaguar), F. c. puma, when hunting, kills a number of animals from a flock or herd. To one only of these kills, however, does it return, and it always makes some pretence of burying the victim singled out for its meal, throwing upon the body in many cases merely a small bunch of thorns. This custom of the puma is frequently taken advantage of by the shepherds, who poison the chosen carcass. The puma, ninety times out of a hundred, makes its first meal upon the entrails of the victim or upon the thigh inside of the groin.

The destruction wrought by pumas upon flocks of sheep is immense. One animal killed upwards of 100 head from among a single flock. One night alone its total amounted to fourteen. Another point in connection with the predatory habits of the puma is that it will travel a long distance, even as much as ten or twelve miles, after killing.

Its method of attack, judging from an examination of its victims, appears to be to spring upon the shoulders of its quarry and to break its neck. Cases are reported of pumas attacking horses, but no instance of this came under my own notice. They generally select a stormy and tempestuous night during which to make their depredations. It is rather curious, as occasionally happens, to see a herd of cows with their calves take up the trail of a puma with a great deal of lowing and fuss, but they do not follow it for any distance.

Darwin writes that the puma is a very silent animal, uttering no cry even when wounded, and only rarely during the breeding season. One moonlight night, in a forest by Lake Argentino, a couple of pumas came out of the dark and began to walk round and round the camp, and continued to do so for more than an hour, all the time keeping up their peculiar cry. On no other occasion—though, as I have said, pumas or rather the evidences of their presence, accompanied us through our long journeys—did I hear them break silence.

PEARSON'S PUMA (FELIS CONCOLOR PEARSONI)

Pumas are more often destroyed in winter, when the snow lies on the ground, and their tracks can be followed to their hiding-places; otherwise they are so marvellously expert in concealing themselves that it is often impossible to find their lair.

Authentic instances of pumas having attacked man are few; but some have certainly occurred.

No. 3. Pearson's Puma (Felis concolor pearsoni).

On my return from Patagonia I brought with me a puma-skin, which seemed to me to differ in some essential respects from any known species. Mr. J. G. Millais, on examining the skin, agreed with me, and pointed out that it possessed several characteristics which do not occur in Felis concolor puma. I took the skin to the Natural History Museum, where Mr. Oldfield Thomas came to the conclusion that the animal was a sub-species of F. c. puma, and named it Felis concolor pearsoni.

The chief points of difference between the two species are as follows: The very different general colour, F. c. pearsoni being reddish-fawn instead of silver-grey. The proportionately very short tail; light instead of dark colour on the backs of the ears, which are, moreover, sharply pointed in the case of the new sub-species, and there is an absence of the dark markings round the digital pads which distinguishes Felis concolor puma.

Several Gauchos, settlers and Indians informed me that there were two kinds of pumas in Patagonia, one being very common, silver-grey in colour and cowardly; the other they described as rare, much fiercer, of a reddish colour, and somewhat smaller than the common grey species. Amongst the seventy-three pumas killed by the English pioneers near Lake Argentino, one, Mr. Cattle told me, differed very much from the ordinary puma, and judging from the description he gave of it, I have no hesitation in concluding that it was a specimen of Felis concolor pearsoni.

No. 4. Guanaco (Lama huanachus).

(Guanaco of settlers, Argentines and Chilians; Rou of the Tehuelches.)

During the whole course of our travels in Patagonia (save when in the forests) a day rarely passed without our seeing guanacos. They may be met within a few hours' ride of any settlement. The range of the guanaco extends all over the plains of Patagonia. In my experience they were most numerous in the Cañadon Davis, in the neighbourhood of Bahia Camerones, and on the high basaltic tablelands to the south of Lake Buenos Aires. At the base of the Cordillera and in some of the river-valleys under the edge of the mountains, the range of the guanaco crosses that of the huemul. I do not think, however, that the guanacos ever enter the forest, although I have seen them in the open patches amongst the lower wooded parts of the Cordillera. As the seasons change they move from higher to lower ground, but these migrations are limited, and a white guanaco has been observed year after year in the same neighbourhood. During the time I spent at Lake Argentino—from February 1 to May 15—I saw but few of these animals, for at that season all the herds migrate to the high pampa. A herd four or five hundred strong inhabited the higher plateaus of Mount Frias.

HEAD OF GUANACO

FitzRoy, in his "Voyages of the Adventure and the Beagle," writes, "Do the guanacos approach the river to drink when they are dying? or are the bones and remains of animals eaten by lions or by Indians? or are they washed together by floods? Certain it is that they are remarkably numerous near the banks of the river (Santa Cruz), but not so elsewhere." It is true that, although one comes upon skeletons of these animals upon the pampas, they are not crowded together as they are in the cañadones of the rivers or by the lakes near water. At the edge of a lagoon at the eastern end of Mystery Plain I saw a great number of skeletons in one place, possibly the very ones noted by FitzRoy. They extended in a wide track down the hillside and to the edge of the water. At Lake Viedma the margins of the lake, near the outflow of the Leona, were covered with their skins and bones. The meaning of this I gathered from Mr. Ernest Cattle. He told me that in the winter of 1899 enormous numbers of guanaco sought Lake Argentino, and died of starvation upon its shores. In the severities of winter they seek drinking-places, where there are large masses of water likely to be unfrozen. The few last winters in Patagonia have been so severe as to work great havoc among the herds of guanaco.

At nightfall guanacos gather into close order, a large herd collecting in a small radius. They seem to choose open spaces in which to pass the hours of darkness. In moments of danger also they pack together densely. At the sound of a shot, the outlying members of a herd will close up and sway their long necks almost to the ground in unison. I see that Darwin says that guanaco are "generally very wild and wary." In places where they are hunted by the Indians this is undoubtedly the case, but on this point no law can be laid down. In some districts the guanaco is very difficult of approach, in others extremely easy. The evidence that I can adduce concerning this point I have given at length in another chapter. Their instinct of curiosity is very largely developed. During our wanderings I studied the habits of the guanaco with ever-increasing interest. In cold weather they become extraordinarily tame, and will permit a man to walk among them as a shepherd walks among his sheep.

The young are brought forth in the months of October, November and the early part of December. In Southern Patagonia some are born as late as the end of December. During the period of copulation the bucks fight a good deal. I never shot an old buck which was not seamed and scarred with the marks of these contests. When fighting they give vent to loud squeals of rage, they strike with their forefeet and bite savagely, mostly at the neck of the antagonist. The marks of these bites are often deep and long. The skin of the neck is luckily very thick, so little harm is done. As has been noted before, the guanacos drop all their dung in one spot, and near these spots their wallows are ordinarily to be found. I saw an old buck spend a long time over his toilette while his wives looked on and waited. He would spend nearly half an hour on his back with his legs in the air, at intervals standing up to neigh and then rolling again.

GUANACO CHICO (CAPTURED WITH LASSOO)

A guanaco descending a hillside is a truly wonderful sight. He proceeds in a succession of bounds, on landing from each of which he dips his head almost to touch his forefeet. The young guanaco keeps up with his elders over bad ground in an extraordinary way.

The power of affection in guanacos towards their young did not appear to me to be very strong. From time to time I had to shoot a young one for food. Out of nine instances which I find in my diary, only twice did the mother halt in her flight to see what had happened to her offspring. On both occasions she stopped within two hundred and fifty yards and stared towards me. If dogs enter into the chase the mother deserts to a greater distance. One day, when I with the dogs had killed a young guanaco, I left it lying and rode away with the dogs. Returning alone, I took up my quarters in the heart of a bush, from whence I observed the herd to which the mother belonged. They did not return nearer than a quarter of a mile to the spot. On another occasion when I shot a young guanaco and concealed myself for the same reason, the whole herd came back and, mounting an eminence in the neighbourhood, scanned the scene of the disaster. They did not, however, venture near the place where the quarry was lying. Curiously enough, wild cattle, though much more difficult of approach than guanaco, often come back in the night lowing and bellowing to visit the spot where a herd-mate has been killed, but before dawn they invariably leave that part of the forest.

The young guanaco is an easy quarry. We caught a considerable number of them for food with the aid of the hounds.

On one occasion a young one was simply headed off from the herd, its portrait taken, and then it was set free again.

No. 5. Patagonian cavy (Dolichotis patagonica).

(Called "cavy" or "hare" indiscriminately by the English residents; liebre by the Argentines and Chilians; Paahi by the Tehuelches.)

The River Deseado forms the southern limit of the distribution of the Patagonian cavy. In 1833 Darwin writes concerning this animal, "They are found as far north as the Sierra Tapalguen (lat. 37° 30′), and their southern limit is between Port Desire and San Julian, where there is no change in the nature of the country." As far as my experience goes, I never observed a cavy after October 23, upon which day I counted fourteen upon the pampa between Lake Musters and the settlement of Colohuapi. The residents of Colohuapi informed me that the place formed the southern limit of the distribution of the cavy. It is, of course, impossible to lay down an exact line, but I think it safe to say that the range of the cavy does not extend south of the 46th parallel. This limit is the more remarkable inasmuch as the country south of lat. 46° does not in any way materially differ from that over which the cavy is commonly to be met with. One most often finds these animals on patches of dry mud. They are comparatively easy to stalk, as easy as an English rabbit. The best method of shooting them is, of course, with the rifle, though occasionally you may start them from a thicket and shoot them as you would an English hare with a shot-gun. They generally weigh between 18 lb. and 25 lb., though I heard of one which I was assured weighed 31 lb.

The cavy will often lead the hounds a good chase, especially where the ground is broken, in such places frequently making its escape.

After being frightened it very soon makes its reappearance, and when it actually takes to flight it rarely goes more than a hundred yards before it turns to see whether it is an object of pursuit. This is only the case when man alone is the pursuer; when dogs are present there is no time to be lost in speculation of any kind.

No. 6. Armadillo (Dasypus minutus).

(Pichy of the Argentines and Chilians; Ano of the Tehuelches.)

This animal is never found south of the River Santa Cruz. During the four months I spent south of that river I did not see one, but when for three days we crossed to the north bank we met with four and killed one, as I have before mentioned. Dasypus minutus is very common in the vicinity of Bahia Camerones. I saw no specimen in the forests of the Andes, but near Lake Buenos Aires and Lake Viedma we found them about the foothills.

No. 7. The Grey or Pampa Fox; Zorro of the Argentines; Paltñ of the Tehuelches.

To the east of the Andes, the pampa fox is to be met with practically everywhere. There are two varieties of foxes upon the pampa. The common pampa variety is a most inveterate thief, and causes endless trouble to travellers by eating all and anything that the wind may blow down from the bushes, upon which one's belongings are generally hung by way of guarding against their depredations. If a horse is sogaed out with a cabresto of hide, the foxes will very often gnaw through the cabresto and set the horse free. This trick has cost the life of more than one Gaucho, who, travelling alone upon the pampa, in some district hundreds of miles away from human habitations, has been left quite helpless without his horse, unable to use his bolas with effect on foot, and so has starved to death.

In my experience the range of the grey fox seems to cease at the foothills of the Cordillera, where the Magellan wolf (Canis magellanicus) is to be found. Of course, in making this statement I am open to correction. I can merely state that, during the time I spent at Lake Buenos Aires and Lake Argentino, I never saw a pampa fox, although evidences of their presence in the way of tracks were frequent, upon the north shore of the former lake. Yet directly one ascended the range of the hills towards the River Fenix, pampa foxes were to be seen. On the top of Mount Frias I saw a pampa fox in the snow. I never came upon the pampa fox in the forests which grow upon the slopes of the Cordillera.

The fearlessness of the grey pampa fox is remarkable, even in districts where it is chased by the Indians and their dogs. The pelts are much used for making capas or fur cloaks. During the early part of January 1901, upon the pampa outside the Cordillera, we continually came upon half-grown pampa foxes in twos and threes. Until they saw the dogs they never took to flight.

No. 8. Cordillera Wolf (Canis magellanicus).

This is the animal locally known as the Cordillera fox. I have elsewhere touched upon its strongest characteristic of courage, and also the dread it inspires among horses. It is, of course, a much larger animal than the pampa fox, which latter can wander about among the troop without causing any disturbance. A single Cordillera wolf will attack young huemules as well as the young of the guanaco. Although found in the forest, this animal also frequents the plains at the foothills of the Cordillera. Personally I never observed it farther east than the River Fenix. In the one case that came under my observation, when sheep had been brought within its range, its depredations among them were considerable.

The measurements which I made of three of these animals were as follows: Female killed at the River Fenix, Lake Buenos Aires, thirty-nine inches; dog-wolf killed at the same place, forty-one inches; dog-wolf killed at the Lake Argentino, forty-one inches. These measurements were taken from the teeth to the end of the tail directly after the shooting of the animals.

When with young the Cordillera wolf, indeed I may say the Cordillera wolves, both male and female, will run growling towards man if he attempts to approach their litter. As far as could be judged from an examination of the lair of one, their bill of fare is very varied. There were the remains of many kinds of birds, as well as the bones of the young of guanaco and huemul.

There is another form of the wolf which I think should perhaps be considered as a sub-species under the name of Canis montanus. Its range is at present undefined. It is a red variety and lacks the dark markings of Canis magellanicus. I hope shortly to have a series of skins of this type. At present my readers can refer to the coloured plate "Camp Thieves," and the photograph on this page. Its general habits seem to be identical with those of Canis magellanicus.

No. 9. Skunk (Conepatus patagonicus).

(Zorino of the Argentines; wikster of the Tehuelches.)

The skunk is to be met with throughout the whole country, but we saw perhaps more specimens of this animal in the neighbourhood of Bahia Camerones than elsewhere. I have also observed it within ten miles of the foot of the Cordillera. The skins are much prized by the Indians for the making of capas.

Besides the animals enumerated above, an otter is common in most of the rivers, but as all the skins I collected have not arrived at the moment of writing, I will hold over any description of this animal until a later date.

RED MOUNTAIN WOLF (CANIS MONTANUS)

FOOTNOTE:
[27] This chapter embodies a paper read before the Zoological Society of London on April 15, 1902, with some additional details.

Rumour of important undiscovered river—Wish to settle question—Dr. Moreno's description of Lake Argentino—Start for Hellgate—Description of Hellgate—Squall—Sunshine—Scenery—Icebergs— Danger-dodging—Absence of life on banks—West channel of North Fjord—Events of voyage—Giant's Glacier—Camera—Second glacier—Deep water—End of west channel—Return to North Fjord— Icebergs—In difficulties with launch—Escape from a reef—Land on peninsula—Guanaco—Fish—Fish and fariña—Heavy gales—Photographs—One more attempt to go up North Fjord—Driftwood—Driven back—Return to Cow Monte Harbour—South Fjord—Storms—Mount Avellaneda—Small fjord— Trouble with launch—Squalls—Launch driven ashore—On fire—Fine weather—Glacier calves— Thousands of square miles of forest unexplored.

"An important river flows into the end of the north fjord (of Lake Argentino) with clear waters—a sure sign that it proceeds from another great lake still unknown."

In these words, taken from the Journal of the Royal Geographical Society for September 1899, under the head of "Explorations in Patagonia," by Dr. Moreno, you have the idea which was the spring of all our efforts in bringing down the launch to Lake Argentino and the aim of the subsequent voyages made in her.

HELLGATE

The opening to the north passage or fjord is locally known as Hellgate, so called on account of the rough weather which usually prevails there. The spot is the opening of a long winding channel that, running up between beetling cliffs and forested mountain-sides as it were into the heart of the Andes, becomes simply a vast funnel through which the winds and storms discharge themselves upon the lake at all times and seasons. I cannot give a better description of Lake Argentino than by using the following extract from Dr. Moreno's account:

"Lake Argentino ... extends sixty miles to the west; and the fjords of the extreme west divide into three arms, which receive the waters of large glaciers from Mount Stokes up to the vicinity of Lake Viedma. An important river flows into the end of the north fjord, with clear waters—a sure sign that it proceeds from another great lake still unknown. The western end is closed by the main chain of the Cordillera with its glaciers, which cross to the Pacific fjords of Peel Inlet and St. Andrew's Sound, and one can distinguish peaks more than 10,000 feet, as Mount Agassiz (10,597 feet)."

On March 11, having mended the launch to the best of our ability, we intended to make a start from Cow Monte Harbour. As we rode down from Cattle's, driving my troop of horses before us, the calm weather which had attended the period of repairs broke up and a strong wind began to blow out of the south-west. A start was, therefore, rendered impossible. We accordingly camped beside the launch, to be ready for an early departure. All night long the wind held, and the sheepskins in the after-hatch, where I was sleeping, took in water. It needed little waking, therefore, to get me out in the morning. The false dawn was still lingering in the sky when the wind fell and we were off in double quick time, heading in a northerly direction, and steering by a clump of Leña dura bushes on a promontory, behind which lay Hellgate.

The swell of the previous night was yet big upon the water, and the launch crawled over it at about three knots. The entrance to Hellgate is possibly one of the most menacing and sinister-looking spots in South America. The great grooved cliffs tower over the yeasty cauldron of water, and down the channel between them, as I have said, the wind hurtles as through a funnel. On this particular morning a squall had darkened the great and houseless unknown beyond. Several icebergs were huddled together, stranded upon the shallows of the eastern shore.

After running through the black throat of Hellgate we put in, beneath a big rock, in order to take shelter from the squall that was fast coming down upon us. We had started on a maté, and so, while we waited, a roast was got under way. As we were eating, the squall that had brooded so ominously in the west broke over the lake, and after raging for a few minutes passed with a shiver that you could follow with the eye, till it lost itself in the distance of the early morning waters. Then the sun glowed out suddenly, as if some gigantic power had lifted an extinguisher from its glory. The farther and middle distances were peopled with snow-peaks, rising in minarets above their girdles of dark forest, which last stretched downwards until they lipped the black water at the mountain bases. For a moment after the outburst of radiance the water alone remained black and angry, and then the squall flicked away its skirts and passed from view, leaving a picture of cold and austere purity extending to the rim of sight. In words I cannot give you any reflection of the scene, and no photograph could ever do more than reproduce its outlines, and yet I suppose few human eyes will ever look upon it.

To describe the kaleidoscope of colours and the scenery through which we passed in that north-west passage of Lake Argentino would merely leave me a beggar in adjectives. Suffice it to say that for that day at least the mist and gloom of the clouds shared short watches with the gold and white of flying sunshine. For the first time in our experience of her the launch played us no tricks, and our progress went on at a steady three knots. Soon a gigantic glacier showed in the channel, seeming to block all farther advance. The Fjord looked full of icebergs; there must have been three thousand of them lying, an inanimate fleet, in their mountain-bound harbour of wind and mist.

A nasty squall caught us as we dodged among the ice, the smallest ripple set us gripping our frail craft, and I am afraid that a moderate sea would have drowned her fires and sent us to explore downwards rather than onwards. Indeed, our entire life on the launch was one long history of danger-dodging. I do not give the details, because some of the same sort have already been written, and repetition is needless. I grant there was more risk in taking the launch and using her in such waters than, perhaps, wisdom would have approved. Without her, however, we could have had no chance of exploring the North Fjord and solving the mystery of the "river with clear waters." Moreover, those who accompanied me went of their own free will, and I must here record my gratitude to Mr. Cattle, who willingly risked his life on our voyages in the launch, and also to Burbury—who accompanied me on my first journey—as well as to Bernardo, who was with me throughout the whole of my Lake Argentino experiences. Wherever I may travel in the future, I can wish for no better companions.

THE NORTH FIORD

Bernardo, the most willing of men, kept our nerves in a state of less than pleasurable excitement. He drove the launch, when I took my eye off him, with 145 lb. of steam in her worn-out boiler—her safety-limit at the best of times had been 130 lb. On shore he succeeded in firing off my jungle-gun by mistake, narrowly missing killing himself at close quarters and myself at some few feet distance. But even after this involuntary attempt at manslaughter one could not be angry with him, he was so genuinely sorry, yet one could not help foreseeing that he was eminently likely to do something of the sort again. He was, to use slang, such a "decent chap," he never grumbled when he had nothing to eat, or a bout of bitter cold labour when we were obliged to turn out in the night to get up the anchor or do some other job. He was also a glutton of the first water for work, but we were all persuaded that he would end by slaying us, in which case I have not the slightest doubt he would have said to me as we were being ferried across the Styx, "By good, Mr. Preechard, I am sorry, the old launch she bust up!" From looking on the launch, as he did at first, with considerable awe and respect, familiarity with her bred contempt, and all her parts lost their novelty to him, save the whistle. When he blew that his face would betoken the intensest satisfaction. In many ways the placid Swede caused us much amusement.

BEYOND MAN'S FOOTSTEPS

One of the most singular things to be observed during that day was the absence of life in the forest which bordered the shore. It was strange to sail along under the vast masses of vegetation and rarely to see or hear any sign of life. On March 12 we continued our advance, and finding that the Fjord here split up into three or four channels, we chose the most westward of them. Our progress was very slow owing to the west wind having packed the ice. In the evening we made our camp among some dead trees upon the margin of the water, and I wandered off into the thickets, where I saw a Cordillera wolf. I picked up a stone and threw it at him, but this had no effect until I hit him with a small twig, which made him growl. Finally he took refuge in a bush.

It was while at this camp that we cut for the first time some Leña dura as firing for the launch. It proved better than califate and gave at least three times the amount of heat to be had from roblé-wood. Afterwards, whenever possible, we burned no other fuel than Leña dura.

The following is from my diary:

"March 21.—During this trip we have had a collapsible canvas boat in tow of the launch, which boat has saved us many a wetting in boarding and in leaving the launch. We go ashore in relays, one man remaining on the launch. This evening, while Cattle, Burbury and I were on the beach wood-cutting and tent-pitching, I heard Cattle shout, and, looking round, saw, to my disgust, the canvas boat already some twenty yards out and drifting quickly away from the beach. The wind had caught her broadside on, and she was being blown out into the current beyond the calm of our sheltering promontory. Cattle and I ran down to the shingle, casting off our clothes as we went. I thought we were in for a long swim, no pleasant prospect in that ice-cold water among the floes. But, as luck would have it, there was a little point of land projecting from the cliff of the promontory, and to this we made our hurried way, leaving behind us a spoor of shed garments. We arrived in the nick of time to secure the boat, and Cattle rowed her round to the beach beyond the camp.

"There is one enormous glacier visible almost due north. It had evidently been throwing many bergs of late. We called it the Giant's Glacier. This glacier is marked with double lines of brown reaching from the clouds right down to the margin of the water, for all the world like the tracks of the chariot wheels of some giant. We are now very much in the kingdom of the ice. Away beyond the immediate foreground of the shores and forests is spread a panorama of unnamed peaks. The silence is seldom broken save by the scream of the wind or the crashing fall of some mass of ice from the glaciers.

"I find my camera has been damaged. This is unfortunate, but hardly to be wondered at. It is a difficult matter to prevent mischief when the launch rolls and everything gets adrift, and one's time is taken up with keeping one's balance, steering, or in doing the myriad little jobs that crowd one upon the other. Although the camera reposed in the sheltering care of various rugs in the after-hatch, the heavy weather defeated all our precautions. In this difficulty a novel of Miss Marie Corelli's has been of the utmost assistance, and saved us from the misfortune of being unable to take photographs. The colonial edition of the 'Master Christian' has a thick red cover, and with the help of some flour paste we have succeeded in making the camera light-proof. Thus I owe a second debt of gratitude to Miss Marie Corelli, beside the pleasure of reading her book."

The next day broke clear and still, raising our hopes as to our progress through the ice. I must say that we took our fine blue weather—little of it as we were blessed with—with a hearty pleasure, and enjoyed it most thoroughly. We might be cold and wet an hour later, but between the squalls it was not so disagreeable, and we made the best of the breaks.

It was not long under these favourable circumstances before we reached the last curve of the channel, and were confronted by another glacier of considerable size, coming down through a depression in the midst of a mountain. Below the glacier the shoulders and base of the mountain were covered with dark forests. All round under the cliffs was, as I have said, deep water, how deep I do not know, as we had no means of taking soundings of such depth.

As there seemed little to be gained by landing at the foot of the glacier we ran back to the camp of the previous night, where the harbourage was at any rate somewhat better. While we were yet ashore, a squall began to grow up in the sky to the west and came down upon the water in an angry spatter of rain. It subsided, however, as quickly as it had arisen, so we got afloat again. Running back through the narrow throat of the channel, we found that the wind, which had veered several points to the north, had almost blocked it with a fleet of icebergs, that were grinding together on the swell of the water. These we managed to make our way through, and it was with some thankfulness that we presently reached the farther shore on the east of the main Fjord. We had no sooner arrived than it began to blow in heavy gusts, and five minutes after the first of them—so quickly do the seas rise upon this lake—we had to shift our anchorage.

In an hour or two, having in the meantime laid in a good store of firewood, and the heavy wind being succeeded by a series of cold showers, we took advantage of the lull and headed up the main Fjord to the north. But the wind, that had temporarily dropped, soon resumed its fury, and the launch was hard put to it to keep her position, far less to make any headway, and then, as was usual in moments of need, the pumps ceased working altogether, and Burbury shouted that no more than ten minutes' steam remained in the boiler. There was nothing for it but to turn her and to run for the land. We found, however, small hope of anchorage, for a bare fifty-foot cliff rose sheer out of the water and so continued for a long distance ahead. Seeing we were unlikely to discover a suitable position, we decided to cross the lake, but we had not gone far when the propeller wheezed into silence. Strong squalls caught us and made the launch roll and heave. Cattle got into the canvas boat with the idea of trying to tow her, and I forward, put out the long oar, which we generally used as one of the bulwarks—and we both endeavoured to keep her from turning broadside on to the waves, in which case she would have been swamped.

Cattle shortly gave up his attempt to tow her; in the sea then running such an effort was hopeless. The wind increased. Cattle came aboard, not without difficulty, and tried rowing with a short oar. Meantime Burbury was baling water into the boiler with a cooking-pot. The launch was rolling in a manner which made rowing a difficult matter. Presently the oar I was using broke off short and the launch was drifting ominously near to a reef. It was a race as to whether we should get up steam before we were cast upon it. We watched the index of the register slowly beginning to quiver, and when it marked 30 lb. we were not much more than a score or so of yards from the rocks. This was, however, enough to enable us to get way on and forge slowly out of danger.

Our steam did not last much longer than to allow us to find shelter under the lee of a line of low rocks, which thrust themselves out and served as a little breakwater in the lake. We remained there while Burbury again filled the boiler, and, having got up steam, we made the mouth of a deep inlet which afforded us good harbourage. Here we landed, and found ourselves upon a peninsula shaped like a spoon, the handle that connected it with the land being very narrow. At its upper end it joined the moraine of the great glacier which I had called Giant's Glacier.

As we came in to the beach, three guanacos cantered down and stared and neighed at us. The sight of these animals brightened the prospect, as it was pleasant to see living creatures in what had hitherto seemed to be an empty amphitheatre of hills. The bay where we had anchored was a shallow lagoon, into which flowed a little stream that wound away out of sight through a thin belt of forest over land comparatively flat. This peninsula carried a light soil and good grass, but bore the appearance of a spot that the winter would strike with peculiar severity. The wood was all roblé and Leña dura and the scrub included califate-bushes, from which last, however, the purple berries had long since departed, much to our sorrow. Huemules, guanacos, pumas, and the red fox gave evident signs of their presence. I observed a pigmy owl (Glaucidium nanum) and several caranchos. In the evening, when speaking upon the subject, Cattle informed me that several kinds of fish were to be found in Lake Argentino. Often as we used to make our meal of fish and fariña (a compound in the concoction of which for good or evil Bernardo stood alone), I used to regret my inability to bring back specimens of the fish from this lake, but I had no means of preserving them.

"Fish and fariña," indeed, became a standing joke with us. We might threaten to blow each other up by the agency of the launch's peculiar engines, and the threats would pass as nothing; but the expressed intention of any one of us who proposed to go and catch fish with a view to preparing a meal of "fish and fariña" soon became too much for the strongest and bravest among us. As a matter of fact, the fish was far from tempting, having a muddy flavour and being full of small bones, which mixed themselves up inextricably with the fariña.[28]

That night shut down with a gale and much rain. The trees groaned, and one close to us was blown down. It was with a very thankful heart that I woke up in the middle of the storm and reflected upon the glorious safety of our new-found harbour. Next morning I was awakened sometime in the dusky grey of dawn because a couple of Chiloe widgeon had come in close to the launch, and roasted duck was voted good by the wakeful Burbury. I sleepily thought the widgeon might have waited, and after all something scared the ducks and they flew off to a distance of a couple of hundred yards. My stalk only resulted in my securing one of the birds.

The ice we had observed earlier in the mouth of the most westerly channel had by this time completely blocked the opening. We spent the day wandering about upon the peninsula, and I tried to get some photographs, but the attempt was rather hopeless in the mist and rain. Indeed, although advantage was taken of every lifting of the weather, four pictures were all that this trip allowed of my completing.

The following day, in spite of bad weather, we made a third attempt to head up the North Fjord, at the end of which we hoped to find the "river with clear waters" mentioned by Dr. Moreno, and at the end of that again the unknown lake. We made two hours very slow progress, the north-west wind quickly beating up a troublesome sea. We observed bits of wood travelling faster than is usual in cases of drift, and now made sure that, could we but reach the end of the Fjord, we should find the river whose current we believed to be responsible for the comparatively rapid movement of the wood.

Our hopes were on this occasion destined to disappointment, for, in spite of all our efforts, we were unable to go forward or to make head against the bad weather, which continued for some days. Besides this, the injector of the launch failed to perform its office, and as the machinery was badly in need of repairs, and the cracked plate was letting in water, I thought it better to run before the wind to Cow Monte Harbour, which was, in fact, our headquarters, and where such tools as we had were stored. One point that was always in our favour while making these attempts to force our way up the North Fjord, lay in the fact that the prevailing winds from north-west or south-west, as the case might be, helped rather than hindered us on our return passages.

OUR LAUNCH AMONG THE ICE

During this interval, while waiting for a second opportunity of attempting to gain the extreme end of the North Fjord of the lake, we arranged to make a short voyage down the South Fjord, or, as it is locally known, to Lake Rica. By doing this, moreover, we should complete our circumnavigation of Lake

Argentino. Before we left, reliable news came up from the settlements with some belated Christmas and other papers. We were very relieved to learn that the Franco-Russian combination was no more than a camp-scare, nor was Russia advancing on India, as the last rumours had told us. When one has lost so large a slice of the general history of the world as we did during the months passed on our expedition, it is hopeless to imagine one can ever make up the loss. The events of that period must always remain blurred and hazy in the mind, only a few ever attaining an accurate outline. And then how greedy one becomes of news after an abstinence so prolonged as ours from that daily mental excitement of civilisation! It is difficult to describe how one grips the strayed journal or periodical when one has been cut off for months from these "curses of modern life."

On April 11 we left Cow Monte Harbour and steamed westwards down the Punta Bandera Channel. In a short time the pump broke down and we had some trouble in putting it right again. In defence of our engineering skill I must say that we had against us the fact that a part of the pump had been taken away for repairs to Buenos Aires by the Commission. We camped at the mouth of a river coming down out of Mount Avellaneda. Above us the bare volcanic summits of the mountains rose starkly out of their circling forests, that were now turning crimson with the brilliant colours of autumn. We could also see the great glacier on the western side of the Canal de los Tempanos. Many deer-tracks were visible, but we saw only one huemul buck in the edge of the forest.

We made an early start next day, which luckily was calm, for the pump gave us a good deal of bother. We proceeded down a smaller fjord lying under Mount Avellaneda, which took us in a westerly direction, but presently curved southwards and ended in a large mountain covered with forest, which I named Mount Millais. The chief hindrances in these winding passages were the constantly veering winds that we encountered. Day and night we were obliged to keep up a constant struggle against them. This was all very well during the daylight, but to anchor the launch snugly and then to be waked by her bumping and straining at her cable perhaps ten times in the night, and to have to turn out in just what you happened to have on in the way of sleeping apparel supplemented only by "the mantle of the night,"—for there never was a moment to be lost at these junctures—was an experience which quickly became monotonous and wearing to strength and temper. During this South Fjord trip the launch certainly did herself proud in this direction; she seldom gave us a couple of hours' quiet rest, often forcing us to face the biting cold a dozen times between dark and dawn.

The forests about this part of the lake were immense, and contained trees and plants unknown in the outer Cordillera or, rather, I should say, the foothills.[29] A bush resembling holly was conspicuous, fuchsias also abounded.

I quote a short description of this region from my diary: "The mountains go in and out of the mist, now seen, now lost. The mist shrouds them at one moment, and the greyness reaches up to heaven and down to earth—into a man's soul it often seems; the next instant there may be gleams of a sad blue sky shining through the torn banners of the haze, and glaciers assume a wonderful goblin hue, a pallid violet." There was some sameness in our days, but the launch kept us alive with anticipation. She seldom lacked the chance of giving us some surprise. Often we asked each other, "Will she drown us after all? And when and where?" A cold death and a deep grave she had it in her power to give. The one good side to the situation was that when we landed, as we often did, in a sleety drizzle on a swampy camp, we forbore to grumble, but were, on the contrary, filled with a strong thankfulness to have escaped from her even for a little time.

We had one particularly bad night, when a series of squalls came down on us, and we spent the greater part of our sleeping-hours in poling the launch off the shore, but at last the wind got the better of us and literally hurled her on the beach.

How we managed to get her off it is impossible to describe; we did it somehow. The next morning was still windy, but we steamed along the Canal de los Tempanos under Mount Buenos Aires, and there it was that a fire broke out on the launch. This was an accident we always dreaded, for, having no room elsewhere, we were obliged to pile the fuel round her engine, with the result that it occasionally became dangerously heated.

GLACIER DE LOS TEMPANOS

Landing at the end of the Canal de los Tempanos we found ourselves in forests of magnificent timber. The vegetation was rank and luxuriant, a mass of decay under a forest of life. From the swampy dank ground tall stems sprang up straight and branchless as palms, while at their feet grew a carpet of ferns.

We had some marvellous days of fine weather in the Cordillera, where on the mountain slopes, as winter drew on, the crimson shades crept deeper to mingle with and finally change the green. In due time we reached the South Fjord by water. The account of a previous visit on horseback has already been told. Then we turned homewards, and on the way I secured some good photos of the great glacier of the Canal de los Tempanos. As we passed down the canal, a big berg broke off from the glacier ahead of us and plunged into the water, sending up a huge wave, which luckily only touched us slightly. It was well we were no nearer. We witnessed after this the fall of several lesser pieces of ice, the noise of which resounded loudly among the gorges.

Our return voyage was eventless. While Bernardo was making our camp-fire upon landing, he called to me to come with my rifle. He said he had been attacked by a large Cordillera wolf, which snapped at his legs. He retaliated with an axe, but it got away. Following in the direction he indicated, I caught a glimpse of the animal crossing a patch of moonlight, and fired, hitting it far back.

There are many thousands of square miles of unexplored forest in Patagonia. It is a region unknown and mysterious, which has never been deeply explored by man. As has been said, no man lives in them, and it is a question whether man has ever lived there, for the one all-sufficient reason—the practical absence of game on which he might subsist.

I well remember my first sight of the forests, and the intense longing that took hold upon me to make my way into their virgin fastnesses. It is one of the traveller's most unquenchable desires, this hankering to go where no other man has yet been. It springs, I suppose, from the undefined thought that in the unknown everything is possible, though few things perhaps come to pass.

ANOTHER VIEW OF THE GLACIER DE LOS TEMPANOS

From afar the forests appear to rim the slopes and spurs of the Cordillera with a seemingly impenetrable mass of blackness, reaching towards and often running up into the snow-line; as you approach the colour assumes its true hue, a deep dense green, a green that seems to have the quality of absorbing light, so that, as you gaze upon the expanse of foliage stretching back into the distances, fold beyond fold, where the valleys and mountain-sides close in behind each other, an impression of gloom and mystery lays hold upon your mind. Upon still nearer inspection you find the trees ranked in heavy phalanxes, while between their close-set trunks has grown up an under-tangle of thorn. Old storms have overthrown many of the giants, so that they lie in tens and twenties, or lean against their yet quick companions awaiting the slow decay of things. But it is very hard to give any adequate idea in words of these vast and nameless tree-kingdoms. Most common among the trees was the antarctic beech. I observed also redwood and cypress.

GLACIER AND GLACIAL DETRITUS

There are some wild cattle and huemules to be found in the outskirts of the woodlands; we also saw parrots, hawks and owls in some of our wanderings, while in other spots there seemed no sign of life at all save a few small rodents, and even those, as we pushed farther into the thicker recesses, disappeared. And then we came under the sway of that curious silence which broods among these forest depths.

The aspects of the various forests and the trees of which they were composed varied greatly. Some were bare and devoid of undergrowth as a northern forest; others were absolutely tropical in their heavy luxuriance. In one, a majestic place, the tall antarctic beeches were draped with long trailing Spanish moss, and on the carpet of moss beneath them lay here and there a dead tree.

Few places are more mournful than this region when rain is falling. After the rain ceases, mists arise and circle round you, shutting you in, these in their turn often being dissipated by a sudden fierce squall. In summer the climate is very humid, and many of the plants have the fat damp aspect seldom observable save in the tropics. The huge masses of rank vegetation seem to stifle you; once you have been in that great black insatiable woodland you can never quite shake off its influence.

In that particular forest was one glade by the outrunning of a little brook where the ground was thick with orchids.[30]

One reads of "virgin forests," but one must behold them to comprehend the reality that underlies the wording. For days you saw no living thing, heard no human tones, nothing but the immense voices of the thunder, the glacier and the everlasting wind. The solitude of Patagonia, its peculiar characteristic of lack of human life in the present and the past, was borne in upon one under that high dome of foliage, and in those aisles abysmally vast, stretching north, south, east and west. In any other country legends would have gathered round these places, some touch of man's presence and adventure humanised them, so to speak. In Patagonia the fancy had nothing to grip, to grow upon, no story of joy or of sorrow. Solitude reigned alone, and nature spoke only by the awful uninterpreted tongues of God's elements.

FOOTNOTES:

[28] Two kinds of fish came under my observation, but I understood there were four.

[29] I hope in a future volume to publish a list of the plants we collected. At the moment of writing all have not reached England.

[30] There were also orchids growing about the foothills of the Cordillera. Those I brought back are now under the care of the Curator of the Royal Botanical Gardens at Kew. They should flower before this book is in print.

CHAPTER XX

DISCOVERY OF THE RIVER KATARINA AND LAKE PEARSON

Fears of winter coming on—Stormy days—Quiet nights—Picnics in Patagonia—Start by night— Hellgate by starlight—Camp on beach—Advance up North Fjord—Approach to River Katarina— Shallow water—Leave launch—Advance with canvas boat—Tameness of huemul—Anecdote of Canoe Indians—White-faced ducks—First sight of lake—Bernardo falls ill—Immoderate bags of so-called sportsmen—Problem of shrinkage of Lake Argentino—Discovery of Lake Pearson—Description— Bernardo better—Comet—Obliged to turn back—Hellgate by firelight.

After our return from our trip to the South Fjord the weather became very threatening, and I was beset with many anxious fears that the winter might set in rigidly, and entirely preclude any attempt to solve the problem of the yet unvisited and unknown river and lake whose existence was conjectured at the end of the North Fjord. Snow fell and blocked the pass to Punta Arenas,[31] which was our south road to the coast, but luckily a milder spell followed, the snow melted and I was encouraged to remain just a little longer to carry out my original idea of making another effort to thoroughly explore the North Fjord.

Storms, however, swept over the lake, and although we undertook a couple of short expeditions in the launch, we waited for better days before again facing the difficulties of the Hellgate passage. Again and again we saw squalls and waterspouts come curling down the channel between the frowning cliffs. Day followed day with heavy winds, the coming of the light seemed to be the signal for the gales to rise, whereas on many nights the weather was fairly still, and the water in consequence calmer. It was during this period of waiting that we arranged the following programme, which I find scribbled upon a page of my diary:

PICNICS IN PATAGONIA

Arranged by the Patagonian Picnicking Company on the most lavish scale.

On the Free Pampas!

Over glorious Lakes!!

Through illimitable Forests!!!!!

Ladies and gentlemen desiring to make this unique trip should communicate at once with the Secretary, Herr Bernardo Hähansen.

Unequalled Scenery!!!   Horse Exercise!!!

Guanaco Shooting!!!   Ostrich Hunting!!!

A special feature will be made of water-trips in the magnificent steam-yacht, the fastest boat on Lake Argentino, commanded by an officer of immense experience and charming manners, who has instructions to do all that he can for the comfort of the passengers.

WRITE EARLY

Applications are pouring in. Only a limited number of passengers can be accommodated. Don't be one of the disappointed! You pay £500. We do the rest!!!!!!!

N.B.—The cultured conversation of the Chief Engineer free of charge. (Gratuities regarded merely as a graceful compliment.)

Passengers are expected to insure their lives in favour of the Company for sums of not less than £1000 each with respectable Insurance Companies.

The engagement of picturesque heathen camp-servants will be made a special study by the Company.

EVENTIDE

At length, weary of waiting on the wind's vagaries, we determined to start by night, during the quieter period we usually then enjoyed, and make what progress we could up the intricacies of Hellgate. Accordingly, at 1 o'clock P.M. on May 3, we began our voyage. We passed through Hellgate and left many silent bays behind us as we kept on our course just outside the inky shadow of the cliffs. The water was still working after the blow of the daytime, but on the whole we had favourable weather and the stars shone brightly. With dawn the wind arose and we were forced to put in to an anchorage on the east shore of the Fjord. Afterwards, travelling by day, we made our way to the peninsula, rocks often jutted out into the fairway, but these were easy to locate, as we had been through the channel before and had some knowledge of its reefs. A number of icebergs had been blown down out of the western channel, but the water had fallen considerably since our last visit, and when we reached the peninsula we found it impossible to resume our former camp there, so we were forced to pass an uncommonly cold night on a bare bit of beach without so much as a bush to shelter us.

From time to time we spent a good while on this peninsula. It was studded with erratic boulders, and the soil on it varied from six to twelve inches in depth. On this visit I saw a red-crested woodpecker. The views from the higher part of the peninsula were infinitely grand. The gigantic glacier, the dark forests, the innumerable icebergs floating below the black cliffs—all these combined to make up pictures which I should like to be able to reproduce.

In time the weather moderated, and we made a last essay to penetrate to the farther end of the main Fjord. As we proceeded the water became shallower, so that it was necessary occasionally to take soundings. There were also many rocks. We once more noticed dry sticks and leaves drifting past, and presently ahead of us, through a gap in the Cordillera, we caught a glimpse of flat country. This time we fulfilled our desire and attained to the termination of the Fjord, where we came to the mouth of a river of considerable size. It swung out from round the base of a cliff, and had thrown up a slight bar where it joined the waters of the lake. I named it the River Katarina.

We camped at this point and began at once to explore the valley of the river. It flowed over a stony bed, presenting much the appearance of a large Scotch trout-stream. The cañadon through which it passed was very wide, and the stream wound greatly. At the time of our visit the river was very shallow, and there was not water enough to float the launch, in fact a stone picked up from the bottom lodged itself between the blades of the propeller and we had to haul up for repairs. This business of repairing was one we often had to perform, and necessity being the mother of invention, the dodges we resorted to were original. The launch, if once hauled up on the beach and sunk in the sand, would have been too heavy for the three of us to get back into the water. On these occasions we therefore used to cut the largest tree-trunks available and roll them under the keel while still half in the water, then the two heaviest of us would go into the bows, which were, of course, in comparatively deep water, and our weight in this position served to raise the stern sufficiently to allow of the third man to execute the repairs needful to the propeller. In the present instance it was found that the machinery was severely strained, though fortunately no damage had been done to the blades of the propeller.

Though the river was shallow in May, we saw abundant evidence that it must carry a greatly increased volume of water in the earlier part of the year. But not finding it possible to take the launch up the channel, we decided on anchoring her as securely as we could and continuing our expedition in the small canvas boat. This we did a day or two later.

Our camping-ground on the bank of the Katarina was among high and rather coarse grass, which would have made excellent feed for horses, but I should not think it possible to keep horses in that cañadon, as, being encircled by hills, the sun would seldom reach it during the winter. There were many patches of wood, composed of rather stunted trees, but it was difficult to penetrate among them, their trunks grew so close together. A certain amount of game lived in the valley, huemules, guanacos, pumas and Cordillera wolves.

The extraordinary tameness of the huemul here was, of course, accounted for by their entire ignorance of man. During my wanderings from the camp I had opportunities of making many interesting observations on this point. They would almost always, if you kept still and made no attempt to approach them, advance timidly towards you. It was in this valley of the Katarina that I met with the most remarkable instance of boldness on the part of these animals. I have given this story in full in another chapter, but I may shortly allude to it here. I was some miles from the camp, among thick grass and scrub, when I perceived emerging from a thicket at a little distance the spiked horns and red-brown sides of a huemul buck; behind him were two does, half hidden in the thicket. Finding that they had perceived me, I lay down on the grass and watched to see what they would do. One could read in their movements and attitudes the battle between timidity and curiosity that was going on within them. A third half-grown doe now appeared, and all four began to drift, as it were, slowly in my direction, keeping their eyes fixed upon me all the time. Now and again they would stop, then move on a few steps nearer, but after a long time they grew courageous enough to come right up to me, and the younger doe sniffed at my boot, then started back some paces, her companions naturally following her example. I could easily have touched her with my hand during a good part of the time. At last the buck lowered his horns as if with the intention of turning me over, but the sun was now sinking, and I was obliged to take my way homewards. As I stirred the huemules made off, but halted at a short distance to stare again at the queer object which had for the first time in their lives entered within their ken.

CAÑADON OF THE RIVER KATARINA

That evening, as we sat round the camp-fire, Cattle told us an amusing story illustrative of the quickness with which the Canoe Indians of the western or Pacific coast pick up the art of bargaining. He with two companions was living in the eternal rain of the Chilian side of the Cordillera, when one afternoon they struck a camp of Canoe Indians, who ran away into the forest on seeing the boat of the white men coming up the fjord. After a time, however, curiosity overcame their terror, and an old woman advanced from under the trees and commenced to open communications with the travellers by means of signs. She was probably sent out on account of her uselessness to the tribe, as, in the event of the white men being evilly disposed, her loss would have been regarded as no great misfortune. By-and-by she was joined by the other Indians, and the party fell to bartering. One of the Englishmen bought a fine sea-otter's skin for a box of matches, and the old lady, who had made the first advances, was asked by signs if she had another to dispose of. She ran back into the forest and presently returned with the half of a skin in each hand. She demanded a box of matches for each piece, for, thinking to improve upon the last bargain, she had cut the otter-skin in two with a bit of glass!

Our next move was to trace the river up to its source. After assuring ourselves that the launch could not go up the stream, we made all ship-shape in the camp and prepared to go ahead by putting our bedding and food in the canvas boat. We set out one grey morning, following the left bank of the Katarina. Parallel with the course of the river ran a chain of small hillocks, and behind these again a series of reedy lagoons. These last were literally black with duck, especially the variety known locally as the "white-faced duck," otherwise the Chiloe widgeon. The lagoons contained brackish water, and I fancy the whole depression in which they lie is flooded in the spring.

On this day Cattle and I, from the top of a hillock, descried what we took to be water in the north end of the cañadon. This was our first sight of the lake the shores of which I afterwards reached.

RIVER KATARINA

In the evening we camped at a spot opposite to the mouth of a tributary of the Katarina that flowed from the hills on the eastern side. At this point Bernardo knocked up. He had had hard work all day with the boat, for the stream was full of shoals, and wind and current were strong against him. He had been in the river off and on, and as he was already suffering from a slight cold when we set out this treatment had not improved it. By night his chest seemed a good deal affected, and his breathing was difficult. The rain of the afternoon turned to snow in the night, and it became very cold, a comfortless position for a feverish man. Our means for dealing with illness were limited, but hot cocoa and rugs seemed the best treatment under the circumstances, and we further sheltered him under the canvas boat, which, being turned over, made a tolerable hut.

Having brought a certain amount of provisions with us, we did not shoot much. There can be little question that, had Patagonia been a country rich in trophies, its less remote valleys would long ago have known the crack of the rifle. Fortunately for its feræ naturæ, the small horns of Xenelaphus bisulcus do not offer sufficient attraction. There is no sport on earth finer than big-game shooting in moderation, but in all parts of the world I should like to see a universal law prohibiting any one sportsman or professional hunter from shooting more than a limited number of a particular animal in a year. This idea, as a universal law, is, of course, impossible of fulfilment, but surely in sport moderation and a due regard for the survival of the various kinds of game should be the guiding rule and principle. However, my pen has carried me away. I merely say that it would be well if public opinion trended more resolutely towards censuring the hunter who selfishly makes immoderate bags. At the present moment he is looked upon as rather a fine fellow by those who lack any real knowledge of the subject, for no man is more strongly opposed to such doings than the true sportsman.

Owing to the unfortunate accident of Bernardo's illness, the general advance of our party was out of the question. It only remained for me to push on alone, and to give up any attempt to take the boat farther. Cattle stayed with Bernardo, to look after him, while I went on up the valley along the banks of the Katarina.

THE LAST REACH

There can be little doubt that all the cañadon of this river formed at one time part of Lake Argentino, and that the hills in the valley were merely small islands in the same. One of the most interesting facts in connection with Lake Argentino is the large volume of water that is precipitated into it by a number of rivers and mountain torrents. Besides the Rivers Leona and Katarina, there are two or three streams of considerable size and countless snow-fed cascades falling from the cliffs. On the other hand, the only large outlet is the River Santa Cruz, and though that river carries off an important amount of water to the Atlantic, the quantity is not sufficient to account for the fact that the great lake is surely if slowly shrinking in size. The North and South Fjords with their adjoining reaches of water at one time formed part of a wide-spreading lake, whose waters washed completely round the bases of the mountains—such as Mount Buenos Aires—and of hills that now stand upon out-jutting points of land or actually upon the present lines of the shores. The reason for this shrinkage of the lake, when appearances would seem to point rather to increase of size, is difficult to discover.

The features of the cañadon of the Katarina changed but little as I walked on deeper into it. I saw two huemul bucks, one accompanied by two, the other by three does; I also saw some guanacos. The Giant's Glacier, which crosses the head of Lake Argentino as far as the peninsula on which we camped, ran parallel behind the cliffs of the western shore, glimmering out palely in the north-west ahead of me. Presently I passed over a stream, and later topping a low bluff I found myself on the shores of a lake, the distant gleam of whose waters Cattle and I had seen on the previous day. I was, of course, very eager to take a photograph of it, but everything around was shrouded in mist, and I had with me only a binocular camera, the mechanism of which did not permit of long exposures.

LAKE PEARSON

I must admit that I was disappointed with the lake when I arrived at it, as I had expected a much larger piece of water. The nearer shores were somewhat low and covered with boulders, while upon the farther sides rose a semicircle of hills whose escarpments fell in places abruptly to the water. About the inferior spurs of a somewhat higher mountain to the north a dense black forest clung. The morning was grey and the water lay dark and ruffled under a chilling wind, while about the distant cliffs of the northern shore wreaths of cloud hung sullenly, only lifting at intervals here and there sufficient to give a glimpse of the bare crags behind them.

Towards the afternoon luck befriended me, for the sky cleared and the sun broke out for a short time, giving me the opportunity I had been hoping for. I made haste to use the camera with such results as will be seen.

This lake I named Lake Pearson.

On my return to the camp I found the sick man improving, which was a relief, as under the circumstances we had very little to give him in the way of comfort. Bernardo was a cheery fellow, who met the disagreeables of his lot good-temperedly, and I have no doubt this helped towards his recovery. Eventually he became quite well.

During the night a comet was visible, hanging in the clear sky like a white sword, hilt downwards. It was very brilliant and very beautiful, seen as we saw it above the dark forest.

There were many reasons why I hoped to be able to push deeper into this region, but it was growing very late in the season, winter with its accompaniment of furious storms was almost upon us, and this fact, joined with the strained and weakened condition of the engine of the launch, compelled us to give up the thought of further exploration. We therefore took advantage of a spell of rather better weather to make our way back down the Fjord. The wind was blowing sulkily out of the north, but this gave us the benefit of a following sea. Once or twice during our passage squalls overtook us, but always blowing mercifully in the direction of our course. Thus we had a following sea right up to the cliffs of Hellgate. In one place a big iceberg had stranded beneath the cliffs.

We landed under the bluffs of Hellgate and lit a fire of Leña dura, which roared and crackled in the dusk, lighting up the gloom of Hellgate with red light. Later we ran across safely to our anchorage off the Burmeister Peninsula.

FOOTNOTE:
[31] Burbury made his way south just in the nick of time. I was obliged to send him to the coast to meet Scrivenor, who was, according to my arrangements, about to leave for England.

CHAPTER XXI

HOMEWARD

Winter comes on—Departure from Lake Argentino—Changed aspect of country—Snow-clouds—Indian encampment—Race with the snow—River Coyly—River Gallegos—Ford—Signs of civilisation—Gallegos—Taking passage in steamer—Lighted street—Good-bye to Bernardo—Meeting with Mr. Waag and Mr. Von Plaaten Hallermund on the Elena—What Patagonia taught me.

A fortnight before we started there was a couple of feet of snow on the high pampa. Beside the lake it had been blowing heavily, and storms of sleet followed each other in dreary succession. Every morning we saw the white cloak of winter throwing its snowy folds lower and lower upon the mountains. The severe season of the Cordillera and Southern Patagonia was fast shutting us in; already the Pass to Punta Arenas was closed feet deep in snow, and our only outlet for the south lay towards Gallegos. It had been my wish to remain as long as possible in the neighbourhood of the Andes, but I had overstayed the utmost limit I originally set myself, and now there was nothing for it but to make a rush for the coast while the journey could still be made.

On May 15 we started in heavy rain. The horses were in excellent condition; indeed, they were too fat, for of late they had not had enough exercise to prepare them for a very trying journey. We took three cargueros besides the horses for riding, and the party consisted of Mr. Cattle's shepherd, George Gregory, Bernardo and myself. At the second camp Gregory was obliged to turn back, as his horses—a troop of colts—had wandered during the night. This was at the River del Bote; from there Bernardo and I went on alone. We found the aspect of the country much changed since we had crossed it three and a half months previously. The green grass had grown yellow, the streams and the lagoons were drying up, numbers of guanaco had descended to the lower grounds. An Indian trader, accompanied by a few tents of Indians, had taken up quarters near the River Califate, a spot formerly inhabited by wildfowl only. For three days we followed the shore of the lake, but then our way led us up on to the high pampa, where we made our camp in a bushless cañadon beside a rocky pool. By this time the horses were beginning to lose their tricks, but at the outset they would hardly allow themselves to be caught, and they wandered every night. The cañadon was clear of snow, but the sky was heavy with the promise of it. We hoped most heartily that it would give us two more days' grace before it fell.

The next day we followed the cañadon, which was a shallow depression running south-west. There was no fuel to be found but the thin roots of the dark bush known as maté negra. The early frosts made travelling difficult, as it was necessary to off-saddle early, that the horses might not be turned out sweating into the cold. We covered sixty miles, changing horses three times, for it was quite clear that we must push on if we hoped to escape the snow. That was one of the most fatiguing marches we had during the whole expedition. About three o'clock I espied some herds of tame cattle in the distance by the side of a lagoon. These proved to belong to some tents of Indians. The men were absent hunting and the camp was given over to the women and decrepit dogs. An enormous china sat in the opening of the largest toldo; she must have weighed twenty odd stone! We learned from her that the season had been a good one for guanaco chicos.

In reply to our question as to how far we might be from the nearest white man's habitation on the next stage of our journey, the fat lady waved her hand picturesquely and vaguely towards the eastern sky but did not commit herself to figures.

The Indian encampment made a singular picture against a somewhat striking background. The western sky was piling up and bulged with snow-clouds, while the sinking sun glowed like a red-hot cannon ball on the rim of the pampa. Against this curtain of colour were set the brown tents of guanaco-skin. In one of these a small fire was burning with little flames about an old meat tin in which water was being boiled for maté. Around the women sat in silence—saving only the fat spokeswoman—inert and apparently content; occasionally one would grunt or shift the child at her breast, but otherwise one heard scarce a sound but the whimpering of the wind from the Cordillera or the plashing of the wildfowl in the swampy margin of the lagoon.

I need not describe at length the days which followed. In due time we came upon a wheeltrack and sighted the first fence. This was in the valley of the River Coyly, a good place for pasturing sheep, but inexpressibly desolate and monotonous in aspect. For two days we held along in this valley or on the pampa immediately above it, but, remembering our experiences near Santa Cruz, I resolved to sleep in no boliche until we reached Gallegos.

The cañadon of the Coyly was fenced at intervals, the grass eaten close to the ground by many sheep. Thousands of wild geese clamoured on the banks of the river. In this river valley we made our last camp in Patagonia. There was no wood for fire, and the horses found but little to eat, the sun set among sickly green lights, and presently rain came on. Altogether it made a dismal good-bye to the life we had led for so many months.

The following day, striking across the pampa for the River Gallegos, we knew ourselves to be entering on the last stage of our wanderings. And here we very nearly had a disastrous accident. Meeting two Gauchos, we asked them about the condition of the ford over the Gallegos, which they told us had been but hock-high when they passed through with their horses. Consequently, when we arrived at the ford half an hour later, we took our troop down into the water, but seeing it looked uncommonly deep for the description given us by the Gauchos, we returned to the shore, and, as there happened to be a house at no great distance, I sent Bernardo to make inquiries. He brought back the news that the tide was running strong and the ford quite impracticable, but it was possible that we might be able to cross higher up at another spot. We followed this advice and crossed in safety, I with my precious photographs tied round my neck; but had we tried the lower ford I am very sure I should have lost them all, which would have been a disappointment indeed, considering the circumstances under which they had been taken and the impossibility of replacing them.

Once across the Gallegos we emerged upon flat ground, and here we found a road with a line of telephone-posts running along one side of it. Gallegos was by that time only eighteen miles ahead, but with our tired horses that appeared a long distance. The country was absolutely featureless, the black posts sticking up against a dull sky, the brown earth absorbing such light as there was. A very cold wind blew across our faces, but there was one thing that cheered us, that told us our wanderings were over— the humming of the wind in the wires overhead.

The road dipped and rose over the long undulations, and at last, as we topped one of the many inclines, Gallegos straggled into sight, obviously a frontier town, all wire fences, wooden and corrugated-iron houses with painted roofs. The emotions with which one returns and feels the long wanderings over are not easy to describe. I rode slowly up the main street and passed the bank—for there is a bank at Gallegos, and the fact gave one a sensation of being very civilised indeed. I dismounted and went into the building to inquire about the steamer for Punta Arenas, where I hoped to pick up a homeward-bound boat. A steamboat was to have started for Punta Arenas that same morning, I was told, but as the captain was in gaol, her departure had been postponed for a day or so. The delay seemed a special dispensation for my benefit, for, had she adhered to her original date, I must have been too late to go by her. I understood that the captain's crime lay in having drawn up his anchor without waiting to receive a written permit.

Luckily I had not been preceded at Gallegos by any "lord," hence I drew the cash necessary for my passage and payments at the bank without any trouble. Then I went on to the hotel and put up my horse, the good little big-hearted Moro, who had carried me a hundred and fifty miles in three days and looked fat on it. Afterwards I bought a cigar, a very bad one, but a cigar for all that, and so proceeded down to the beach to secure my passage. Up on the shingle were several ships high and dry, and out in the fairway about the very smallest steamer I have ever seen, yet a good sea-boat, as I afterwards proved. She rejoiced in a brilliant green deck-house two storeys high, and the funnel was almost on top of the propeller!

When it grew dark it was strange to walk through the lighted streets and to see the faces pass and repass beneath the lamps. There was a delightful sense of newness about it all. But perhaps the most strange sensation was produced by a visit to the hairdresser's shop, where one could watch in the glass the swift transformation. Afterwards it was quite good to smoke a second execrable cigar, and to listen to the hotel-keeper in another room telling some of his friends how he had mistaken me for a camp-loafer owing to my patched clothes and the ragged remnants of my boots, and had, in consequence, led me to an outhouse, proposing to allow me to sleep there!

Best of all, perhaps, was the civilised dinner, despite the attentions of an intoxicated itinerant dentist, who kept on reiterating the same question, "Have you ever been to Nahuelhuapi?" the huapi ending in a wail—"w-a-a-a-pi." Bernardo had not turned up from the farm where we had left the horses, and a gentleman connected with the Government who was present, understanding that I wished to see him before sailing, offered to send a file of soldiers to look for him. Presently Bernardo arrived, and then we went away and lit our pipes for a last talk over it all.

PUNTA ARENAS

Next morning on the wet shingle I said good-bye to him, and there he stood for a while as the boat shoved off and we rowed away. A wild figure was Master Bernardo, for he had not yet had time to clothe himself in the garments of civilisation. With his ragged blue jersey and his big boots of potro hide, surmounted by his pleasant bearded face, he watched us through the wind and the rain, and then he turned and walked away, passing out of sight among the sheds. He was going to Santa Cruz by the horse-track. Good luck to him, and may we meet again!

I went aboard, little guessing the pleasure that awaited me, for at the gangway-head I met Mr. Waag and Mr. Von Plaaten Hallermund, of the Boundary Commission, who were on their way down from Santa Cruz to Punta Arenas. Mr. Waag and I had just missed each other by a couple of hours on the pampa up country some months earlier. We were soon deep in talk about the Cordillera, and all that had happened to the three of us since we last met at the Hotel Phœnix in Buenos Aires. Mr. Waag had had a successful time about Lake Puerrydon, and Mr. Von Plaaten Hallermund at Lake San Martin. Meantime the Elena got in her anchor, and we were in the Magellan Straits by nightfall.

And so we reached Punta Arenas, where I was shown much hospitality by Mr. Perkins, and where I had the pleasure of meeting Mr. Fred Waldron, in whose company, as well as that of Mr. Waag and Mr. Von Plaaten Hallermund, I made the passage to Buenos Aires by the Pacific Company's steamship the Orellana, and so home.

To turn for a moment to the personal point of view. I had landed in Patagonia with enthusiasm, and I left it not in the least damped or disheartened in that enthusiasm, but very much the opposite. I had learned many lessons of life, passed through many experiences, explored a small part of the earth's surface, and made some original observations with regard to the zoology of the country and other matters, but I am inclined to think that the most useful lesson to myself was one that sank deeper and deeper into my mind, I might say heart, with every day lived in these great solitudes—and that was the knowledge of my own ignorance. The long solitary days in the forests, on the pampas, and about the stormy fjords of the Cordillera brought me face to face with Nature. There are many voices in the silence of Nature. The stars above, the waters beneath, and the earth all spoke in a hundred tongues, and little enough of it all could I, with my lack of knowledge, interpret. "There are many kinds of voices in the world, and none of them is without signification," but so long as they spoke to me in unknown tongues how much was I the better? And there it was I learned the useful truth that, to be a traveller of any value, a man must also be an adequate interpreter.

THE AUTHOR

A FEW WORDS ABOUT THE FUTURE OF PATAGONIA

It would be possible to write a very long chapter about the future of Patagonia. I do not, however, propose to do this, but to write what I have to say as briefly as possible.

To begin with, Patagonia can boast of a fine climate, for, though the winters are certainly hard, no endemic disease exists. The country is exceptionally healthy, nor are there any poisonous reptiles to endanger life on its far-reaching pampas. There are few parts of the earth of which so much can be said.

A large portion of the land is eminently suited for the support of sheep, as the enormous and prosperous sheep-farms to be found along the east and south coasts bear witness. Cattle and horse-breeding are also successfully carried on, and although a portion of the country is unsuited for agricultural purposes, it is equally certain that large expanses of ground of great fertility and rich promise are to be found here.

The tide of pastoral life from the thriving southern farms round and about Punta Arenas on the Straits of Magellan, and Gallegos on the Atlantic coast, is setting strongly north and west. The crying want of the country is capital to open up means of communication with the interior. At present there are no railways or other settled lines for the transport of produce, although I believe a steam-launch has lately been placed upon the River Santa Cruz. In consequence of this lack some farmers have to carry wool two hundred miles by bullock-cart to the coast; a few cover even a greater distance. To send wool two hundred miles in bullock-carts means at least three weeks of travel. To go and come from the farm to the coast would thus take up about two months of a farmer's time. Peones are necessary to look after the carts, and their wage is at least £5 a month and their keep. Then carts not infrequently break down upon the rough surfaces of the pampas and in the cañadones, hence more delay. Even when the port is reached difficulties have to be surmounted, for none of them, with the exception of Punta Arenas, are served by any steamship lines. This was so at the time of my being in Patagonia last year (1901). Government transports from Buenos Aires had the whole of the coast service of Argentine Patagonia in their hands, and these could boast of only very uncertain dates of departure and still more uncertain dates of arrival.

All these difficulties of transit do not make for prosperity. I understand that of late a German line has undertaken to call at some of the ports, and if they carry out their contract it should help events in Patagonia to get into the stride of success.

On the coast-farms, where ships could and did occasionally put in, especially in the wool season, money was made and men began to see fortune ahead. But far away in the interior, where a very few pioneers have made their homes beside a lake here and there, the wide and uninhabited pampas lie between the producer and his market. Until railways open up the land the position of these people cannot much improve. They are too heavily handicapped in the race.

It is almost impossible to tell what enormous numbers of sheep and cattle Patagonia could produce for the providing of the world if capital and enterprise would but pave the way. In the meantime the country remains the paradise of the middleman. At present there is little money in hand, much of the trade is carried on by barter, and on this system there is always an evil tendency towards profits accruing mostly to the storekeepers, who gradually become more or less masters of the situation. Many of the small farmers are deeply in debt to this class. A hard winter—and there are often very hard winters—fills the pocket of the storekeeper, for they advance provisions, without which no man can continue to live, and they, of course, thus secure mortgages on the farms.

This same unfortunate liability is observable in other countries where similar conditions obtain, but the opening up of the interior of Patagonia and the introduction of capital in the hands of employers of labour would probably lessen the pressure of hard times on the poorer farmers.

Beyond the pampas again tower the unnumbered peaks of the Cordillera, and among them all things, minerally speaking, are possible. Perhaps the future of Patagonia is to be found there. In a few years the Patagonian Andes may be as commonly known a seeking-place for fortune as Klondyke is to-day. But concerning this part of the subject I have nothing to say, being no prophet of El Dorados.

Although during our travels we had little time to spare for prospecting, or searching for the mineral wealth which may lie hidden in the Cordillera, yet there was one obvious source of riches that was always before our eyes in those regions.

The coast-towns of Patagonia are supplied with wood by sea from the woodlands of Tierra del Fuego, and this while many square miles about the bases of the Andes are covered with dense forests of magnificent growth. Here are to be found beech, cypress and redwood, not to speak of other trees, but the absolute absence of any means of conveying logs to the coast has so far left this store of wealth untouched. Until better means of transport can be developed, there are certainly one or two rivers which might be made use of in this connection.

I can only insist upon the fact that Patagonia is a great though at present undeveloped land; that it cries aloud to railway enterprise to become its salvation. Nevertheless, it is even now a good country for the man ready and able to work. A capable man will make £6 a month and his keep, but he must know the work required of him; a considerable time has to be spent in learning the skilled labour of camp life, and very hard labour that sometimes is. An emigrant does not consequently find it so easy to get employment. But, given vigorous health, an aptitude for hard work, and a small sum in hand to keep him going until he is broken in to the necessities of the life, and I know of few countries more favourable to the unmarried working man.

There is something further which I should like to suggest to intending emigrants of my own nation.

The greatest of British exports is, one might contend, Britishers.

The attitude of the young Britisher abroad towards the rest of the world in general is at once a source of great national strength and of serious national weakness.

First, as we know, he is a poor linguist, who prefers to go on speaking his own language, and, when not understood, attempting to enforce comprehension by the very simple expedient of shouting louder. The result of this uncompromising attitude, backed by a good national financial status, is that as the mountain will not go to Mahomet, Mahomet must needs come to the mountain, and the foreign Mahomet does come, wrestling his way through difficulties of pronunciation. By his attitude in this matter—an attitude dictated partly by a too common lack of the linguistic faculty and partly by a certain rooted conviction that a man who cannot speak English is a man of "lesser breed"—the Britisher has to a certain extent forced English upon a very unwilling world.

But whether this question of the one-language system is a loss or a gain to the country, it is very certain that there is another idiosyncrasy of the Englishman abroad which is an undoubted loss. Every country has its own ways and methods, not only peculiar to its inhabitants but adapted to their special needs. And here the brusque unadaptability of the Englishman becomes pitifully apparent.

He loses immensely by it. He will ride on his English saddle because he has been used to ride on it at home; he will wear his pigskin leggings for precisely the same reason.

You cannot teach him that he who walks in a noontide sun in latitudes near the equator is sometimes apt to contract a fever. Of course I refer chiefly to the "new chum," but we have an unfortunate gift of remaining new chums for an indefinite period.

Our young blood is very sure of himself, which is a first-rate national trait, and one to which as a nation we, no doubt, owe much. But it has its drawbacks. Thus, although he is physically excellent beyond his fellows, his death-rate is usually heavier, which in the nature of things it ought not to be.

But in cases where adhesion to the methods of the country to which he has migrated touches not himself but his goods and his work he needlessly—indeed, almost mischievously—handicaps himself. He takes pride in occupying a position of more or less splendid isolation.

The Britisher lacks adaptability. He lacks suavity. He often lacks common politeness. In fact, he is a good fellow when you know him, but you have got to know him first. An excellent reputation to possess, perhaps, apart from business, and when your position is assured. But in foreign countries, and in the case of dealing with strangers of other nations, who are very apt to like or dislike at first sight, its results are disastrous, for they rarely reconsider their first opinion.

The Continental races, on the other hand, aim at merging their individuality in that of their temporary hosts. Actuated by a sense of politeness or of self-interest—I do not know which—these peoples do not thrust forward the fact that they are aliens, but rather try to foster the idea that the land of their adoption is their own. But when the young Englishman comes along, his manner placards him with his nationality. He seems to say, "You fellows, I've got to live here, Fate orders it. But I am not of you. Apart from business, leave me alone."

He and his compatriots are sufficient unto themselves. And not infrequently also, though strangers in a strange land, they are a law unto themselves. Now this is all very well in its way, and we would not, I suppose, have it otherwise; yet, if the English youth abroad would modify their attitude towards the works of the alien, even while, if they so choose, preserving it towards the alien himself, they would rise to greater heights of success than they at present touch.

The fact is that the alien thinks the Englishman is a fool of a very notable kind, and in many cases he is right.

It is not in the excellence of their goods, or even in the cheapness of their tariff, that the Germans are forging ahead of us in trade. It is in their attitude towards those with whom they deal. They make an art of selling a yard of red flannel to an elderly negress. The negress feels the compliment, rather despises the complimenter, but likes it on the whole—and comes again.[32]

While the German studies the people who are to buy his goods in a spirit of subtlety, the Englishman makes up his mind without considering anybody save himself and his own ideas. In the days before competition assumed its present proportions this was all very well, perhaps; or at least it was not the commercial suicide that it certainly is to-day.

From the standpoint of the employer, the Englishman does not know his work. He has no money. He must, therefore, earn something. He expects to be allowed to earn and learn at one and the same time, which is an absurd notion.

The cause of all this is the same as that which sends out first-rate goods but to the wrong market.

The fact is, we do not study our markets seriously either for mercantile or for human exports.

If the South Sea Islanders want red cloth we send them yellow, and if in Patagonia there is an opening for men who are decent practical blacksmiths, we send them a stream of youths who have never fullered a shoe, but who are well up in the rudiments of Greek.

FOOTNOTE:
[32] I have watched with considerable interest the methods adopted by the Germans as opposed to those of the young man of our own race. I remember an instance of a German who set up as a chemist in a town out Central America way, and whose chief source of income came from the sale of drugs to rather impressionable negroes. In his place the Englishman would have laid in decent English drugs, would have sat behind his counter, and would have dispensed in stolid fashion to the limit of the abilities with which he was blessed. Not so our German friend. His drugs were good, but not supremely so; his prices were cost prices, with a mere shaving of profit.

But his method was excellent.

He made a character-study of each of his customers. He sold a fine tonic, coloured red and reported invincible. He put the title of Dr. before his name, and advertised free consultations, provided the patients bought their medicines at his store. He throve.

The expedition sent out to Patagonia under my charge by Mr. C. Arthur Pearson owed its origin to the discoveries made in that country by Dr. F. P. Moreno of certain remains of an animal, the Pampean Mylodon or Giant Ground Sloth, long believed to belong to the category of extinct prehistoric mammals. The marvellous state of preservation of the remains found at Last Hope Inlet seemed to give some ground for the supposition that the animal might possibly have survived to a recent period. Professor Ray Lankester, the Director of the British Museum of Natural History, in commenting upon the chance of the Mylodon being still alive in some remote and unknown region of Patagonia, said: "It is quite possible—I don't want to say more than that—that he still exists in some of the mountainous regions of Patagonia." These words from such an authority carried weight, and the question assumed an importance that made it worth all practicable examination. I have in the following pages put the whole case as clearly and as definitely as lies in my power.

To begin with, I give the story of Dr. Moreno's discovery as he himself told it to the Zoological Society, and the description of the remains by Dr. A. Smith Woodward, LL.D., F.R.S.

I. ACCOUNT OF THE DISCOVERY by Dr. MORENO

In November 1897 I paid a visit to that part of the Patagonian territory which adjoins the Cordillera of the Andes, between the 51st and 52nd degrees of South latitude, where certain surveyors, under my direction, were carrying out the preliminary studies connected with the boundary-line between Chile and Argentina; and in the course of this expedition I reached Consuelo Cove, which lies in Last Hope Inlet. In that spot, hung up on a tree, I found a piece of a dried skin, which attracted my attention most strangely, as I could not determine to what class of Mammalia it could belong, more especially because of the resemblance of the small incrusted bones it contained to those of the Pampean Mylodon. On inquiring whence it came, I was informed that it was only a fragment of a large piece of skin which had been discovered two years before, by some Argentine officers, in a cavern which existed in the neighbouring heights. Immediately on receiving this news, I hastened to the spot, guided by a sailor who had been present when the original discovery had been made. As, at that moment, I had no means of making more than a few hurried excavations, which gave no further traces of the discovery, I left orders that the search should be continued after my departure; but this once more also failed to give any ultimate results. Nothing could be found but modern remains of small rodents, and these chiefly on or near the surface of the ground. From the most careful inquiries which I set on foot, it appeared that, when the first discovery was made, no bones were found, the skin being half buried in the dust which had accumulated from the gradual falling away of the roof of the cavern, composed of Tertiary Conglomerate. It was only in the broad entrance to the cavern that were found a few human bones, borne thence to the shore of the Cove and afterwards broken up.

As already stated, the skin here presented to you formed but a small part of a larger one. One small piece had been carried off by Dr. Otto Nordenskjöld, and others by officers of the Chilian Navy, who later on had visited the spot. The inhabitants of the locality looked upon it as an interesting curiosity, some of them believing that it was the hide of a cow incrusted with pebbles, and others asserting that it was the skin of a large Seal belonging to a hitherto unknown species.

In Consuelo Cove, I embarked on board a small Argentine transport, which had been placed at my disposal to carry out the study of the western coast as far as Port Montt, in lat. 42°. At this latter place I left the steamer, which then proceeded to make a series of surveys. These lasted until her return to La Plata, at the latter end of July 1898, when she brought back to me the fragment of skin in question.

This is an accurate and true version of the discovery of this skin, which gave rise to the publication of Señor Ameghino's small pamphlet,[33] in which he gave an account of the discovery of a living representative of the "Gravigrades" of Argentina, distinguishing it by the name of "Neomylodon listai".

I have an idea that Señor Ameghino never saw the skin itself, but only some of the small incrusted bones, of which he had obtained possession. The vague form in which he draws up his account compels me to believe this suspicion to be true.

My opinion is that this skin belongs to a genuine Pampean Mylodon, preserved under peculiar circumstances resembling those to which we owe the skin and feathers of the Moa. I have always maintained that the Pampean Edentates, now extinct, disappeared only in the epoch which is called the "historical epoch" of our America. In the province of Buenos Aires, buried chiefly in the humus, I have found remains of Panochthus, and others of the same Mylodon from the seashore, all of which present the same characteristic marks of preservation as the remains of human beings discovered in the same spot. In this identical layer of the sea-shore, close to the bones I have also found stones polished by the hand of man, and flints cut like those found in the Pampean formation. In 1884, in a cavern near to the Rio de los Patos, in the Cordillera, I discovered some paintings in red ochre, one of which, in my opinion, resembles the Glyptodon on account of the shape of the carapace.

Ancient chroniclers inform us that the indigenous inhabitants recorded the existence of a strange, ugly, huge hairy animal which had its abode in the Cordillera to the south of lat. 37°. The Tehuelches and the Gennakens have mentioned similar animals to me, of whose existence their ancestors had transmitted the remembrance; and in the neighbourhood of the Rio Negro, the aged cacique Sinchel, in 1875, pointed out to me a cave, the supposed lair of one of these monsters, called "Ellengassen"; but I must add that none of the many Indians with whom I have conversed in Patagonia have ever referred to the actual existence of animals to which we can attribute the skin in question, nor even of any which answer to the suppositions of Señor Ameghino according to Señor Lista. It is but rarely that a few Otters (Lutra) are found in the lakes and rivers of the Andes, as in the neighbourhood of Lake Argentino, in the "Sierra de las Viscachas," and in the regions which I believe Señor Lista visited, there are only a few scarce Chinchillas (Lagidium), which have a colouring more dark greyish than those found to the north, and are in every case separated from these by a large extent of country.

The Pampean Edentata have in former days certainly existed as far south as the extreme limit of Patagonia. In 1874, in the bay of Santa Cruz, I met with the remains of a pelvis of one of these animals in Pleistocene deposits, and also remains of the mammals which are found in the same formation, such as the Macrauchenia and Auchenia. It would not be astonishing that the skin of one of these should have been preserved so long, because of the favourable conditions of the spot in which it was found.

The state of preservation of this piece of skin, at first sight, makes it difficult for one to believe it to be of great antiquity; but this is by no means an impossibility, if we consider the conditions of the cave in which it was found, the atmosphere of which is not so damp as one might at first imagine it to be, although it is situated in the woody regions near to the glaciers and lakes. It is well to mention that in 1877, under similar conditions, and in a much smaller cave, scarcely five metres from the waters of Lake Argentino, situated sixty miles more to the north, I discovered a mummified human body painted red, with the head still covered in part with its short hair wonderfully preserved, and wrapped up in a covering made of the skin of a Rhea, and holding in its arms a large feather of the Condor, also painted red; this was all covered up with a layer of grass and dust fallen from the roof of the cave. In another cave in the neighbourhood I discovered a large trunk of a tree, painted with figures in red, black, and yellow. The sides of the rock close to the entrance of the cave were covered with figures, some representing the human hand, others combinations of curved, straight, and circular lines, painted white, red, yellow, and green. Now, this mummy, which is preserved in the Museum of La Plata, does not belong to any of the actual tribes of Patagonia. Its skull resembles rather one of those more ancient races found in the cemeteries in the valley of the Rio Negro—a most interesting fact, since they belong to types which have completely disappeared from the Patagonian regions, and it is well known that the actual Tehuelches may be considered to have been the last indigenous races which reached the territory of Patagonia. Many a time the Tehuelches have spoken to me of these caves as abodes of the evil "spirits," and of the enigmatical painted figures they contained: some attributed the latter to these same "spirits," others to men of other races, of whom they have no recollection. In another cave, four hundred miles farther to the north, in 1880, I discovered other human bodies, more or less mummified and in good preservation, but of a different type, and beside them some painted poles which served to hold up their small tents, the use of which had already disappeared more than three centuries ago; together with the upper part of the skull of a child perfectly scooped out like a cup. And yet the historical Tehuelches, the same as all the indigenous races in the southern extremity of South America, hold their dead in great respect, and never use such drinking-vessels.

These proofs of the favourable conditions of the climate and of the lands near to the Cordillera, which are revealed to us by the preservation of objects undoubtedly dating from very remote epochs, strengthen my opinion that this skin of a huge mammal, which has long since disappeared, may well have been preserved till the present time.

I may add that a further careful search is now being made in the earth forming the floor of the cave, and I hope in due time to have the honour of communicating the results to this Society.

II. DESCRIPTION AND COMPARISON OF THE SPECIMEN by A. SMITH WOODWARD

(a) Description.

The problematical piece of skin discovered by Dr. Moreno measures approximately 0.48 m. in the direction of the main lie of the hair, while its maximum extent at right angles to this direction is about 0.55 m. The fragment, however, is very irregular in shape; and it has become much distorted in the process of drying, so that the anterior portion, which is directed upwards in the drawing, is bent outwards at a considerable angle to the main part of the specimen which will be claimed to represent the back. The skin, as observed in transverse section, presents a dried, felt-like aspect; but there is a frequent ruddiness, suggestive of blood-stains, while the margin exhibits distinct indications of freshly dried once-fluid matter, which Dr. Vaughan Harley has kindly examined and pronounced to be serum. Its outer face is completely covered with hair, except in the region marked C and above B, where this covering seems to have been comparatively fine and may have been accidentally removed. The inner face of the skin is only intact in a few places, the specimen having contracted and perhaps been somewhat abraded, so that a remarkable armour of small bony tubercles, irregularly arranged and of variable size, is exposed over the greater part of it. At one point there is an irregular rounded hole about 0.02 m. in diameter, which might possibly have been caused by a bullet or a dagger, but in any case was probably pierced when the skin was still fresh. Owing to its direction, this hole is partly obscured by the overhanging hair.

The skin in its dried state varies in thickness in different parts. The average thickness of the flattened portion, which must be referred to the back, is shown by the cleanly-cut right margin of the specimen to be 0.01 m. This is slightly increased towards the posterior (lower) end of the border, while above it the thickness becomes 0.015 m. The latter thickness also seems to be attained in the much-shrivelled corner marked C—a circumstance suggesting bilateral symmetry between at least part of the two anterior outer angles of the specimen. The thinnest portion preserved is the border above B; and the skin must also have been comparatively thin in the region of the accidental notch to the left, considerably below C.

The portion of skin above B is interesting not only from its relative thinness, but also from the occurrence of an apparently natural rounded concavity in the margin. This excavation, which measures

0.05 m. along the curve, is marked by the remains of a thin flexible flap, which is sharply bent outwards, and is covered with short hairs on its outer face. It is especially suggestive of the base of an ear-conch; and if this appearance be not deceptive, it is worthy of note that the dried skin hereabouts and in the region which would have to be interpreted as cheek (C) is much more wrinkled than elsewhere.

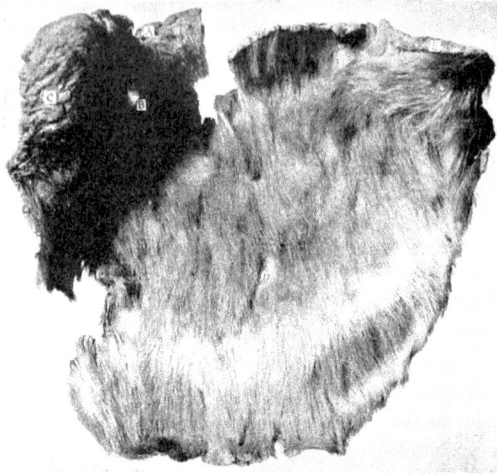

SKIN OF GRYPOTHERIUM, OUTER VIEW. ¼ NAT. SIZE

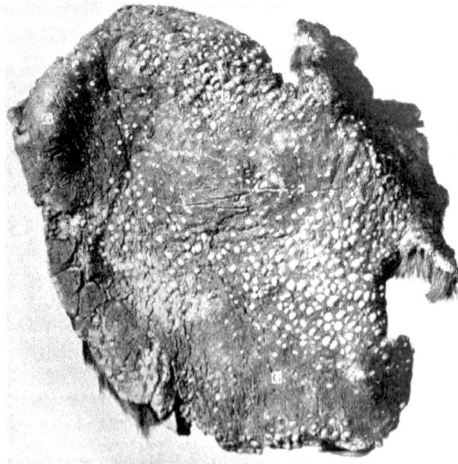

SKIN OF GRYPOTHERIUM, INNER VIEW. ¼ NAT. SIZE

As already mentioned, the outer aspect of the skin is completely covered with hair, which is very dense everywhere except on the left anterior corner. Here it seems to have been removed by abrasion. A small patch of hair has also clearly been pulled out near the gap in the left border of the specimen; and close to the middle (where marked D) there is a small hairless depression which may perhaps be interpreted as a wound inflicted and healed during life. The hair is only of one kind, without any trace of under-fur, and it is still very firmly implanted in the skin, without signs of decay. Its arrangement seems to be quite regular, there being no tendency towards its segregation into small groups or bundles. It is of a uniform dirty yellowish or light yellowish-brown colour, and, making due allowance for slight ruffling and distortion of the specimen, it may be described as all lying in one direction, vertically in the photograph, except at the two upturned anterior corners of the specimen, where there is an inclination from the right and left respectively towards the centre. The longest hairs, which usually measure from 0.05 m. to 0.065 m. in length, are observed in the half of the specimen in front of (above) the letter D. Those in the middle of the extreme anterior (upper) border measure from 0.03 m. to 0.05 m. in length, those at the hinder (lower) border about the same; while some of the comparatively small and delicate hairs on the supposed cheek are not longer than 0.01 m. The hairs are stiff, straight, or only very slightly wavy, and all are remarkably tough. Examined under the microscope, their cuticle is observed to be quite smooth, while the much-elongated cells of the cortex are readily distinguishable. Mr. R. H. Burne has kindly made some transverse sections, which prove the hairs to be almost or quite cylindrical, and none of the specimens examined present any trace of a medulla.

The dermal ossicles are very irregular in arrangement, but are to be observed in every part of the specimen, even in the comparatively thin region near the supposed ear. They form everywhere a very compact armour, and some of them are quite closely pressed together; rarely, indeed, there is a shallow groove crossing a specimen, possibly indicating two components which were originally separate. As shown by every part of the cut margin, and especially well in a small section prepared by Prof. Charles Stewart, they are all confined to the lower half of the dermis, never encroaching upon the upper portion in which the hair is implanted. It is also to be observed that, where the inner surface of the skin is intact, the ossicles are completely embedded and only faintly visible through the dry tissue. The exposure of a considerable number of them, as already mentioned, is due to the rupture and partial abrasion of this surface. No tendency to arrangement in parallel lines or bands can be detected; and large and small ossicles seem to be indiscriminately mingled, although of course allowance must be made, in examining sections and the abraded inner view of the skin, for differences in the plane of adjoining sections and varying degrees of exposure by the removal of the soft tissue. The largest ossicles are oblong in shape when viewed from within, and measure approximately 0.015 m. by 0.010 m.; but the majority are much smaller than these. They are very variable and irregular in form; but their inner face is generally convex, sometimes almost pyramidal, while the outer face of the few which have been examined is slightly convex, more or less flattened, without any trace of regular markings.

In microscopical structure the dermal ossicles are of much interest, and I have examined both horizontal and vertical sections, one of the former kindly prepared by Prof. Charles Stewart. The tissue is traversed in all directions by a dense mass of interlacing bundles of connective-tissue fibres, which exhibit an entirely irregular disposition, except quite at the periphery of the ossicle. Here they are less dense, and are arranged in such a manner as to form at least one darkened zone concentric with the margin in the comparatively translucent border. Occasionally, but not at all points, the fibres in this peripheral area may be observed to radiate regularly outwards. Numerous small vascular canals, frequently branching, are cut in various directions; and the bony tissue, which is developed in every part of the ossicle, exhibits abundant lacunæ. Nearly everywhere, except in the narrow peripheral area just mentioned, it is easy to recognise the bony laminæ arranged in Haversian systems round the canals; and most of the lacunæ between these laminæ are excessively elongated, with very numerous branching canaliculi, which extend at right angles to their longer axis. Near the margin of the ossicle, especially in its more translucent parts, the bone-lacunæ are less elongated, more irregular in shape, and apparently not arranged in any definite order. There is no clear evidence of bony laminæ concentric with the outer margin, though appearances are sometimes suggestive of this arrangement. A vertical section of an ossicle presents exactly the same features as the horizontal section now described. It is thus evident that the vascular canals with their Haversian systems of bone have no definite direction, but are disposed in an entirely irregular manner.

Taking into consideration all characters, and making comparisons with the aid of my friend Mr. W. E. de Winton, I am inclined to regard the fragmentary specimen as the skin of the neck and shoulder-region with part of the left cheek. The apparent bilateral symmetry between at least part of the thickened anterior outer angles of the specimen has already been noted; and if this observation be well founded, the middle line of the back extends vertically down the middle of the photograph, p. 306. If the rounded notch above B be the base of the external ear, as seems probable, the thick wrinkled skin (C) with fine short hair still further to the left must be the cheek. The ear and cheek on the right side have been removed; but at the base of the outwardly-turned angle on this side of the specimen there are the very long hairs which occupy a similar position on the left. It thus seems possible to estimate the transverse measurement between the ears as from 0.25 m. to 0.30 m., which corresponds with a tentative estimate of the same distance in Mylodon robustus based on a skull in the British Museum.

(b) Comparisons and General Conclusions.

The skin now described differs from that of all known terrestrial Mammalia, except certain Edentata, in the presence of a bony dermal armour. There can therefore be little doubt that the specimen has been rightly referred to a member of this typically South American order. Even among the Edentates, however, the fragment now under consideration is unique in one respect; for all the ossicles are buried deeply in the lower half of the thickened dermis and the hairs are implanted in every part of its upper half, whereas all the forms of bony armour hitherto described in this order reach the outer surface of the dermis and are merely invested with horny epidermis. This is the case, as is well known, in the common existing Armadillos, in which the hair is only implanted in the dermis between the separate parts of the armour. Even in the unique and remarkable skin of an Armadillo from Northern Brazil, described by Milne-Edwards under the name of Scleropleura bruneti[34] the bony plates and tubercles are still covered only by epidermis, although most of them are reduced to small nodules and might well have sunk more deeply into the abnormally hairy skin. There is also reason to believe that in the gigantic extinct Armadillos of the family Glyptodontidæ the same arrangement of dermal structures prevailed; for one specimen of Panochthus tuberculatus obtained by Dr. Moreno for the La Plata Museum actually shows the dried horny epidermis in direct contact with the underlying bone, and seems to prove that the numerous perforations in the Glyptodont dermal armour were not for the implantation of hairs (as once supposed), but for the passage of blood-vessels to the base of the epidermal layer. Similarly, among the extinct Ground-Sloths of the family Mylodontidæ dermal ossicles have been found with the remains of Cœlodon[35] and various forms (perhaps different subgenera) of Mylodon; but the only examples of this armour yet definitely described[36] exhibit a conspicuously sculptured outer flattened face, and it thus seems clear that Burmeister was correct in describing them as originally reaching the upper surface of the dermis and only covered externally by a thickened epidermis. It is, however, to be noted that Burmeister himself actually observed armour of this kind covering only the lumbar region of the trunk. He believed that the other parts of the animal were similarly armoured, because he had found "the same ossicles" on the digits of the manus, where they were "generally smaller and more spherical"; but he unfortunately omits to make any explicit statement as to the presence or absence of the characteristic external ornamentation on the latter.

The omission just mentioned is especially unfortunate, because on careful comparison it is evident that the irregular disposition of the small ossicles in the piece of skin now under consideration is most closely paralleled in the dermal armour of the extinct Mylodon, as already observed by Drs. Moreno and Ameghino. There is obviously no approach in this specimen to the definite and symmetrical arrangement of the armour such as is exhibited both by the existing Armadillos and the extinct Glyptodonts. There are, then, two possibilities. Either the dermal armour of Mylodon varied in different parts of the body, being sculptured and covered only by epidermis in the lumbar region, while less developed, not sculptured but completely buried in the dermis in the comparatively flexible neck and shoulder region—in which case Dr. Moreno may be correct in referring the problematical specimen to Mylodon; or the dermal ossicles of this extinct genus may have been uniform throughout, only differing in size and sparseness or compactness—in which case Dr. Ameghino is justified in proposing to recognise a distinct genus, Neomylodon.

To decide between these two possibilities, it is necessary to wait for additional information concerning the anterior dorsal armour of Mylodon as precise as that published by Burmeister in reference to the lumbar shield. Meanwhile it must suffice to compare the microscopical structure of the ossicles from the new skin with that of the small sculptured tubercles of undoubted Mylodon. It must be remembered that the specimen has been buried in the Pampa Formation for a long period, and that the oxides of iron and manganese have infiltrated the margin of the bone, rendering the structure of its outer border more conspicuous than that of its central portion. It must also be noted that some of the manganese has assumed its familiar "dendritic" aspect, in this respect presenting appearances not due to original structure. The calcified interlacing fibres of connective tissue are as abundant here as in the ossicle of the so-called Neomylodon; but in a very wide peripheral area they exhibit a marked radial disposition, nearly everywhere extending in bundles at right angles to the border. Rather large vascular canals, infiltrated with the oxides of iron and manganese, are observed in places, often bifurcated and usually bordered by a transparent zone free from the connective-tissue fibres. Well-developed bone-lacunæ are very abundant, many exhibiting short branching canaliculi, and most of the others very irregular in shape, evidently furnished with canaliculi which cannot be seen from lack of infiltration. The lacunæ are never much elongated, and are not arranged in distinctly differentiated Haversian systems in any part of the section; while the only regular disposition of the bony laminæ is traceable near the circumference, where the lacunæ are frequently arranged or clustered in parallel zones concentric with the border. A vertical section of one of the same specimens shows the connective-tissue fibres radiating outwards towards the lateral margins, but not directly towards the upper sculptured face. There are no bony laminæ clearly parallel with the latter face, and at least one vascular canal in transverse section seems to be the centre of a Haversian system.

The histological structure of the ossicles in the skin now under consideration thus resembles that of the sculptured tubercles of Mylodon in all essential features, but differs in two noteworthy respects. In the ossicles of the so-called Neomylodon, as already described, the fibres of connective tissue do not exhibit much definite radiation towards the lateral margin; while the bony tissue at most points is disposed in definite Haversian systems. There is thus enough discrepancy to justify the suspicion that the new and the old specimens do not belong to the same animal. In fact, so far as the differentiation of the dermal bone is concerned, the so-called Neomylodon is precisely intermediate between Mylodon and the existing Armadillo (Dasypus); sections of the scutes of the latter animal, both in the Royal College of

Surgeons and in the British Museum, showing that in this genus nearly the whole of the osseous tissue is arranged in Haversian systems, although abundant interlacing connective-tissue fibres are still entangled in it, at least near the border.

If the characteristic dermal armature does not suffice for the definite expression of an opinion as to the precise affinities of the specimen, a still less satisfactory result can be expected from a comparison of the hair. For, in the first place, no hair has hitherto been discovered in association with the skeleton of any extinct Ground-Sloth; while, secondly, the hairy covering of a mammal is perhaps that part of its organisation most readily adapted to the immediate circumstances of its life. So far as their endo-skeleton is concerned, the extinct Mylodonts and their allies are precisely intermediate between the existing Sloths and Anteaters; they combine "the head and dentition of the former with the structure of the vertebral column, limbs, and tail of the latter."[37] It might therefore be supposed that the hair of this extinct group would exhibit some of the peculiarities of that in one or other of its nearest surviving relatives. The epidermal covering of the piece of skin now described, however, entirely lacks the under-fur which is so thick in the Sloths; while the structure of each individual hair, with its smooth cuticle and lack of a medulla, is strikingly different from that observed both in the Sloths and Anteaters, and identical with that of the hair in the surviving Armadillos. The large hair in the Sloths and Tamandua exhibits a conspicuously scaly cuticle; while that of Myrmecophaga is remarkable for its very large medulla. All these animals now live in the tropics, either in forests or swamps, whereas the Patagonian animal must have existed under circumstances much like those under which the Armadillos still survive. Hence the characters of the hair of the so-called Neomylodon may be of no great importance in determining the affinities of the animal, but may represent a special adaptation to its immediate environment.

Finally, there is the question of the antiquity of the problematical skin. On two occasions I have examined the mummified remains of the extinct Mammoth and Rhinoceros from Siberia in the Imperial Academy of Sciences at St. Petersburg; I have also carefully studied the remains of the neck and legs of the Moa from a cavern in New Zealand, now in the British Museum. Compared with these shrivelled and dried specimens, the piece of skin from Patagonia has a remarkably fresh and modern aspect; and I should unhesitatingly express the opinion that it belonged to an animal killed shortly before Dr. Moreno recognised its interest, had he not been able to give so circumstantial an account of its discovery and strengthened his point of view by recording the occurrence of a human mummy of an extinct race in another cavern in the same district. The presence of an abundant covering of dried serum on one cut border of the skin is alone suggestive of grave doubts as to the antiquity of the specimen; but Dr. Vaughan Harley tells me that similar dried serum has been observed several times among the remains of the Egyptian mummies, and there seems thus to be no limit to the length of time for which it can be preserved, provided it is removed from all contact with moisture. I may add that I have searched in vain in the writings of Ramon Lista (so far as they are represented in the Library of the Royal Geographical Society) for some reference to the statement which the late traveller made verbally to Dr. Ameghino; and as the piece of skin now described certainly represents an animal almost gigantic in size compared with the Old-World Pangolin, I fear it cannot be claimed to belong to Lista's problematical quadruped, whatever that may prove to be.

The final result of these brief considerations is therefore rather disappointing. There are difficulties in either of the two possible hypotheses. We have a piece of skin quite large enough to have belonged to the extinct Mylodon; but unfortunately it cannot be directly compared with the dermal armour of that genus, because it seems to belong to the neck-region, while the only dermal tubercles of a Mylodont hitherto definitely made known are referable to the lumbar region. If it does belong to Mylodon, as Dr.

Moreno maintains, it implies either that this genus survived in Patagonia to a comparatively recent date, or that the circumstances of preservation were unique in the cavern where the specimen was discovered. On the other hand, if it belongs to a distinct and existing genus, as Dr. Ameghino maintains—and as most of the characters of the specimen itself would at first sight suggest—it is indeed strange that so large and remarkable a quadruped should have hitherto escaped detection in a country which has been so frequently visited by scientific explorers.

[P.S.—At the reading of this paper Prof. Ray Lankester remarked that he should regard the characters of the hair as specially important, and would not be surprised if the problematical piece of skin proved to belong to an unknown type of Armadillo. This possibility had occurred to me, but I had hesitated to mention it on account of the considerable discrepancy observable between the arrangement of the bony armour in Neomylodon and that in the known Glyptodonts and the unique Brazilian Armadillo (Scleropleura), which happen to exhibit an incompletely developed (incipient or vestigial) shield. In each of the latter cases, the armour is not subdivided into a compact mass of irregular ossicles, but consists of well-separated elements which could only become continuous by the addition of a considerable extent of bone round their margins, or by the special development of smaller intervening ossicles.

Since the paper was read, I have had the privilege of studying Dr. Einar Lönnberg's valuable description of the pieces of the problematical skin mentioned by Dr. Moreno as having been taken to Upsala by Dr. Otto Nordenskjöld.[38] It appears that with the skin was found the epidermal sheath of a large unknown claw, which may have belonged to the same animal. This specimen proves to be different from that of any existing Sloth, Anteater, or Armadillo, and is considered by Dr. Lönnberg to belong probably to the hind foot of a Mylodont, which did not walk on the exterior, lateral surfaces of the toes to the same extent as Mylodon. In a section of the skin provisionally ascribed to the leg, he observes that the small ossicles are very irregular, and shows two instances in which two are placed one above the other. In microscopical sections of the ossicles, however, he does not find the distinct Haversian systems of bone so conspicuous in my slides; and hence he fails to remark the differences between the structure of the armour in Neomylodon and Mylodon, which seem to me to be particularly noteworthy. His so-called "pigment cellules" in Mylodon are the dendritic infiltrations of oxide of manganese and stains of oxide of iron, to which I have made special reference. His observations as to the absence of a medulla in the hair confirm my own; but I have not seen any evidence of the suspected loss or disintegration of the hair-cuticle. Finally, Dr. Lönnberg has boiled a piece of the skin, thereby extracting glue, "which proves that the collagen and gelatinous substances are perfectly preserved." The latter observation confirms the evidence of the serum recorded above, and indicates that if the specimen is "of any considerable age, it must have been very well protected against moisture and bacteria."—A. S. W.]

III. DESCRIPTION OF ADDITIONAL DISCOVERIES by A. SMITH WOODWARD[39]

Last February, when presenting to the Zoological Society an account of the skin of a Ground-Sloth discovered in a cavern in Southern Patagonia, Dr. Moreno mentioned that further excavations were being made in the hope of finding other remains of the same animal. The task referred to was undertaken by Dr. Rudolph Hauthal, geologist of the La Plata Museum, who met with complete success.[40] He not only found another piece of skin, but also various broken bones of more than one individual of a large species of Ground-Sloth in a remarkably fresh state of preservation. Moreover, he discovered teeth of an extinct horse and portions of limb-bones of a large feline carnivore, in association with these remains; he likewise met with traces of fire, which clearly occurred in the same deposits as the so-called Neomylodon. All these remains were found beneath the dry earth on the floor of an enormous chamber which seemed to have been artificially enclosed by rude walls. In one spot they were scattered through a thick deposit of excrement of some gigantic herbivore, evidently the Ground-Sloth itself; in another spot they were associated with an extensive accumulation of cut hay. Dr. Hauthal and his colleagues, indeed, concluded that the cavern was an old corral in which the Ground-Sloths had been kept and fed by man.

As the result of these explorations, Dr. Moreno has now the gratification of exhibiting to the Society complete proof that the piece of skin described on the former occasion belongs to a genuine Pampean Ground-Sloth, not Mylodon itself, but a very closely related genus Grypotherium, of which skulls are already known from Pampean deposits in the Province of Buenos Aires.[41] The collection which we now have the privilege of examining distinctly supports his contention that the large quadruped in question belongs to an extinct fauna, though contemporary with man. The discovery is thus unique in the history of palæontology, on account of the remarkably fresh state of preservation of all the remains. Some of the new specimens exhibit no indication whatever of having been buried. Many of the bones retain their original whitish colour, apparently without any loss of gelatine; while both these and other bones, which have evidently been entombed in brownish dust, bear numerous remnants not only of the dried periosteum, but also of shrivelled muscles, ligaments, and cartilages. Very few of the bones are fossilised, in the ordinary sense of the term.

An admirable brief description of this collection has already been published (op. cit.) by Dr. Roth, who was the first to recognise the generic identity of Neomylodon with Grypotherium. Some of the specimens, however, are worthy of a more detailed examination; and Dr. Moreno has kindly entrusted them to me for study in connection with the collections in the British Museum and the Royal College of Surgeons. The following notes, supplementing Dr. Roth's original memoir, are the result of this further investigation.

1. REMAINS OF GRYPOTHRIUM LISTAI.

Number of Individuals.

Among the fragmentary bones of the Ground-Sloth, it is easy to recognise evidence of three individuals, which do not differ much in size. There are three distinct examples of the occiput and fragments of the dentigerous portion of three mandibles. It is also noteworthy that the three malar bones preserved are all different in shape, while three corresponding fragments of the acromial process of the scapula differ in size. One portion of maxilla seems to represent a fourth individual, being probably too small for either of the skulls to which the occiputs belong. Finally, as Dr. Roth has pointed out, one shaft of a humerus, which appears to be the bone of an adult, belongs to a much smaller animal than is indicated by any other specimen in the collection.

Remains of three individuals are thus recognisable with certainty; two others can probably be distinguished; while some of the fragments may even belong to a sixth specimen. It must also be noted that other portions of jaws are said to have been discovered by E. Nordenskjöld.[42]

Skull and Mandible.

The largest portion of cranium (No. 1) is not stained in any way, and does not retain a trace of the material in which it was buried in any hollow or crevice. It does not appear to have been damaged during excavation, but exhibits fractures which were almost certainly made when the animal was freshly killed. The cranial roof near the occipital region is battered in four places, though the injuries do not affect the brain-case itself; while the right occipital condyle is partly removed by a sharp, clean cut. There can, indeed, be no doubt that the animal was killed and cut to pieces by man.

This skull is evidently that of an adult animal, all the sutures in the hinder region being closed. The inner wall of the temporal fossa is much flattened, without any irregular convexities, but marked with the characteristic reticulately-decussating, fine ridges of bone, and studded with adherent patches of muscle-fibre. The upper border of the fossa is a remarkably sharp edge, while the narrow flattened cranial roof is only marked by a faint longitudinal median furrow and by a diminutive tuft of fibre in a small median pit near the occipital edge.[43] The fractures exhibit the very large cancelled chambers surrounding the brain-case dorso-laterally; while a median longitudinal section shows both these cells and others in the basi-sphenoid. The basi-cranial axis is nearly straight, inclining a little upwards in front. The anterior condyloid foramina piercing the basi-occipital are remarkably large, as usual; the basi-sphenoid is very long and narrow, flattened mesially on its lower face, but with one slight median prominence near its hinder end; the pre-sphenoid forms a short acute rostrum, above which there are remains of the vomer. The hinder ends of the pterygoids are shown to be inflated with large cancellæ, but the sides of the base of the skull are somewhat obscured by the dried soft parts. The mastoid process of the periotic, with its articular facette for the stylohyal, seems to be rather smaller than in Mylodon. The tympanic bone is preserved on the right side, though wanting on the left. It is an irregular curved plate only slightly bullate, but forming a complete floor to the tympanic cavity. As usual in Edentata, it is not produced into an auditory meatus.

The right maxilla (No. 4) is in precisely the same state of preservation as the specimen just described, and probably belongs to the same skull. Its anterior margin is perfectly preserved, indicating that the facial region is very short in front of the anterior end of the zygomatic arch, which is pierced by a rather large suborbital canal. Its upper border proves that the nasal region was raised into a slightly convex dome; while its antero-superior angle is not rounded as in Mylodon, but curves upwards and forwards and ends in a point as in Grypotherium. At the oral border there are the shattered bases of four teeth.

A fragment of the nasal region (No. 13) may also have belonged to the same skull, but its state of preservation is a little different from that of the two specimens just described. It has clearly been buried in a powdery deposit, which has stained it brown; but the enveloping dust must have been extremely dry, for fragments of cartilage adhere to it, as well preserved as in the nasal chamber of the cranium itself (No. 1). It also bears traces of the integument.

Judging by the figures of the skull of Grypotherium published by Reinhardt (loc. cit.), this specimen seems to have occupied an anterior position in the nasal region. It is thus of great interest, because the three known skulls of Grypotherium leave the precise nature of the bony arcade separating the narial openings undecided. According to Reinhardt, the nasal bones terminate as in Mylodon, and the arcade is an element interposed between them and the premaxillæ. According to Burmeister, the nasals themselves extend forwards and constitute the greater part, if not the whole, of the problematical bar. The fragment now under consideration is clearly in favour of the latter interpretation. Its lower thickened end is a massive bone, not bilaterally symmetrical, and not showing any trace of a median suture. Its inferior face is irregular and roughened, and can scarcely be regarded as an articular facette. Its upper portion consists of a pair of bones separated by a very well-marked median longitudinal suture. These are not thickened at their contracted upper end, where they have evidently been broken, and are not quite bilaterally symmetrical. They doubtless fuse at their lower end with the problematical azygous bone already mentioned, but the arrangement is obscured by the enveloping soft parts. A pair of bones, which may be regarded as nasals, thus extend forwards in a narrow arch to a point just above the anterior end of the premaxillæ; while the massive bone effecting a union between the two normal pairs of elements is probably an ossification in the internasal septum. It is interesting to note that there is an incipient trace of a similar forward production of the nasals in the genus Scelidotherium; while there is sometimes an ossification of the internasal septum in Megatherium.[44]

The three specimens now described, when placed approximately in their natural positions, afford a very satisfactory idea of the form and proportions of the skull when complete. The malar bone is the only important part to be added; but unfortunately it is impossible to decide which of the three specimens of this element in the collection belongs to the individual now under consideration. As already mentioned, these three bones are all different in the shape and proportions of the hinder bifurcated end. They are all very fresh in appearance, but have been stained reddish-brown by the earth in which they must have been buried.

The hinder portion of the second skull already mentioned (No. 2) comprises the occiput and brain-case as far forward as the front of the cerebral hemispheres. It is much battered and broken, and in quite as fresh a state as the cranium already described, with a considerable investment of dried soft parts on its base. It is only very slightly smaller than No. 1, but is of interest as exhibiting some of the sutures, besides a roundness and smoothness indicative of immaturity. The supraoccipital is shown to be very large; a small median point of it enters the foramen magnum, while the suture separating it from the parietals and squamosals extends along the rounded lambdoidal ridge. The horizontally extended suture between the squamosal and parietal on the inner wall of the temporal fossa is seen in the position where Owen determined it to occur in Mylodon.[45] Both tympanics are preserved, but they are more obscured by soft parts than in No. 1.

To this cranium probably belongs a detached portion of the left side of the facial region (No. 5), in a similar state of preservation and slightly smaller than the maxilla (No. 4). The suture between the frontal and the maxilla still persists, while the oral border is preserved farther forward than in the last-mentioned specimen, showing a fragment of the much-reduced premaxilla united with the maxilla by a jagged suture.

The third imperfect occiput is about as large as the immature specimen No. 2, but does not exhibit any features worthy of special note.

The largest and most important portions of the mandible are Nos. 9 and 11, which evidently belong to the right and left rami of one and the same jaw. They are much broken and are in the same fresh condition as the skulls, with traces of the periosteum and even considerable portions of the soft parts of the gum. The right ramus is preserved sufficiently far forwards to show that there was no caniniform tooth in front of the series of four ordinary molars. Judging by the extent of the latter series, the specimen probably belongs to the same individual as the skull No. 1.

Another portion of a mandibular ramus (No. 10) of the left side is slightly smaller than the last and may well have belonged to the immature individual No. 2. It is similarly quite fresh in appearance, and bears the shrivelled remains of the gum. It is interesting as exhibiting the two posterior molars slightly different in shape from those of the former mandible. In this specimen the longer axis of the third molar is oblique, whereas in No. 9 it is coincident with the axis of the mandible; while in the former the fourth molar is not so long in proportion to its width as in the latter. Such slight differences, however, cannot be regarded in the Edentata as more than individual variations.

Brain-cavity and Cerebral Nerves.

By the kind permission of Dr. Moreno, the cranium No. 1 has been vertically bisected to display the character of the cranial cavity and the nerve-foramina. An instructive plaster-cast of the cavity has thus been made by Mr. C. Barlow, the Formatore of the British Museum.

The olfactory lobes are shown to have been well developed, projecting a little in front of the cerebral hemispheres. These hemispheres are together somewhat longer than broad, slightly broader behind than in front, and a little constricted in the middle. They do not overlap the cerebellum, which is relatively large. The origins of the nerves are very imperfectly shown in the cast; only their exits from the cranial cavity are clear. The most interesting are the optic and trigeminal nerves, which pass out of the cranial cavity at first by a common exit, which is soon subdivided by a bony partition into two canals, the former no less than 0.08 m., the latter 0.045 m. in length. The fourth, seventh, eighth and twelfth nerves are also recognisable on the cast; and one prominence of plaster has filled the foramen lacerum posterius.

Compared with the brains of Mylodon and Scelidotherium, so far as known from casts of the cranial cavity,[46] that of Grypotherium is observed to be more elongated, with less divergent and prominent olfactory lobes, less constricted cerebral hemispheres, and a larger cerebellum. In the form and proportions of the cerebrum and cerebellum, it similarly differs from Megatherium.[47] The cerebral hemispheres of the existing Cholœpus didactylus and Bradypus tridactylus[48] are more tapering forward, and their cerebellum is relatively smaller than in Grypotherium.

Auditory Ossicles.

The auditory ossicles were preserved in the tympanic cavities of both skulls, Nos. 1 and 2, being retained by the dried soft parts. They were detected by Prof. Charles Stewart, who kindly extracted them, with great skill, from both sides of each skull. Comparing these ossicles with the fine collection in the Royal College of Surgeons, they prove to be closely similar to those of all the existing Sloths, but most nearly resembling those of Cholœpus didactylus. The malleus is bent exactly as in the latter species, and is of similar shape. As observed by Prof. Stewart, it is remarkable in articulating with the incus not only by the head, but also by a diminutive lower facet, which is in contact with a small facetted process on the anterior arm of the incus. A feeble indication of the same secondary articulation is also observable in Cholœpus; but it is curiously absent in the second specimen of Grypotherium. The two divergent arms of the incus are equal in length, as usual in the Sloths. The stapes is only very slightly perforated in both specimens; while a small circular disc firmly fixed to the incus represents the orbicular bone in the second skull. The auditory ossicles of Grypotherium, therefore, are very different from those of Myrmecophaga, in which the malleus is less sharply bent, the incus has divergent arms of unequal length, and the stapes exhibits a large perforation.[49]

Vertebræ and Limb-bones.

Nearly all the remains of vertebræ and limb-bones are in the same state of preservation as the portions of skull and mandible already described, with adherent cartilage and traces of muscles and ligaments. With some of the ungual phalanges there are also well-preserved examples of the epidermal sheath. As already remarked by Roth, the edges of one sheath probably belonging to the fourth digit of the manus, are quite sharp, and indicate that if the animal walked on its fore feet it resembled Myrmecophaga in the peculiar twist of the manus.

All the specimens in this series seem to have been accurately determined and sufficiently described by Roth. It is only necessary to emphasise the fact that the two shafts of humerus with abraded, not sharply broken, ends have a much more fossilised appearance than any other specimen in the collection, and are deeply stained throughout by ferruginous matter. The small shaft, No. 22, certainly seems to have belonged to an adult animal, as remarked by Roth, and it was probably much smaller than any individual indicated by the other remains.

Skin and Hair.

The new piece of skin, which is stated by Hauthal to have been found in the deposit of excrement, is not quite so well preserved as the original piece. It is much folded in an irregular manner; and the hair, which is yellower than in the previous specimen, is preserved only in patches on the outer face. It must have been stripped from the body of the animal by man; but the only distinct marks of tools, which were evidently made when the skin was fresh, are a few indents and small pits on the outer face. The indents must have been made by oblique thrusts of a stick, or a small, blunt, chisel-shaped instrument. The small pittings are nearer the middle of the specimen and less conspicuous. A vacuity in the skin seems to be due to accidental tearing or to a thrust after it was dry: it may even have been caused by the fallen blocks of stone found lying upon it.

The specimen, as preserved, measures about a metre across in one direction by 93 centimetres in another direction. As already observed by Roth, its irregular folding makes the determination of its position on the trunk very difficult; but I am convinced that its state of preservation is not sufficiently good to justify an attempt to unfold the skin by the ordinary method of steaming. Taking all facts into consideration, Roth seems to be correct in ascribing it to the right flank and the postero-superior part of one of the limbs. It most probably belongs to the fore limb, as Roth supposes; but there is no clear proof that it is not referable to the hind-quarters.

The original situation of the piece of skin being thus determined, it is interesting to observe the disposition of the ossicles in the lower layer. Owing to abrasion, contraction, and partial disintegration, they are conspicuous in most parts of the specimen. They are very irregular in shape and size, and closely compacted together, as in the previous specimen. It is, however, to be noted that in some parts there is a distinct tendency to arrangement in regular, straight, parallel rows. The long axes of the elongated ossicles are nearly always coincident with the direction of these rows. They are especially well shown on the middle of the flank; and, as might be expected, the rows are here disposed vertically, parallel with the ribs.

In some parts of the skin the ossicles are exposed on their outer face; but appearances render it almost certain that this exposure is due to the disintegration and abrasion of the specimen. In one patch thus uncovered by the removal of the soft parts, the ossicles are seen to form a closely arranged, flattened pavement; and their outer face is much more conspicuously marked by pittings than that of any ossicle extracted from the first discovered piece of skin. In fact, as Roth remarks, the pitting is here quite similar to that observable on many ossicles dug up in association with the fossil skeletons of Mylodon; though it does not form so regular a reticulate pattern as that of the dermal ossicles of Mylodon in the British Museum figured on the former occasion.[50]

Another interesting feature of the new piece of skin consists in the dwindling and even total absence of the ossicles towards the ventral border. A section along the edge exhibits only two diminutive nodules of bone in a length of 0.1 m.; while another similar section taken vertically from the skin of the limb shows no trace of ossicles, except perhaps two little specks. It must, however, be noted that the limb was not entirely destitute of armour; for on the border the bones are as well developed and conspicuous as on the middle of the flank. In the newly-cut sections the skin has a translucent aspect, showing that it is merely dried and not tanned in any way.

The hair on the new specimen varies in length from 0.07 m. or 0.10 m. to 0.15 m. or 0.22 m. It is thus longer than that of the previous piece of skin. Masses of still longer hairs—some 0.30 m. in length—were found detached among the excrement, and these are also believed by Roth to belong to the same animal. His determination is probably correct; for, when examined microscopically, these long hairs are observed to have a perfectly smooth cuticle, while some transverse sections (kindly made by Mr. R. H. Burne) demonstrate the complete absence of a medulla, exactly as in the short hairs. The latter feature proves that they cannot be referred either to the horse or to the guanaco.

Excrement.

The large cylindrical pieces of excrement, which may be referred to Grypotherium without any hesitation, have already been described and figured by Dr. Roth. They consist of irregular discoids of herbaceous matter closely pressed together, the largest measuring no less than 0.18 m. in diameter. Mr. Spencer Moore has kindly examined them from the botanist's point of view and reports that they are composed "in large part apparently of grasses, as the haulms, leaf-sheaths, fragments of leaves, &c., of these plants are frequent in the mass. A spikelet, almost entire, of what seems to be a species of Poa, and the flowering glume of another grass, probably avenaceous, have also been found. Besides these there are at least two dicotyledonous plants, one herbaceous and the other almost certainly so, the latter having a slender greatly sclerotised stem. Unfortunately, as no leaves have hitherto been observed attached to the fragments of stem, their affinities are altogether doubtful. There are numerous silicious particles in the excrement, and there are many pieces of the underground parts of the plants, suggesting that they have been pulled out of the ground. A few pieces of stems are sharply cut, not bruised or torn at the end." The latter fact is especially important in connection with Dr. Hauthal's discovery of cut hay in the cavern, and his theory that the Grypotherium was kept in captivity and fed by man.

Generic and Specific Determination.

The fortunate discovery of all parts of the skull and dentition renders the generic determination of this Ground-Sloth now quite certain. The teeth show that it belongs to the family Mylodontidæ; the presence of only four instead of five upper molars separates it from the genera Mylodon, Lestodon, and Scelidotherium; the forward production of the nasals and the ossification of part of the internarial septum place it definitely in the allied genus Grypotherium, as originally diagnosed by Reinhardt. The only question needing consideration is, whether the fragment of cranium described by Owen in 1840 as the type of the genus Glossotherium[51] is really identical with that subsequently described by Reinhardt under the name of Grypotherium darwini, as now seems to be commonly believed.

Darwin's original specimen, on which the genus Glossotherium of Owen was founded, is preserved in the Museum of the Royal College of Surgeons. It has thus been possible to compare it directly with the undoubted cranium of Grypotherium from the Patagonian cavern. The specimen is merely the left half of the hinder part of the cranium, and is therefore very inadequate for discussion; but several features seem worthy of note. Compared with the new skull No. 1, the fragment named Glossotherium has (i.)

the inner wall of the temporal fossa less flattened, (ii.) the digastric fossa deeper in proportion to its width, (iii.) the hinder border of the inflated pterygoid vertical, instead of sloping downwards and forwards, (iv.) a much larger and deeper pit for the articulation of the stylohyal, and (v.) a longer canal penetrating the base of the occipital condyle for the passage of the hypoglossal nerve. In all these respects the so-called Glossotherium agrees much more closely with the typical Mylodon; and Owen was probably correct in 1842 when he expressed the opinion that the two are at least generically identical.[52]

I am therefore of opinion that Grypotherium is the correct generic name for the Ground-Sloth from the Patagonian cavern, while Glossotherium must be relegated to the synonymy of Mylodon.

The specific determination of the new specimens is more difficult. As remarked by Roth, only two species of Grypotherium seem to be already known from the Pampa formation—G. darwini by three skulls[53] and G. bonaerense solely by a maxilla.[54] The portions of skull and dentition now under discussion indicate an animal much larger than G. bonaerense (assuming the original maxilla to be that of an adult); while they are considerably smaller than any known specimen of G. darwini. Moreover, the nasal arcade now described is narrower and more concave on its outer face than that of G. darwini, as already observed by Roth. It thus seems very probable that the animal from the Patagonian cavern represents a distinct species, which must bear the name of G. listai. This specific name was given by Ameghino to a fragment of the first-discovered piece of skin, and the curious argument which leads Roth to propose the substitution of a new name for it does not affect its validity.

It may be added that Dr. Erland Nordenskjöld has recently compared his specimens from the Patagonian cavern with the skull of Grypotherium darwini at Copenhagen, and finds no specific difference.[55] No particulars however, have yet been published.

2. ASSOCIATED MAMMALIAN REMAINS.

Felis, sp.

A feline carnivore larger than the existing Jaguar (Felis onca), but about the same size as an average Tiger (F. tigris), is represented in the collection by the distal half of a right humerus (No. 44), a left fourth metatarsal (No. 46), and the distal end of another metatarsal (No. 47). These bones have evidently been buried in dust, but are in the same fresh state of preservation as those of Grypotherium.

Careful comparison of these bones shows that they are undoubtedly feline; and there is no difficulty in determining that they belong to Felis rather than to the extinct Machærodus. A humerus of M. neogæus, from a Brazilian cavern, now in the British Museum (No. 18972 b), is readily distinguished from the new Patagonian humerus by the remarkable lateral compression of its shaft and the much greater downward extension of its prominent and sharp deltoid ridge. The humerus in all the large species of Felis, on the other hand, only differs from the fossil now under discussion in very small particulars. In fact, the humerus and metatarsals of the existing Felis onca are essentially identical with the bones from the Patagonian cavern, except that they are rather smaller. I am therefore inclined to regard the newly discovered remains as indicating a comparatively large variety of F. onca, which once lived in the temperate regions of Patagonia, beyond the present range of this species. Such an occurrence would be a precise parallel to that of the Cave-Lion in Europe. It is well known that nearly all the remains of F. leo found in the Pleistocene formations of the temperate parts of the Old World indicate animals of somewhat larger size than any surviving in the warmer regions to which the species is now confined.[56]

It may be noted that bones of the Jaguar of ordinary dimensions have been recorded from the Pampa formation of the Province of Buenos Aires.[57]

Arctotherium, sp.

With the bones of Felis just noticed, Roth provisionally associates the imperfect distal end of a remarkably large right femur. He is thus induced to suppose that the carnivore represented by the fragments will prove to be a new genus and species of the Felidæ. He suggests for it the name of Iemisch listai, on the assumption that it is the mysterious quadruped which Ameghino states is known to the natives as the Iemisch.

A comparison of the distal end of the femur in question with the femora of Felidæ in the British Museum seems to prove conclusively that it cannot be referred even to the same family. Its width across the condyles is much greater, compared with its antero-posterior diameter, than that observed in any feline. Moreover, the pit for the tendon of the popliteus muscle below the external condyle is unusually deep. In both these respects the bone closely resembles the distal end of the femur of a Bear. I have been therefore led to compare it with the corresponding part of the extinct Bear of the Pampean formation, Arctotherium.

Fortunately, the fine and nearly complete skeleton of Arctotherium bonaerense in the Bravard Collection in the British Museum comprises the right femur and enables direct comparison to be made. The fragment lacks the inner condyle; but enough of the trochlea remains to show its broad and gently-rounded form, with a wide and deep intertrochlear notch, precisely as in Arctotherium. It has the same development of the external condyle as in the latter, while the fossa for the popliteal tendon is equally deep, only slightly differing in shape. In fact, there is very little discrepancy, except in its smaller size; and species of Arctotherium smaller than A. bonaerense are already known both from the Pampa formation of Argentina[58] and the caverns of Brazil.[59]

The fragment just described has evidently been severed from the rest of the bone by a sharp, clean cut made by man; and Dr. Hauthal is quite certain that this was not done by one of his workmen during excavation (op. cit. p. 59). At least one medium-sized species of Arctotherium must therefore have survived until the human period in Southern Patagonia.[60]

Onohippidium saldiasi.

A horse is represented in the collection by an upper molar, a fragment of premaxilla with two incisors, an imperfect atlas and two well-preserved hoofs apparently of a fœtus or perhaps of a newly-born animal. Of these remains only the upper molar is capable of satisfactory determination.

This tooth is the second upper molar of the left side, and has been exhaustively compared with corresponding teeth by Dr. Roth, who gives a good series of figures. It is readily distinguished from the homologous molar in the genus Equus by the peculiar form of its two inner columns—a fact which I have been able to verify by the examination of an extensive series of specimens, both recent and fossil, in the British Museum. Further comparison, indeed, shows that it must be referred to the extinct Pampean genus Onohippidium.[61] Roth assigns it, apparently quite rightly, to the same species as a maxilla from the Pampean formation of the Province of Buenos Aires, for which he proposes the name of Onohippidium saldiasi.

Large Extinct Rodent.

The proximal end of the femur of a large rodent has already been recognised by Roth, and compared with the extinct Megamys. It cannot be more exactly determined.

Existing Species.

One imperfect fragment of pelvis and sacrum seems to belong to a puma (Felis concolor) of rather large size; but it is not sufficient for precise determination.

The small mandibular ramus of a musteline referred by Dr. Roth to Mephitis suffocans, does not pertain to this genus and species. Mr. Oldfield Thomas determines it to belong to the rare Lyncodon patagonicus, which still lives in Patagonia and has not hitherto been found fossil. A slightly larger extinct species of the same genus has been described by Ameghino on the evidence of a skull from the Pampean formation near Lujan, in the Province of Buenos Aires.[62]

A cranium, some vertebræ, and a tibia and fibula appear to represent the existing Ctenomys magellanicus, as noted by Roth.

The remains of the Guanaco (Lama huanacos) do not present any features worthy of special remark.

Man is represented by a diseased scapula and by two bone awls, which are clearly made from the tibia of a species of Canis intermediate in size between C. jubatus and C. magellanicus.

3. RELATIVE AGE OF THE REMAINS

As the result of Dr. Roth's researches, supplemented by the additional observations now recorded, it is evident that the majority of the mammalian remains from the cavern near Last Hope Inlet belong to the extinct fauna which occurs in the Pampean formation of more northern regions. To this category are referable the genera Grypotherium, Onohippidium, Megamys, and Arctotherium; also Macrauchenia, which is said to have been discovered in the same deposit on the floor of the cave by Dr. E. Nordenskjöld. The large Felis likewise probably belongs to the same series. Remains of mammals of the existing fauna, on the other hand, are comparatively few and insignificant, referable to the genera Ctenomys, Cervus, Lama, Lyncodon, and Felis.

Although Dr. Hauthal's explorations were rather hurried and Dr. Nordenskjöld's results have only been published hitherto in abstract,[63] their account of the deposits on the floor of the cavern seem to confirm the suspicion that the remains of these two faunas were introduced at two successive periods. According to Hauthal, the remains of the Guanaco were found along with fragmentary bones of Deer, shells of Mytilus chorus, branches of trees, and dried leaves, in the superficial dust of the cavern near the outer wall. The skin of Grypotherium and all the other remains of this and the associated Pampean genera were discovered in the deeper layer of excrement and cut hay between the mound and the inner wall of the cavern. According to Nordenskjöld, three distinct strata can be recognised on the floor of the cavern as follows:

A. A thin surface layer, containing ashes, shells, and bones of recent animals broken by man.

B. A middle layer, containing numerous branches of trees and dried leaves, with remains of Lama and the extinct horse, Onohippidium. Said to be probably the stratum in which the original piece of skin was found.

C. A bottom layer, usually about a metre in thickness, without any traces of branches or leaves, but only dried herbs. Remains of Grypotherium numerous and confined to this stratum, associated with its excrement and hair, also with remains of a large variety of Felis onca, Macrauchenia, and Onohippidium.

It is unfortunate that the question of the contemporaneity of the various bones cannot be tested by the ingenious method of chemical analysis which has been applied with success to similar problems by M. Adolphe Carnot in France. The French chemist has shown that when bones are buried in ordinary sediments they undergo changes which gradually cause the percentage of contained fluorine to increase. According to him, the longer a bone has been buried, the greater is the percentage of fluorine found in it on analysis. In one case[64] he examined the scapula of a deer and a human tibia, discovered together in fluviatile sand near Billancourt (Seine); he found that the former had seven or eight times its usual percentage of fluorine, while the human bone did not differ in any respect from the normal in this constituent. He therefore concluded that the latter bone was not of the same age as the former, but had been introduced comparatively recently by burial. In this and the other recorded cases, however, it is to be observed that the sediment was of a uniform character and admitted of free percolation of water. In the Patagonian cavern, on the contrary, the bones occur partly in dust, partly in dried herbage, partly in dried excrement, and partly in the burnt residue of the same. Moreover, they must always have been subjected to intense dryness, and the usual process of chemical alteration cannot have taken place.

Considering all circumstances, I think that, even without chemical evidence, zoologists and geologists cannot fail now to agree with Dr. Moreno and his colleagues of the La Plata Museum, that the remarkably preserved Grypotherium from the Patagonian cavern belongs to the extinct Pampean fauna of South America, and need not be searched for in the unexplored wilds of that continent. If we accept the confirmatory evidence afforded by Mr. Spencer Moore, we can also hardly refuse to believe that this great Ground-Sloth was actually kept and fed by an early race of man.

IV. NOTE CONCERNING TEHUELCHE LEGENDS by HESKETH PRICHARD

I now proceed to give the testimony of Dr. F. Ameghino, whose brother Carlos was well acquainted with the country and who early gave it as his opinion that the animal, which is named the Neomylodon listai, was still living in Patagonia. In support of his opinion he adduced tales which Carlos Ameghino had gathered from the Indians, who roam the pampas, of a vast mysterious beast said by them to haunt the distant lagoons and forests of the unexplored regions near the Andes. These stories had, moreover, been confirmed in Dr. Ameghino's opinion by the experience of the late well-known geographer and traveller, Señor Ramon Lista, who verbally told both Dr. Ameghino and his brother that he had seen and fired at a mysterious creature, which, however, disappeared in the brushwood and could not afterwards be traced. He described it as being covered with reddish-grey hair, and he believed it to be a pangolin or scaly-anteater.[65] Taking all things into consideration, Dr. Ameghino announced his conviction that the mysterious animal referred to was the last representative of a group, long believed extinct, related to the Mylodon.

According to Dr. Ameghino the Indians had bestowed upon the mysterious animal the name of Iemisch. Nothing would induce them to penetrate into the supposed haunts of this monster. It was described as amphibious, equally at home on land or in the water; in remote mountain recesses it lurked in caves, or had its lairs by the shores of lonely lagoons and rivers, or at times lay in wait among the lower passes of the Cordillera. In habits it was nocturnal, and its strength so great that it could seize a horse in its claws, and hold itself down to the bottoms of the lakes! The head was supposed to be short and without external ears, but showing enormous dog-teeth: the feet short and bear-like, armed with formidable claws united by a swimming membrane; the long tail, tapering and prehensile, the hair hard and of a uniform yellowish-brown. In size it far exceeded any creature they knew of, its legs, though short, being almost as great in girth as its body. It followed, naturally that narratives of personal experiences and encounters with this terrific animal were varied.

These data, it must be confessed, were bewildering. In fact, as described by the Indians the Iemisch was scientifically absurd; but the Indian is like a child in many ways and would naturally endow a creature he feared with extraordinary attributes.

I will quote here an extract from Winwood Reade's "Savage Africa," one of the finest books of travel ever written.

"It must be laid down as a general principle that man can originate nothing; that lies are always truths embellished, distorted, or turned inside out. There are other facts beside those which lie on the surface, and it is the duty of the traveller and the historian to sift and wash the gold-grains of truth from the dirt of fable.... It is true that some of the ancient myths have been sobered down to natural beings. The men with dogs' heads of whom Herodotus speaks are the barking baboons which I saw in Senegal: the men with their head under their shoulders, their eyes in their breast, are the ill-formed negroes, whose shoulders are shrugged up, and whose heads drop on their breasts: the mermaids of the Arab tales are the sea-cows of the African rivers, which have feminine dugs and a face almost human in expression: the huge serpent which opposed the army of Regulus is now well known as the python: the burning mountains which Hanno saw, and the sounds of the lutes which were believed to proceed from the strife of the elements, are only caused by the poor negroes burning the grass of their hill-tops: the music being that of their flutes, as I have heard it often in those long and silent African nights far away.

"Incredulity has now become so vulgar a folly, that one is almost tempted, out of simple hatred for a fashion, to run into the opposite extreme. However, I shall content myself with citing evidence respecting certain unknown, fabulous and monstrous animals of Africa, without committing myself to an opinion one way or the other; preserving only my conviction that there is always a basis of truth to the most fantastic fables, and that, by rejecting without inquiry that which appears incredible, one throws away ore in which others might have found a jewel. A traveller should believe nothing, for he will find himself so often deceived: and he should disbelieve nothing, for he will see so many wonderful things; he should doubt, he should investigate, and then, perhaps, he may discover."

It was in this spirit that I set out for the interior of Patagonia. Although the legends of the Indians were manifestly to a large extent the result of imaginative exaggeration, yet I hoped to find a substratum of fact below these fancies. After thorough examination, however, I am obliged to say that I found none. The Indians not only never enter the Cordillera but avoid the very neighbourhood of the mountains. The rumours of the Iemisch and the stories concerning it, which, in print, had assumed a fairly definite form, I found nebulous in the extreme when investigated on the spot.

Finally, after much investigation I came to the conclusion that the Indian legends in all probability refer to some large species of otter. Musters, in his book "At Home with the Patagonians," makes mention of an animal much feared by the tribe with whom he travelled, which they called "water-tiger," and which they said lived in a rapid and deep river near to Nahuel-huapi, a lake the name of which lends colour to the tale, for it means Tigers' Island. Musters says he himself saw two ostriches, that, being considered in too poor a condition to be worth taking to camp for food, were left on the bank of the river referred to, torn and partly devoured when on the following day he and his party revisited the spot. Tracks of an animal were also plainly visible leading down into the water.

Compare this with a story told me by Mr. Von Plaaten Hallermund. He described the case of a mule which had fallen over a precipice in the vicinity of the River Deseado. When on the following day the peones climbed down to salve its cargo, they found the animal on the edge of the water half eaten, and in its neighbourhood were tracks strange to them. "Like those of a puma, yet not those of a puma," as they said.

The manager of Messrs. Braun and Blanchard's store at Santa Cruz gave me a description of a skin brought in by Indians which, though not a puma-skin, was quite as large as the skin of the common silver-grey puma generally is. I myself saw a very large otter in the River Senguerr, but unluckily had not my rifle with me, and although I returned as quickly with it as I could, all trace of the otter had vanished.

Taking into consideration the amphibious nature attributed by the Indians to the Iemisch, there seems to be little reason to doubt that the real animal underlying the rumours of a mysterious monster is a sub-species of the large Brazilian otter (Lutra brasiliensis).

To return to the possible survival of the Mylodon, as far as our travels led us both north and south on the eastern side of the Cordillera, we could discover no trace whatever either by hearsay or from the evidence of our own experience to warrant the supposition that it continues to exist to the present day. But there are hundreds of square miles of dense forest still unexplored along the whole length of the Patagonian Andes, and I do not undertake to declare positively that no such animal exists in some unknown and hidden spot among their recesses. Roughly speaking, there are many thousand square miles of snowy summits, ravines, high plateaus and valleys in this region. The task of finding a final answer to the Mylodon problem on the drag-net principle of passing to and fro throughout the whole district would be so gigantic and prolonged where the natural difficulties are great, as to be practically impossible. Such an answer must be left to time and the slow process of things. In the meanwhile I can merely state my own conviction that the odds are very heavily against the chances of such a survival. The probable habitat of the Mylodon would naturally be the forests. I penetrated these in more than one direction, and one of the most striking characteristics of the forests was the absence of animal life, evidence of which grew less and less the farther we forced our way into their depths. It is a matter of common knowledge that, where the larger forms of life are to be found, there also a liberal catalogue of lesser creatures co-exist. The conditions which favour the life of the greater favour also the existence of the less. This is presumptive evidence only, and though it has certainly influenced my own conclusions, I do not wish to force it upon others. I have stated the case as fairly as I can, and I leave my readers to form their own opinions.

FOOTNOTES:

[33] F. Ameghino, "Première Notice sur le Neomylodon listai, un Représentant vivant des anciens Edentés Gravigrades fossiles de l'Argentina" (La Plata, August 1898); translated under the title "An Existing Ground-Sloth in Patagonia," in "Natural Science," vol. xiii (1898), pp. 324-326.

[34] A. Milne-Edwards, "Note sur une nouvelle Espèce de Tatou à cuirasse incomplète (Scleropleura bruneti)," Nouv. Arch. Mus., vol. vii. (1871), pp. 177-179, pl. xii.

[35] P. W. Lund, K. Dansk. Vidensk. Selsk. Afhandl., vol. viii. (1841), p. 85 (footnote).

[36] H. Burmeister, Anales Mus. Publico Buenos Aires, vol. i. (1864-69), p. 173, pl. v. Fig. 8.

[37] Flower and Lydekker, "Introduction to the Study of Mammals," p. 183.

[38] E. Lönnberg, "On some Remains of 'Neomylodon listai," Ameghino, brought home by the Swedish Expedition to Tierra del Fuego, 1895-1897, Wissensch. Ergebn. schwedisch. Exped. Magellansländ, unter Leitung v. Otto Nordenskjöld, vol. ii. pp. 149-170, pls. xii.-xiv. (1899).

[39] "On some Remains of Grypotherium (Neomylodon) listai and associated Mammals from a Cavern near Consuelo Cove, Last Hope Inlet, Patagonia." Proc. Zool. Soc., 1900, pp. 64-79, pls. v.-ix.

[40] R. Hauthal, S. Roth, and R. Lehmann-Nitsche, "El Mamifero Misterioso de la Patagonia, Grypotherium domesticum," Revista Mus. La Plata, vol. ix. pp. 409-474, pls. i.-v. (1899).—F. P. Moreno, "Note on the Discovery of Miolania and of Glossotherium (Neomylodon) in Patagonia," Geol. Mag. [4] vol. vi. pp. 385-388 (1899).

[41] J. Reinhardt, "Beskrivelse af Hovedskallen af et Kæmpedovendyr, Grypotherium darwinii, fra La Plata-Landenes plejstocene-Dannelser," K. Dansk. Vidensk. Selsk Skr. [5] vol. xii. (1879), pp. 353-380, pls. i. ii.—H. Burmeister, "Atlas de la Description physique de la République Argentine," sect. ii. (1881), p. 119, woodc. (Mylodon darwinii),—R. Lydekker, "The Extinct Edentates of Argentina," Anales Mus. La Plata—Paleont. Argentina, vol. iii. pt 2 (1894), p. 85, pl. liv.

[42] R. Hauthal, op. cit. p. 4.

[43] See S. Roth, op. cit. pl. ii. Fig. 1.

[44] R. Lydekker, Anales Mus. La Plata—Paleont. Argentina, vol. iii. pt. 2 (1894), p. 73, pl. xlv. Fig. 1.

[45] R. Owen, "Description of the Skeleton of an Extinct Gigantic Sloth, Mylodon robustus, Owen" (1842), p. 18.

[46] P. Gervais, "Mémoire sur les Formes Cérébrales propres aux Édentés vivants et fossiles," Nouv. Arch. Mus., vol. xv. (1869), p. 39, pl. iv. Figs. 1, 2.

[47] P. Gervais, loc. cit. p. 39, pl. v.

[48] Ibid. p. 38, pl. iv. Figs. 3, 4.

[49] J. Hyrtl, "Vergleichendanatomische Untersuchungen über das innere Gehörorgan des Menschen und der Säugethiere" (1845), p. 135, pl. v. Fig. 6.

[50] P. Z. S. 1899. pl. xv. Figs. 4-6.

[51] R. Owen, "The Zoology of the Voyage of H.M.S. Beagle.—Part I. Fossil Mammalia" (1840), p. 57, pl. xvi.

[52] R. Owen, "Description of the Skeleton of an Extinct Gigantic Sloth, Mylodon robustus, Owen" (1842), p. 154, foot-note.

[53] Described respectively by Reinhardt, Burmeister, and Lydekker, loc. cit.

[54] F. Ameghino, "Contribucion al Conocimiento de los Mamiferos de la Republica Argentina" (1889), p. 738, pl. xliv. Fig. 8.

[55] E. Nordenskjöld, "La Grotte du Glossotherium (Neomylodon) en Patagonie," Comptes Rendus, vol. cxxix. (1899), p. 1217.

[56] Dawkins and Sanford, "The British Pleistocene Mammalia" (Palæont. Soc., 1869), p. 150.

[57] F. Ameghino, "Contribucion al Conocimiento de los Mamiferos de la Republica Argentina" (1889), p. 342.

[58] F. Ameghino, op. cit. (1889), p. 317.

[59] H. Winge, "Jordfundne og nulevende Rovdyr (Carnivora) fra Lagoa Santa, Minas Geraes, Brasilien" (E. Museo Lundii, 1895), p. 31.

[60] Dr. Moreno has lately received reports of bear-like tracks in remote parts of the Cordillera, which he thinks may imply that a species of Arctotherium still lives in Patagonia.

[61] F. P. Moreno, "Revista Mus. La Plata," vol. ii. (1891). p. 56, R. Lydekker, "Anales Mus. La Plata—Paleont. Argentina," vol. ii. pt. 3 (1893), p. 77. pl. xxix.

[62] F. Ameghino, op. cit. (1889), p. 324.

[63] E. Nordenskjöld, "La Grotte du Glossotherium (Neomylodon)en Patagonie" Comptes Rendus, vol. cxxix. (1899), pp. 1216, 1217.

[64] A. Carnot, "Sur une Application de l'Analyse chimique pour fixer l'Age d'Ossements humains préhistoriques," Comptes Rendus, vol. cxv. (1892), pp. 337-339.

[65] Pangolins, armadillos, and sloths are more or less related.

On a new Form of Puma from Patagonia by OLDFIELD THOMAS, F.R.S.

The National Collection owes to the generosity of Mr. C. Arthur Pearson the skin of a fine puma, obtained by Mr. Hesketh Prichard during the recent Daily Express expedition to Patagonia. The skin is remarkably unlike any known form of puma, and appears certainly to represent a new sub-species.

Dr. Matschie has already shown[66] that the red puma of the tropics to which he restricts the name Felis concolor, is replaced south of 25° S. lat. by the silver-grey form for which Molina's name, F. puma, is used.

Now, again, south of about 44° S. lat., there proves to be another form, represented in the British Museum not only by Mr. Prichard's skin from Santa Cruz, but by a second much younger specimen from the Rio Senguerr. Both show the same characteristics, and are equally different from the Argentine silver-grey form.

In commemoration of Mr. Pearson's scientific spirit in sending out the expedition, and in presenting the specimen to the National Museum, I would propose to call it

Felis concolor Pearsoni, sub-sp. n.

General build thick and sturdy, with comparatively short limbs and tail. Fur thick and woolly, the specimens evidently in winter pelage. General colour nearest to Ridgway's "clay-colour," therefore exceedingly different from the nearly "drab-grey" of F. c. puma. This colour is most vivid along the back, paler laterally on the sides, but there is nothing that can be called a distinct dorsal dark line. Undersurface whitish-fawn, the hairs sandy at their bases, whiter terminally. Face very much like back, darker markings practically obsolete; the usual lighter markings near the eye present but not conspicuous. Ears of normal length, their backs uniformly whitish-fawn, without darker markings. Outer sides of limbs like back, inner sides like belly; ends of fingers and toes whitish, without any darker markings round the pads. Tail proportionally very short, brownish clay-colour above, whitish below, the tip not or scarcely darker.

Dimensions of the typical skin, which has been tanned and stretched, so that the measurements are merely approximate:—Head and body 1370 millim., tail 530, ear 80.

Hab. Santa Cruz, Patagonia; about 70 miles inland.

Type. Female. B.M. No. 1. 8. 12. 1. Brought home by Mr. H. Prichard and presented by Mr. C. Arthur Pearson.

The skin was bought by Mr. Prichard from Indians in the region mentioned, so that neither flesh-measurements nor skull were obtained.

The second skin is that of a young male, killed on the Senguerr River, in March 1897, by one of the collectors from the La Plata Museum, by whom it was presented to the British Museum. Owing to its youth, its peculiarities had not been previously noticed.

F. c. Pearsoni is distinguished from F. c. puma not only by its very different general colour, but also by its shorter tail, light-coloured ear-backs, and the absence of the dark markings round the digital pads.

FOOTNOTE:
[66] SB. Ges. nat. Fr. Berlin, 1892, p. 220; 1894, p. 58.

LIST OF PLANTS.[67] **BY JAMES BRITTEN, F.L.S., AND A. B. RENDLE, M.A., D.SC.**

Hamadryas Kingii, Hook. fil.	Top of mountains.
Ranunculus peduncularis, Sm.	Low slopes of mountains.
Anemone, cf. lanigera, Gay.	Low slopes and pampa.
Berberis buxifolia, Lam.	
Berberis empetrifolia, Lam.	Slopes of mountains.
Senebiera pinnatifida, DC.	Low slopes of mountains.
Thlaspi gracile, Phil.	Swamp.
Draba Gilliesii, Hook.	High slopes and top of mountains.
Cardamine pratensis, L. var.	Swamp.
Nasturtium, aff. palustre, L.	Sheltered slopes of mountains.
Viola maculata, Cav.	Sheltered slopes and forests.
Polygala Salasiana, Gay.	North slope of Mount Frias.
Lychnis magellanica, Lam.	High slopes of mountains.
Stellaria debilis, D'Urv.	Low slopes of mountains.
Cerastium arvense, L.	Low slopes of mountains.
Cerastium var.	Low slopes of mountains.
Arenaria serpens, H.B.K., several forms	Low slopes of mountains, beach, lake and sheltered pampa.
Calandrinia cæspitosa, Gill.	Top of hills among stones.
Geranium magellanicum, Hook. fil.	Low slopes of mountains.
Erodium cicutarium, L'Herit.	Low slopes of mountains.
Oxalis enneaphylla, Cav., var. pumila, Hook, fil.	High slopes and top of Mount Frias.
Oxalis sp.	Bare sandy ground.
Colletia discolor, Hook.	Low slopes of mountains.
Adesmia boronoides, Hook. fil.	Low sandy ground.
Astragalus cf. alpinus, L.	High slopes of mountains.
Lathyrus nervosus, Lam.	Low slopes of mountains.
Lathyrus cf. pubescens, Hook. & Arn.	Low slopes of mountains.
Vicia, aff. bijuga	Low slopes of mountains.
Vicia sp.	Low slopes of mountains.
Anarthrophyllum desideratum, Benth.	Top of Mount Frias.
Potentilla anserina, L.	Swamps in open places of forests.
Geum magellanicum, Comm.	Slopes of Punta Bandera.
Acæna adscendens, Vahl.	By springs and streams.
Acæna cuneata, Hook. & Arn.	Low sandy soil.
Acæna sp. aff. multifida, Hook. fil.	Pampa slopes and low slopes.

Saxifraga Pavonii, D. Don.   On rocks, low slopes overhanging lake.
Donatia fascicularis, Forst.   Top of mountain.
Escallonia macrantha, Hook. & Arn.   Low slopes, Mount Buenos Aires.
Escallonia cf. alpina, Poepp.   Low slopes, Mount Buenos Aires.
Ribes cuneifolium, Ruiz & Pav.   Valleys and low hillsides.
Hippuris vulgaris, L.   Standing water.
Œnothera odorata, Jacq.   Mountain slope and low slopes.
Fuchsia coccinea, Ruiz & Pav.   Low slopes and Punta Bandera.
Epilobium, cf., densifolium, Haussk   Bed of dried up stream.
Epilobium sp.   Punta Bandera.
Grammatocarpus volubilis, Presl.   Low slopes, Mount Buenos Aires.
Azorella trifurcata, Hook. fil.   Top of mountain.
Azorella sp. aff. bryoides, Phil.   Mountain tops.
Azorella cf. trifoliolata, Hook. fil. Shingle on beach.
Mulinum spinosum, Pers.   Pampa under Mount Buenos Aires and low slopes.
Osmorrhiza chilensis, DC.   Forests of Mount Buenos Aires.
Bowlesia, sp.   Low slopes of mountains.
Sanicula macrorrhiza, Colla.   Top of Mount Buenos Aires.
Oreopolus glacialis, Schlecht.   Tops of mountains.
Galium Aparine, L.   Forest, Mount Buenos Aires.
Galium sp.   Mountain slopes and low slopes, shingle banks of stream.
Valeriana carnosa, Sm.   Low slopes, Mount Buenos Aires.
Boopis sp.   Nitrate pampa.
Boopis sp.   Top of mountains and shingle beach.
Nardophyllum Kingii, A. Gray.   Mountain tops.
Chiliotrichum amelloides, Cass.   Springs in slopes of mountains.
Erigeron alpinus, L.   Low slopes of mountains.
Erigeron sp.   Mountain slopes, Mount Buenos Aires.
Baccharis sp.   Beach, Punta Bandera.
Antennaria sp.   Pampas.
Gnaphalium spicatum, Lam.   Low slopes of mountains.
Madia, cf. viscosa, Cav.   Slopes of mountains.
Matricaria Chamomilla, L.   Low slopes of mountains.
Senecio magellanicus, Hook. & Arn. Among stones, top of Mount Buenos Aires.
Senecio albicaulis, Hook. & Arn. Mountain slopes.
Senecio Kingii, Hook. fil.   High slopes of mountains.
Chabræa purpurea, DC.   Pampa and high slopes of mountains.
Chabræa multifida, DC.   Low slopes of mountains.
Chabræa sp.   East slope of Mount Frias.
Perezia linearis, Less.   High slopes of mountains.
Panargyrum Darwinii, Hook. & Arn.   Tops of mountains.
Nassauvia, sp.   Tops of mountains.
Nassauvia, sp.   Beaches and mud flats.
Nassauvia pygmæa, Hook. fil.   Top of mountains.
Hieracium patagonicum, Hook. fil. Low slopes of mountains.
Achyrophorus tenuifolius, DC.   Low slopes of mountains.
Taraxacum officinale, Wigg., var.   Low slopes of mountains.
Sonchus asper, Vill., var.   Punta Bandera.

Pernettya pumila, Hook.   Mountain tops.
Pernettya mucronata, Gaud., 2 forms   Low slopes of mountains, high & wooded slopes of Mount Buenos Aires.
Primula magellanica, Lehm.   Swamp.
Samolus spathulatus, Duby.   Swamp on pampa.
Armeria chilensis, Poepp.   Low slopes of mountains.
Phacelia circinata, Jacq., two forms   North slope Mount Frias.
Collomia coccinea, Lehm.   Low shingly ground.
Collomia gracilis, Dougl.   Low slopes of mountains.
Amsinckia angustifolia, Lehm.   Forest on mountain slope and low ground.
Calceolaria Darwinii, Benth.   High slopes of mountains.
Calceolaria sp. aff. lanceolata   Low slopes of mountains and banks of streams, low ground.
Veronica peregrina, L.   Sheltered pampa.
Verbena aff. microphylla, Phil.   Mount Buenos Aires.
Micromeria cfr. Darwinii, Benth.Pampa.
Scutellaria nummulariæfolia, Hook. fil. Shingle beach.
Plantago uniglumis, Wallr.   Stony top of mountains.
Plantago maritima, L.   Nitrate pampa.
Rumex crispus, L.   By water slopes of pampa.
Rumex magellanicus, Griseb.   Shingle beach.
Embothrium coccineum, Forst.   Low slopes of mountains.
Myzodendron punctulatum, Soland.   Forests on mountains; parasitic on Fagus antarctica.
Myzodendron quadriflorum, DC. Forests, parasitic on Fagus antarctica.
Arjona patagonica, Hombr. & Jacquem.   Low slopes and pampas.
Quinchamalium procumbens, Ruiz & Pav. Pampa.
Euphorbia portulacoides, Spreng. Pampa.
Urtica magellanica, Poir.   Low slopes of mountains.
Fagus antarctica, Forst.   Forests and mountains.
Empetrum nigrum var. andinum, DC. Grassy top of mountain.
Chloræa magellanica, Hook. fil. Slopes of Mount Buenos Aires.
Asarca araucana, Phil.   Slopes of Mount Buenos Aires.
Asarca cf. cardioglossa, Phil.   Slopes of Mount Buenos Aires.
Stipa sp.   Sandy slopes of foothills.
Phleum alpinum, L.   Mountain slopes.
Alopecurus alpinus, Sm.   Springs.
Arundo pilosa, D'Urv.   Low slopes of mountains.
Poa pratensis, L.   Sheltered pampa.
Festuca sp.   Pampa.
Bromus sp.   Pampa.
Hordeum jubatum, L.   Slopes of mountains.
Carex Banksii, Boott.   Swampy springs in forest on mountain slope.
Sisyrinchium filifolium, Gaud.   Pampa.
Aspidium mohrioides, Bory.   Low slopes.
Aspidium coriaceum, Sw.   Punta Bandera; mountain slope; bush slope.
Lomaria alpina, Spreng.   Swamp.
Cystopteris fragilis, Bernh.   Forest.
Bryum sp. (immature)   Wet forest.
Marchantia polymorpha, L.   Forest swamp.

| Usnea barbata, Ach. | Growing on Fagus antarctica. |
| Usnea melaxantha. Ach. | On rocks. |

FOOTNOTE:

[67] Owing to the very short time allowed before going to press we are unable to furnish a complete list. We hope, however, to give in a future number of the Journal of Botany a full list with notes on critical or otherwise interesting species.

GLOSSARY

Alazan, a chestnut horse.
Alpargatas, shoes made of canvas with jute or hemp soles.
Asado, roast meat. In the camp cooked on a spit over the fire.
Asador, the spit on which meat is roasted.
Asulejo, a blue-eyed, grey and white horse.

Bandurria, an ibis.
Barranca, cliff-like banks of river or lagoon.
Bayo, a cream-coloured dun horse.
Blanco, white; a white horse or cow.
Bocado, a thong of raw hide passed twice round the lower jaw of a young horse as a bit.
Bolas, Boleadores, three balls of stone covered with raw hide and attached to one another by twisted thongs of raw hide; used for catching wild animals.
Boliche, a small drinking-store.
Bombilla, a metal tube for sucking the tea from the maté cup.
Bozal, a halter.

Cabresto, a leading rein always attached to the bozal for tying up the horse; from the Spanish word cabestro.
Cacique, an Indian chief or leader.
Cañadon, a dale or dip of low land between stretches of high land.
Capa, a cape or cloak.
Carancho, the large, eagle-like carrion hawk (Polyborus tharus).
Carguero, a pack-horse or mule.
Carpa, a tent, or shelter of a movable kind.
Casa, a house, even if only a mud hut.
Cebruno, a dark mouse-coloured horse with a reddish tinge.
Chico, little.
Chimango, a harrier-like carrion hawk (Milvago Chimango).
China, Indian woman; also a native Criska woman.
Chiripá, a loin-cloth the size of a poncho, and worn so as to form loose, baggy trousers.
Cinch, English spelling of "Cincha," the raw-hide girth used with native saddles.
Colorado, red; a bay horse.
Cordillera, the chain of mountains called the Andes.
Cruzado, a horse having crossed white feet—i.e., one fore-foot white and one hind-foot of opposite sides; always expected to be good horses.

Estancia, a farm in Argentina.
Estanciero, a stock-farmer in Argentina.

Gateado, a yellow dun horse with a black stripe down the back.
Gaucho, the Argentine cowboy.

Horqueta, a fork; the separation of two streams forming a fork; name of a horse with a forked cutting in the ear.

Macho, a male animal; especially a mule.
Madrina, the bell-mare followed by all the horses or mules of a tropilla.
Manada, a herd of mares.
Manea, hobbles for a horse made of raw hide generally.
Mañero, a cunning, tricky horse or person.
Martineta, the "large partridge" (Calo dromas elegans).
Maté, the small gourd in which the Yerba tea is made; also the tea itself.
Moro, a dark blue roan horse.
Mula, female mule.
Muy limpio, literally "very clean."

Oscuro, a dark or black horse.
Overo, a spotted or splashed horse.

Palenque, posts or rails put up for tying-up horses.
Pampa, the great plains of South America.
Pampero, the south-west wind, often a hurricane in South America, blowing across the Pampas.
Pangaré, a bay horse, with the peculiar mule-like colouring of the nozzle.
Pantano, a mud hole; a sticky muddy place.
Peon, a working man or porter.
Picaso, a black horse with white feet and face.
Plaza, open square in a town.
Poncho, the rug or shawl, with a hole in middle, to slip over the head.
Potro, a colt or wild horse.
Puchero, mutton or beef boiled with rice, and vegetables when there are any.

Rincon, a corner.
Rosado, a light strawberry roan horse.
Rosillo, a red-roan horse.

Soga, a cord or strip of hide.

Toldo, an awning; the Indian tent of raw hides.
Tordillo, a grey horse.
Tostado, a dark chestnut horse.
Travesia, a desert.
Tropilla, the troop of horses or mules driven in front of travellers in South America.

Vaqueano, a guide.
Vega, a valley.

Yerba, the Paraguayan tea, universal in Argentina.

Zaino, a brown horse.

www.ingramcontent.com/pod-product-compliance
Lightning Source LLC
Chambersburg PA
CBHW060504090426
42735CB00011B/2108